" . . . then left round the minefield and over the wire, you can't miss it!"

THE WILDEST TESTS

THE WILDEST TESTS

Ray Robinson

PELHAM BOOKS

First published in Great Britain by PELHAM BOOKS LTD
52 Bedford Square, London, W.C.1
1972

© 1972 by Ray Robinson

Set and printed in Great Britain by
Tonbridge Printers Ltd, Peach Hall Works, Tonbridge, Kent
in Baskerville eleven on twelve point on paper supplied by
P. F. Bingham Ltd, and bound by James Burn
at Esher, Surrey

CONTENTS

1	The Noble Game	11
2	Home and Hosed	15
3	Igniting the Fuse	19
4	The Battle of Adelaide	26
5	Flying Bottles	39
6	Turmoil in Trinidad	54
7	Up in Flames	73
8	Teargas Panic	83
9	Be England what she will . . .	94
10	Don't Spare the Horses	100
11	Captain Besieged	113
12	Aussies, go Home!	124
13	Woe, Calcutta!	139
14	Bouncers and Beercans	160
	Index	181

ILLUSTRATIONS

Between pages 48 and 49

1. Woodfull ducks to a Larwood bouncer, Brisbane, 1933
2. Georgetown, 1954. Mounted police try to control crowd
3. Len Hutton says his team wants to stay on the field
4. Chester Watson relaxes
5. Ted Dexter leaves the field after a riot had stopped play, Trinidad, 1960
6. Rioting spectators invade the field amidst smoke and tear gas bombs, Calcutta, 1967

Between pages 80 and 81

7. Cricket's most savage riot
8. Bengali rioters retaliate against the police
9. Onlookers hurl chairs and benches on to a mid-field blaze
10. High-speed bowler Wesley Hall airborne
11. Cowdrey and Sobers try to calm the crowd, Kingston, 1968
12. Tom Graveney drives
13. Graveney and Milburn surrounded by milling spectators, Karachi, 1969
14. Student demonstrators swarm on to the playing area, Karachi, in the Pakistan-England test, 1969
15. The Pakistan team head for the safety of the dressing room Karachi, 1969

Between pages 112 and 113

16. Demonstrators set fire to stands at Brabourne Stadium, Bombay, 1969
17. 'Garth' McKenzie, often a match-winner

18. Clive Loyd's drive, packed with power
19. Gary Sobers' inimitable square cut
20. Lawry and Stackpole wait for police to clear playing area, Calcutta, 1969
21. A photographer watches Lawry and Stackpole
22. The incident when another photographer fell

Between pages 144 and 145

23. Coils of barbed wire at Headingley
24. Crowds congratulate Greg Chappell at Perth
25. A bouncer from Alan Thomson strikes Luckhurst on the back
26. Terry Jenner collapses on the pitch
27. Illingworth hurries over to Jenner
28. Snow and Illingworth argue with the umpire
29. A spectator grabs John Snow's shirt

Grateful thanks are due to the following, whose photographs are reproduced in this book :

Associated Press Ltd.: 5, 13, 14, 15; *Universal Press International*: 6; *Truth, Brisbane*: 10; *Statesman Bengal*: 21, 22; *The Gleaner, Jamaica*: 11; *Sport & General*: 12, 17, 19; *Central Press*: 1, 24; *Press Association*: 18, 23; *Australian Cricket*: 25; *G. C. Dixit*: 7, 8, 9; *F. W. Bennett*: 16, 20; *Melbourne Sun*: 26, 29; *Sydney Sun/Herald*: 27, 28.

ACKNOWLEDGEMENTS

The author and publishers wish to thank Paul Rigby (*The Sun*, London), Jeff Hook, (*The Sun*, Melbourne) Frank Benier (*The Sun*, Sydney) and *Daily Mirror*, London, for kind permission to republish their cartoons.

For bibliography and quotations we are grateful to Alex Bannister (*Daily Mail* and author of *Cricket Cauldron*), J. S. Barker (*In The Main*), Ken Barrington (*Running Into Hundreds*), Richie and D. E. Benaud, Brian Close (*M.C.C. Tour of West Indies, 1968*), Gerald Gomez, Derek Leon and Philip Thomson of Port of Spain, Brian Johnston (BBC), Harold Larwood and Kevin Perkins (*The Larwood Story*), Arvind Lavakare of Bombay, Norman May and Alan McGilvray (ABC), K. M. Meher-Homji, Michael Melford (*Sunday Telegraph*), Keith Miller and Crawford White (*Daily Express*), Rusi Modi, V. Pattabhiraman, Madras, Ian Peebles (*Bowler's Turn*), Niran Prabhu (*The Times of India*), Norman Preston (editor of *Wisden's*), Alan Ross (*Through The Caribbean*), Gordon Ross (editor of *Playfair Cricket Monthly*), P. N. Sundaresan of Madras (editor of *Indian Cricket*), E. W. Swanton (*Daily Telegraph, West Indian Adventure, West Indies Revisited* and *The World of Cricket*), C. S. A. Swamy (*Sunday Standard,* Delhi), Clive Taylor (*The Sun*), John Thicknesse (*Evening Standard*), Clyde Walcott (*Island Cricketers*), E. M. Wellings (*Evening News*), Phil Wilkins (*Sydney Morning Herald*), John Woodcock (*The Times*), Ian Wooldridge (Bagenal Harvey Organisation).

For co-operation with scores and statistics we thank Irving Rosenwater, Bill Frindall (BBC), Anandji Dossa of Bombay and David Sherwood of Sydney.

Also many cricketers for confirming or debunking, discounting or amplifying events, not always to their own personal advantage.

Chapter One

THE NOBLE GAME

AMONG the charms of cricket, to many, are that it is usually pleasant to play and often relaxing to watch, free from rat-race taints. In the only sport ever called 'the noble game' centuries are frequent, coronaries few.

Since the world-wide convulsions of Hitler's War, followed by a train of upheavals around the globe, international cricket has been subjected to pressures and strains it had never known. After 400 years of the game's more or less peaceful spread from the cricket-a-wicket of Tudor England to torrid Guyana, sweltering Singapore and other points west and east, the curtain began to rise on dramatic and upsetting events, foreign to the game's village origins.

Restive onlookers flung bottles, cans and stones on to hitherto-sacred turf. Demonstrators surged on to grounds. Umpires feared assault. Audience participation was getting out of hand. Protesting students stopped a Test match. Police in three cities discharged teargas against cricket crowds, a distinction until then reserved for soccer partisans and, away from grounds, political, racial or religious fanatics. Infuriated rioters piled benches on a midfield fire. A chair spared from the flames at another ground hit an Australian captain.

Stop the World, I Want to Get Off was the title Leslie Bricusse and Anthony Newley gave one of the wittiest musical shows of the 1960s. Cricket devotees felt their world was falling apart. Their first reaction was to try to keep their beloved game as they had known it. The wish was to insulate cricket from the disturbing influences rampant in the surrounding world, to give it a separate existence, a dreaming detachment from an age of political cross-currents, racial and social spasms, civil war, anti-war agitation, disarmament marches, demonstrations of dissent and demands for reform.

11

The diehard cliché, *law and order,* once uttered like an incantation to stifle or suppress opposition, has lost some of its old magic in an age which no longer gives blind allegiance to all laws but bucks some of them as hangovers from a period left behind by time's onward march. This ferment increases as the generation gap widens into a chasm between those accepting things as they have been and those demanding something better, if not sure what. Politicians heeded dissatisfied students enough to lower the voting age in some countries to 18, thus giving them a chance to use the ballot box better than their conformist elders.

Gradually it is being recognised that cricket, a team game played and watched by people of dissimilar races and creeds, cannot be isolated from everyday life. It was idle to imagine that it could remain a solitary unaltered segment in the post-war pattern . . . that the winds of change noted by Prime Minister Harold Macmillan in 1960 could blow everywhere except through the W. G. Grace memorial gates, rattle all windows except those of the Melbourne pavilion . . . that gusts would not tear branches from samans around Queen's Park Oval, Trinidad, ruffle the turquoise pool alongside the Bombay clubhouse or fan smouldering embers at Calcutta.

Yet cricket's worries have been dwarfed by those plaguing

'You don't run into as much
apathy as you used to.'

football, especially soccer, the world's favourite spectator sport. Children who should be alive today were among 318 people trampled to death after police mishandling of a disturbance about a neutral referee's decision at Lima national stadium in 1964. What began as a match between Peru and Argentina ended with a casualty list like a weekend's warfare in Vietnam. Public indignation compelled the police chief to resign.

At an Italian match, Napoli v. Modena in 1963 a rioting mob tore down goalposts to use as clubs in a battle against truncheon-swinging police. More than 100 were arrested. Again the rioters were protesting against a referee's decision.

Without attempting to belittle the Latin Americans and the Italians' well-earned reputation for volatility, I mention a few incidents to show that they have no monopoly of this attribute. Unable to get into Stamford Bridge ground to see a Russian team play Chelsea soon after the war, London soccer fans wrenched gates off. Thousands wedged into the packed ground, iron railings gave way and swarms of people spilled on to the field. Angry seat-holders in the grandstand threw stones, clods and scraps of wood at those on the touchline spoiling their view. In Yarra Park six years later, thousands of Australian Rules fans, locked out of the vast Melbourne ground as Geelong played Essendon, threw stones at House Full signs on the fortress-like walls. An impromptu storming party lifted an old tree-trunk and, like a platoon of Roman Legionaries, used it as a battering ram to smash down a gate. The insurgents forced hundreds of the 84,000 paying customers forward over the pickets to the chalk-line of the playing area. Taking the hint, the Melbourne Cricket Club has since increased accommodation to more than 122,000 and since 1957 tickets for the finals have been sold in advance.

Even the most law-abiding people on earth, the New Zealanders, were guilty of a lapse when more than 60,000 rugby fans tried to see the All Blacks play British Isles at Wellington in 1959. Some of the thousands locked out of Athletic Park smashed two gates and tore gaps in the fence to force entry.

Since a grenade was thrown into Millwall's goalmouth in 1966 British authorities have made greater efforts to combat the menace of soccer hoodlums whose afternoon at the football seems incomplete without studded gloves, knuckle-dusters and steel-capped boots you wouldn't kick a horse with. One London magistrate, Seymour Collins, suggested segregating rival supporters, saying: 'It seems to me they should be put in cages.' In 1970 the Law Society's *Gazette* called on courts to impose heavier penalties, including longer jail terms, to stamp out senseless outbursts. A Law Society memorandum to the Home Office and the Lord Chancellor recommended that football hooligans and vandals be compelled to repair public property, trains and buses they damaged.

Ill-feeling about Honduras's treatment of poor settlers from El Salvador lay behind violence at two World Cup elimination matches in 1969 which provoked war between these two Central American republics. Bombers and tanks were in action for five days before the anxious Organisation of American States could negotiate a cease-fire. Cricket still has some way to go.

Chapter Two

HOME AND HOSED

WHAT can be done to head off a worsening trend? We can't all be Bertrand Russells but we don't have to be so dumb that we fail to recognise basic truths, though they may be obscured by a camouflage of dissimilar customs, regional chauvinism, blind patriotism, touchy pride and other human weaknesses.

A game spread by imperialism (before it became a discredited word) appealed so much to the colonised in both hemispheres that it lived down its murky association with occupying troops. It has robustly survived the decay of colonialism to win more fans than it ever attracted in the Golden Age which we all respect so much. Millions feel there is too much at stake for drawbacks and frictions to be taken lightly, yet better learn this way than take them too seriously; that way leads to irritation, brush-offs, recriminations, patronising self-righteousness, even jingoistic utterances, resulting in resentments deeper and wider than a moat.

A four-sided challenge confronts ground managements, police, the crowds and, not least, the players they pay to watch.

Ground managers should be busy re-thinking crowd arrangements, correcting those which have failed in seven Test matches since 1954 and several other games. Above all, they must assure that players will not be molested. Phoning the police for a riot squad that will turn rumblings into ructions is the last thing they should think of.

If police chiefs value their jobs, the disastrous results of existing strong-arm crowd-control methods in most places around the world should be impelling them to confer urgently to devise something less calamitous.

Until teargas is eliminated by the Geneva Convention outlawing asphyxiants, they could restrict it to such justifiable acts as subduing desperate criminals shooting from hide-outs. Events show that, if discharged into crowds, teargas is pre-eminent at causing panic and starting stampedes in which nothing spares innocent people. This has happened whether it has been loosed with the notion of quelling sport disturbances, or to disperse anti-war demonstrators in American cities or against religious rioters in Londonderry and Belfast street fights – the first citizens in the British Isles exposed to teargas. Chemical experts reported to the United Nations that ill-considered civil and military use of chemical agents could turn out to be highly dangerous and result later in asthmatic and bronchitis attacks among persons with impaired health.

Difficulties for police have increased, making fresh thinking necessary since the days when they could simply use violence to disperse disapproved assemblies. Television films of posses breaking up anti-war demonstrations in Australia and Japan had unforeseen effect. A Sydney magistrate rejected police versions of a street mêlée when they were disproved by cameramen's films. Next, TV viewers wrote to newspapers protesting against 'disgusting scenes in Canberra as security forces manhandled young people'. Fukuoka Court seized from four Japanese television channels films of police clashing with students demonstrating against a visit by a U.S. nuclear aircraft-carrier. Newsreels of mounted troopers' charges into a hostile crowd of anti-apartheid campaigners outside the Springboks' rugby match in Melbourne caused bitter controversy. As arrests were made in other States demonstrators called : 'The world is watching !'

Fire-hoses have a much better record than teargas or charges with batons or lathis. Sydney accidentally discovered this before World War I when fight fans, disagreeing with a Stadium referee's decision, set fire to the bleachers. In putting out the blaze firemen found that the jet from their hose had the spraying side-effect of cooling the mob's fury. Insufficient use has been made of the discovery. The cost of equipping every Test match ground with fireplugs at strategic points would be trifling compared with the futility of more violent attempts to subdue out-of-control crowds.

Public relations, the most neglected element in the whole cricket set-up, could be used to encourage self-discipline. All-out efforts are needed to make cricket-goers fully aware that pelting at players or interrupting a match will be penalised by loss of the game they love to watch, that it is up to them whether their city will be allotted a Test match next time around. Give a crowd a vested interest in ensuring an unmarred Test and hooligans would transgress at their peril. The worst job for police, perhaps, would be to remove half-lynched hoodlums to an ambulance instead of dragging them to a lock-up. If spectators near a troublesome group also knew that an outbreak could bring a retributive jet from an undiscriminating fire-hose nozzle this ought to contribute powerfully to self-discipline, the only thorough-going solution to crowd problems.

Leads well worth following have been given by the European Football Union (UEFA). After a goalkeeper was felled in a 1969 semi-final, UEFA warned three clubs that their grounds would be barred from European Cup football for a set period if missile-throwing did not stop. Wisely, the club managements were told they must inform their supporters of the warning – a far-seeing attempt to enlist the well-behaved majority in a protective alliance against the clots. A German soccer club planned a civil legal action against an uncivil fan to recover the equivalent of £3,000 in fine and costs the club had to pay because a flying can injured an Italian forward.

A dig into history, 2,000 years back, turned up the time a team of Nucerian athletes came to compete in Pompeii. A brawl between athletes became a riot when fans joined in, several people were killed and the city was damaged before troops asserted control. It was the last day of Pompeii athletic contests for ten years; by Rome Government decree all games were banned there from 59AD to 69AD.

Depriving unruly fans and players of their sport can be likened to depriving dangerous motorists of their driving licences – a penalty that hits home hardest. The cancelled Test could be transferred to the ground of the best-behaved crowd as a reward for their sportsmanship. After political turmoil caused a cricket Test to be taken away from one city (Georgetown in 1962), Australian, English and Indian teams played Tests there without interruption, despite one stone-throwing incident after the 1968 match by louts resentful of persistent pad-play. A 20-minute stoppage in New Zealand's Test in 1972 was caused by ire against a partner who ran out a local hero.

Moats may sound medieval but evidence suggests that for

the worst trouble-spots modern moats like that at the Maracana Stadium, Rio de Janeiro, would be a long way ahead of the barbed wire strung around English Test grounds in 1970 and some Australian grounds in 1971. Anti-apartheid demonstrations during the Springboks' rugby tour of Britain were estimated to have cost £50,000 for police protection. The Maracana moat, three metres wide, keeps hotheads in sport's largest crowds from mobbing players and manhandling referees. (At the risk of seeming flippant, cricket's moats could be stocked with trout, for people who would rather fish than watch some strokeless bore.)

Chapter Three

IGNITING THE FUSE

NOTHING ignites the fuse for a riot so quickly as foul or unfair play – as the masses view it – or an umpire or referee's decision, especially if this is mingled with bitter disappointment at a team's imminent defeat. Deplorable as this is, it is one of the failings in the jigsaw of human make-up which mankind has yet to overcome. In their *Lessons of History* Will and Ariel Durant have worked out that in more than 3,400 years of recorded history the world has known only 268 years of peace. In the present enlightened century alone International Red Cross reports show wars have killed more than 90 million people in 130 conflicts on five continents.

People so open to evil impulses do not shed these defects when they pass through turnstiles or, as players, fight, kick or bite opponents. Commenting on the crippling of Brazil's wonder-footballer Pele in a World Cup incident the *Football Association Year Book* said: 'What is required at all levels is an awareness that those who break the laws of football on the field and the laws of society off it should be branded criminals . . .' In fact, after violence on the field in the 1969 World Club Cup final in Buenos Aires some Estudiantes players were jailed for having assaulted AC Milan players.

A brawl on the field at Springs, Eastern Transvaal, led to the first British Lions player ever sent off, prop-forward John O'Shea, being attacked by incensed spectators near the grandstand. Non-playing Lions rushed to aid him and fighting raged for ten minutes before police could stop it.

The scene caused by an Argentine captain's refusal to go when a neutral German referee ordered him off in a World Cup match in 1966 so roused an 88,000 crowd at Wembley that police had to join hands to prevent them from swarming on to the field. Britain's former Minister with responsibility for Sport, Denis

Howell, was speaking of soccer when he expressed the following opinion, but other sports could well examine their own consciences about the tendency: 'I feel the standard of sportsmanship has dropped. A win is everything. An honourable defeat or draw is not part of things.'

This is a long way from the spirit evident when both sides risked honourable defeat in West Indies' cricket Tests in Australia. The ultimate losers' spectacular batting and acceptance of difficult decisions brought them the most grateful ticker-tape farewell ever accorded visiting sportsmen anywhere. Don't tell me it can't happen again!

Sir Neville Cardus's statement that it's usually the losing side that complains about umpiring was smilingly corrected by Bradman; Sir Donald said: 'Not usually, always,' Stating a case for a later generation, Bob Simpson has pointed out that nothing upsets a touring side quicker than inconsistent umpiring and that players generally remember only the poor decisions. He adds: 'It is all right to say forget them and accept what comes along. In the pressure of international cricket this is almost impossible to do.'

These words from a frank ex-captain show a pronounced shift in approach. In international careers linking on from 1928 to 1963, Bradman, Lindsay Hassett and Neil Harvey played 286 Test innings, Harvey in six countries. They were no more exempt than anyone else from the risk of judicial error. I saw most of their 260-odd dismissals and not once did they fail to quit the wicket immediately an umpire raised his finger. No meaningful stare, no scanning the skies, no tapping the pitch, no reluctant departure, no looking back. I did not even detect a momentary start of surprise if they felt sure an umpire was mistaken. As a witness of most of Sir Leonard Hutton's innings against Australian bowling, all Peter May's except a handful and every one of Sir Frank Worrell's, I cannot recall a single shadow on their acceptance of decisions. May's demeanour was more admirable in the high-pressure period of the throwing controversy, when he must have felt several times that he was out to illegal deliveries. Cricket-goers know these six men were not exceptions to the prevailing standard of behaviour. Flip through *Wisden's* pages of birthdays and you will see the names of hundreds of others.

A dozen years brought two instances of team managers ordering players to apologise to umpires – Walter Robins at Port of Spain in 1960 and the Duke of Norfolk at Brisbane in 1962 – and in Adelaide captain Ray Illingworth apologised to an umpire on behalf of Geoffrey Boycott, who had thrown his bat down and disputed a run out decision. I do not believe this means that players in the game today are inferior in character to their predecessors and less capable of doing the right thing in trying moments, if they set their minds to it. Many of them never do otherwise, though rubbing shoulders with others who have been caught up in the tide. Looking back on the Port of Spain stresses, Ken Barrington was man enough to praise and thank Walter Robins, himself an ex-captain, for his 'sharp, constructive words'.

When experienced Test players of the highest repute differ about a point of fact, witnessed at close range, no man's version can be accepted as conclusive. Indeed, the evidence might convince a Solomon that all mistakes are not made by umpires.

Barely a dozen yards separated Gary Sobers and Wesley Hall from Ken Mackay in Adelaide when the Queenslander played forward to a well-up ball from Worrell. Stooping at silly mid-off, Sobers grabbed the shot and the West Indians began moving off, believing it was a catch, which would have decided the Test. Mackay was just as sure he had played down a bump-ball. 'Fair go!' he said to the nearest fieldsman. A belated appeal failed, as in Umpire Egar's opinion the ball went from the bottom of the bat to the ground. A year later, playing for Queensland, Hall repeatedly said to Mackay : 'Come on Slash, you can admit you were out now', but Ken always replied he was sure the ball came off the floor.

When Peter Burge dived at cover for a dropping shot by Ted Dexter off Neil Hawke's hard-to-pick slower ball at Old Trafford, the batsman turned a couple of yards away, then paused to ask : 'Did you make a clean catch?' Peter replied : 'I really don't know.' Yet Umpire Buller was expected to know. To Simpson's appeal he replied 'Not out'.

As David Brown's seventh ball to Bill Lawry at Brisbane was deflected to leg, to be caught by wicket-keeper Jim Parks, the three men with the nearest unobscured views were the still-running bowler, Umpire Egar, front on, and a short-leg fieldsman, Mike Smith, from side-on. Bowler and fielder thought the ball went off a glove, the umpire's 'Not out' showed he did not agree and the batsman said later it had gone off his body.

As Basil Butcher, 98, stretched forward to Derek Underwood at Headingley in 1969, his top hand holding the bat defensively, did the ball scrape its outer edge before Alan Knott's gloves reached low for it or did it brush Butcher's sleeved forearm, as West Indians believe? This time Umpire Elliott's view coincided with the fieldsmen's.

Experienced players' counts of bouncers per over in Tests in Australia in 1971 differed so much that it almost sounded like a game of bingo or housie. Some of the 19,000 onlookers at the Newlands Test, 1970, shouted rebukes to Australian captain Bill Lawry who had thrown his cap to the ground after an adverse decision and snatched the ball from umpire Bill Wade, who had been South Africa's wicket-keeper in eleven Test matches. A couple of other fieldsmen performed too. Watching similar dismay on the previous tour of South Africa had caused ex-captain Richie Benaud to say the Australians virtually threw away a Durban Test by playing with half-an-eye on an umpire instead of concentrating both eyes on the ball. (If any appealer under Benaud's captaincy looked like making a fuss about a decision Richie immediately used to wave or beckon him a couple of yards – unnecessary yards – to snap the thread of dissent.)

Raising the standard of umpiring – Bob Simpson emphasises this most of all – would help reduce the risk of contentious decisions and players' unsporting reactions causing a turbulent crowd to erupt. No workable way of achieving this perfection has emerged but the International Cricket Conference and umpires' associations should keep trying.

I have yet to meet a cricketer who has toured Britain without ranking England's general umpiring standard as the highest. It is upheld by fulltime men who mostly had years of grounding as players in first-class cricket before putting on white coats to umpire six days a week for a living. Yet if part-time umpires in other countries could be raised to such an exalted level would this mean players would accept all decisions as correct? I leave the answer to spectators who were at Edgbaston or the Oval in

1968 and Headingley in 1969, and Sydney in 1971.

Glib talk of neutral umpires may not sound nonsensical until you picture England playing Australia with, say, a Jamaican umpire at one end and a Pakistani at the other, or a South African, Indian or New Zealander. Impartial as High Court judges, to be sure, but all from countries where umpires have fewer opportunities to gain experience in long matches and build up powers of concentration. Would they have as much chance of satisfying the players' demand for perfection as say, Elliott and Fagg at Leeds or Rowan and Brooks at Perth?

Could the theory of choosing an elite panel of men to umpire Tests in all countries stand the strain of England playing Australia with an English umpire at one end and an Australian at the other? In the 1970's the glare of publicity and a less-tolerant atmosphere would make this a more explosive mixture than when men from each country, William Gunn and Charles Bannerman, stood in a Sydney Test in 1887. With such a pair, would peace reign if a Meckiff or a Rhodes were no-balled for throwing from one end and passed by the other? Or if either umpire had to rule on a case like one in Melbourne when the stumps were hidden by a batsman's legs and no bail fell until after he started to run?

If little new is being attempted just now to bring less-efficient pockets of umpiring to more satisfactory levels there is one thing cricketers can do immediately : lift the standard of their own behaviour when decisions go against them. Some seem no longer to consider it unsportsmanlike to show dissent, as if unaware of the harm this does. Although international players who have not fallen from grace still form a majority, it is distasteful to see the insidious habit taking such a hold that five men captaining their countries have been guilty of glaring, staring or otherwise acting as if adverse decisions were incredible errors, or of petulantly snatching the ball or hotly disputing a ruling in the middle. Onlookers at Kingston in 1965, Durban in 1967, Port of Spain in 1968, the Oval in 1968, Cape Town in 1970 and Sydney in 1971 were left in less doubt about the affronted skippers' displeasure than they were about the reasonableness of the decisions.

As from 1971, following bat-throwing in Adelaide and uproar in Sydney; the Cricket Council and Test and County Cricket

Board are regarding dissent from umpires' decisions, whether by word or deed, as a breach of discipline to be penalised by suspension or disqualification through termination of a player's registration. No period is laid down, unlike the eight weeks mentioned in the International Lawn Tennis Federation management committee's proposal to punish players' misbehaviour on court. Captain Ray Illingworth's first reaction to the Cricket Council announcement was: 'If it means that by showing dissent to an umpire a player can have his career finished I think it's a bit harsh.' Yet in the long view if action never becomes necessary to enforce the warning nobody will have more to gain than the cricketers from what premiers and presidents call 'a relaxation of tension'. Scoring runs and taking wickets in international cricket are hard enough without the triple handicap of having rattled umpires, players approaching the wicket in fearing-the-worst mood and being guilty of resentful actions that incur hostility of crowds.

Once a touring captain's duties lay along a path not much wider than to have his men playing well and doing their best to win without infringing the Laws of Cricket. It was all as simple and elemental as, say, Adam and Eve's existence in the Garden of Eden. Like the figleaf in their paradise, public relations had yet to intrude on the scene as an addition to things a skipper must have on his mind. Not now. Press, radio and television play garish floodlights on a Test tour. Any captain failing to give full attention to this side of his increased responsibilities will be fortunate to escape doing disservice to himself, his side and the game.

Whatever their feelings about a crowd's conduct, captain and players now have to make sure they do nothing arrogant, unsporting or unthinking that would add fuel to the fire. The more trying the situation the more blameless their own actions must be. Unless they want to fulfil Oscar Wilde's glum line that 'each man kills the thing he loves' the players' first contribution should be to uphold the spirit of the game and restore respect for umpires' decisions.

Another hoot-rousing custom which official complacency allows to persist, despite demonstrations, is one permitting stoppages for dull light. At such times any fielding captain can end play prematurely by bringing on bowlers fast enough to put batsmen in danger of injury. Yet officials fail to give umpires power to tell captains that if the light becomes too dim for pace bowling they must use slow bowlers, so that the arranged hours can be played. This is not so revolutionary as some might imagine, as some English umpires got fairly near it when county cricket was resumed after the 1939-45 War.

If lessons derived from matches interrupted by riot and commotion enable cricketers and ground authorities to adjust to the irreversible tide of change the game will emerge from the wildest Tests better able to move with the times.

Chapter Four

THE BATTLE OF ADELAIDE

IN the year 2010, I wonder, will Wesley Hall and Frank Tyson be remembered with the awe evoked by the name Harold Larwood 40 years after his bowling demoralised Australia's batting in the bodyline Tests of 1932-33? Why, it seemed to take almost that long for batsmen's nerves to settle down again!

Men who faced one of these high-speed bowlers find it hard to credit that either of the other two was faster. It is rather like an argument whether the north, south or west wind can blow hardest. Facing these human cyclones, merely to take block was rather an act of bravado before three ashen stumps.

What was the secret of Larwood's ability to bowl at terrifying speed when he stood only 5 feet $8\frac{1}{2}$ inches and weighed less than 175 pounds? Harold has since revealed that, through his 14-stride run-up, he felt relaxed right up to the high lift of his forward foot which gave batsmen a last warning of the wrath to come. The gift of co-ordinating balanced momentum and sudden muscular thrust into an explosive climax was his to a degree nobody has equalled, though Ray Lindwall got too close to it for batsmen's peace of mind. Harold was the smallest of captain D. R. Jardine's ballistic battery. Yet the perfection of his side-on delivery, the torque from an ex-miner's strong back and the downthrust of a high arm enabled the one-time pit-boy to make the ball rear from the earth more abruptly than his taller and stronger allies, Bill Voce, 6 feet 1 inch, and Bill Bowes, 6 feet 4 inches, each around 200 pounds.

The Adelaide match was the third of five Tests in which Larwood totalled 33 wickets, still an unsurpassed feat for a fast bowler anywhere and equalled only by left-hander Alan Davidson against West Indies in Australia in 1961.

When Jardine won the toss from W. M. Woodfull at Adelaide Oval on 13th January, 1933, the happiest faces were in the

Englishmen's room, as batting last had cost them the second Test by enabling O'Reilly and Ironmonger's spin to equalise the rubber. Soon the happiest expressions were worn by Australia's fieldsmen. Pleasure at capture of four good wickets for 37 in 90 minutes before lunch was exceeded by relief at being spared having to stand up to Larwood, Allen and Voce on a responsive wicket. 'Luckiest toss we ever lost,' one Australian told me.

Australia's sole fast bowler, Tim Wall, a 6 feet Adelaide school-master went into action and bowled like a man sensing a chance to take five wickets, if the catches would stick. Douglas Jardine's mastery of defensive batting could not save his leg stump from a breakback. England's finest batsman, Walter Hammond, made only two before a jumping outswinger edged from his bat into the gloves of Oldfield, one of the central figures in the most bitter Test match ever played, if played is the word. After 45 minutes, a fleeting stay for him, Herbert Sutcliffe (9) fell to a one-hand catch at silly-leg by Wall off Bill O'Reilly, an even taller school-master (6 feet 3 inches). O'Reilly was a bowler of genius so versatile that he could be called on to help open the attack, though it was his artifice with spin that caused Sir Donald Bradman to rank him as the greatest bowler he ever faced. Tilting back the middle stump of Leslie Ames (3) left-hand spinner Bert Ironmonger lowered the fourth wicket at 30.

To halt the inroads, England had Yorkshire left-hand Maurice Leyland, a commonsense batsman if ever there was one, solidly supported by studious Bob Wyatt. Leyland counter-attacked as soon as the sun removed residual moisture from the pitch. His compact strokes made Wall's bowling look tamer. With well-muscled forearms he off-drove O'Reilly, Ironmonger and Grim-mett in a manner to which they were not accustomed. In his chanceless 83 of a 156 stand in three hours Maurice hit 13 fours before O'Reilly bowled him off the inside edge. On his way to 78 Wyatt survived a low slipchance. He picked the safest direction – over the narrow side boundaries – for a hook off Wall and two sweeps off Grimmett to make himself the only English-man who has hit three sixes in a Test innings in Australia. Artful flight brought Grimmett revenge when a mishit was caught by Richardson.

Seven out for 236 on the day (98 eight ball overs) left Eddie Paynter only tailenders for company in his first Test innings against Australia. Jardine had chosen the Lancashire left-hander to replace the Nawab of Pataudi, although a few weeks earlier the Indian prince had scored 102 on his five-hour Test début. Pataudi later joked: 'It's a dangerous thing to score a century in our team – you'll get yourself dropped.' Some thought Jardine felt the Nawab too slow a scorer (a fine distinction!) or it might have been because of another witticism. To maintain maximum pressure in the leg-trap wing of the bodyline attack Jardine had directed that, if a batsman hit a ball hard to leg, there must be no flinching among the arc of close fieldsmen. Once Jardine himself had involuntarily flinched, causing Pataudi to say: 'Skipper, you seem to have forgotten your own instructions!' Such an undiplomatic shaft was not good for the discipline the iron-willed captain thought necessary to carry through his strategy in the face of resentment from the batsmen, tirades from several critics and vituperation from crowds enraged by the frequency of bouncers.

Smallest of England's team, Paynter, 5 feet $5\frac{1}{2}$ inches, had the nimblest footwork. Twinkling feet often carried him along the track to combat Grimmett, O'Reilly and Ironmonger, all at a disadvantage against a quick-footed left-hander (it was four years before the leg-before-wicket law was extended to balls pitching outside the off stump). Eddie's drives, hooks, cuts and glances, nine of them to the fence, earned a Saturday crowd's unstinted applause in his three-hour innings of 77 before Fingleton caught his attempted hook off Wall. Nobody had expected Hedley Verity to stay $2\frac{1}{2}$ hours and make 45, aided by a couple of chances. He was one of Wall's five victims in England's total of 341, made in $7\frac{1}{4}$ hours.

The match was almost eight hours old before anything caused an outbreak of ill-feeling that had been festering for two months since the first trial of bodyline – which had been primarily designed to bring Bradman's excessive scoring back to a more reasonable level. In a Melbourne match in November five fielders had been posted behind the batsmen's legs before bouncers struck Woodfull's chest and rattled Bradman. Don looked as if he thought Larwood and Bowes were trying to skewer him to the sightscreen. The word bodyline had been coined in December in an attempt to label a type of direct attack as different from traditional leg-theory as an inter-continental missile from a boy's paper dart. At practice two days before the Adelaide Test the sight of Bowes skittling Jardine's stumps brought a loud cheer from watchers behind the nets, followed by heckling and jeering. As the noise upset concentration, the captain curtailed the spoilt practice and complained to the Board of Control. Next day locked gates and police guards kept out all 'except officials whose presence was indispensable'. So fuel was heaped on smouldering acrimony! All around Australia on the morning of the match, reports about locked gates and police guards pushed into the background what normally would have been the barred reporters' Test previews.

After his first over toward the cathedral end Larwood saw Fingleton touch Allen's third ball into Ames' gloves. As spearhead of the bodyline attack, Larwood's pattern was to bowl to four slips while the shiny ball would swing out for him. When it lost its gloss he would run wide of the stumps to deliver shorter breakbacks that leapt at right-hand batsmen trying to protect their bodies without popping catches to five leg-trap fieldsmen, backed by two leg outfields.

The fifth ball of Larwood's second over bounced inches from Woodfull's head. Moving across for back-foot defence as the next pitched short outside the off stump, the captain was struck over the heart when the ball broke in. The bat fell from his hands and he clutched his chest as he doubled up in pain. An angry hoot exploded from the outer crowd, most of whom had seen photographs of Woodfull suffering a similar blow in Melbourne. Allen, Jardine and other fieldsmen ran to offer sympathy to the stricken skipper and booing continued for three minutes before he recovered enough to resume. Meanwhile Jardine had walked down to Larwood, whom Hammond was encouraging to take no notice of the trouble brewing at the ringside.

In his book *The Larwood Story* the bowler recalls that Jardine said to him: 'Well bowled, Harold!' Larwood knew what this meant, as Bradman was standing only a few feet away and Jardine was trying to unsettle him by making him believe the ball was being bowled intentionally to hit the man. The roar the blow caused was mild compared with the sequel when, as Larwood began to run up for his next over, Jardine clapped his hands to stop him and motioned slipfielders across to the leg trap, leaving Voce alone at deep backward point. At the sight of the hateful bodyline field-setting being used against a batsman who had just been shaken by a severe knock a thunderous bellow burst from the crowd, not only those on the open green mounds but many in the shaded stands lining the western side of the oval. The noise, growing louder as Larwood ran to the crease, doubled when the next ball, a bouncer, knocked the bat from Woodfull's hands.

Everyone who knows the Notts speedman is aware that the combative side of his nature contains nothing vindictive or spiteful. Somebody even said he wouldn't hurt a fly. Perhaps so, but he wasn't bowling against flies, and barrackers' howls spurred him to a high pitch of hostility. Savage roars started up every time he bowled. Seeing Bradman evade several bumpers in the seven balls after Woodfull was hit, Larwood bustled Don (8) into spooning a catch to silly-leg, Allen. McCabe (8) uneasily deflected the last ball of his seventh over to fine-leg, Jardine. His dominance disturbingly asserted on a now-dull pitch, Larwood was rested after eight overs.

Several shortish balls from the three fast bowlers rapped Woodfull around the haunches – an occupational risk against pacemen – while he hung on for three-quarters of an hour before Allen bowled him via the bat for 22. Four were down for 51 but England missed Voce's left-hand skip-bombing when an ankle strain put him off the field for the last hour of the second day. A loudspeaker call for a doctor set the crowd thinking aid was needed for Woodfull, instead of Voce. Fresh taunts were hurled at Larwood. Whenever his captain fielded near the boundary jeers came from some of the crowd. The politest remarks heard were: 'Do you call this sport?' and 'Why don't you play cricket, Jardine?'

Woodfull, who to that stage had not resorted to newly-created anti-bodyline chest pads, was lying on a massage table receiving treatment for a livid bruise on the breast when MCC manager P. F. Warner walked in to express sympathy. Woodfull replied: 'I do not wish to discuss it, Mr Warner.'

Warner: 'Why, what is the matter?'

Woodfull: 'There are two sides out there. One is playing cricket and the other is not. The game is too good to be spoilt.

It is time some people got out of the game. Good afternoon.'

From later talks with Woodfull I gathered that he felt his words might bring home to the team managers the necessity for them to do something about tactics that threatened to ruin the game. In this his utterance was ineffective, but news of it had an impact on public opinion like a flour-bomb on a university chairman. Half-a-dozen players had heard their skipper's words. When these became known outside, 'Plum' Warner jumped to the conclusion that they had been divulged by Fingleton, a journalist. This deduction by Sir Pelham (as he became three years later) ran counter to a well-founded belief in the Australian team that another batsman with quick perception, realising the full significance of his captain's reproof, thought it would be a mistake if the truth were hushed up. The players heard that the news was imparted next day at a rendezvous in a car on North Terrace with a pressman he could trust to keep the source confidential. So as not to leave an obvious trail, Claude Corbett did not keep the facts for a scoop in his own paper alone but shared some of them with other writers when they returned from Sunday cricket in the hills.

Numbers of people who had not seen the tactics had, like the folk at home, regarded it as inconceivable that an English team could resort to the methods reported. That such an eminently fair-minded man of Woodfull's high principles should have been moved to speak so, caused many of them to take a closer look, among them Sir Robert Menzies.

As Bill Ponsford walked from the stand stairway to the arena gate a friend in the crowd, wishing to know the name of his hotel, called: 'Where are you staying, Ponny?' The sturdy Victorian answered: 'Out in the middle for as long as I can.' Three-and-a-half hours he stayed. His 85 contained a few chances but eight fours came from the middle of his heavy bat and he endured punishment in a manner that gave the attackers no encouragement. In Larwood's words, Ponsford suffered more than anybody in the match and showed he could take a hiding. On his doings in the heat of the battle, Harold could have been barred for life from the Anti-Vivisection Society! Padding saved Ponsford's torso from the full force of many blows but 11 bruises

31

were visible when he changed. (A newcomer under a shower in a later match, seeing purple blotches with yellow haloes on Bill's side, back and hip, wondered was he suffering from some strange disease!) Australia's hopes of matching England's 341 faded when Ponsford, trying to glance Voce, was bowled behind his well-nourished calves after lunch on the third day.

Billy Woodfull came hurrying out in civvies to where I lay. Though naturally a mild-mannered, scholastic type of man he came out in a way clearly indicating that one of his men had been hurt and he was going to take over. He helped me up, saying 'Come along, Bertie'. With his arm supporting me I was able to walk off, although still dazed and shaken by the shock.'

Six were down for 194 but Oldfield produced his most stylish strokes for 41 before he was accidentally knocked out by a ball from Larwood. Here is the dapper player's recollection of how it happened: 'After I glanced a ball to the boundary Larwood dropped the next one short, almost a foot outside the off stump. I think I could have hit it to the off for maybe two but – as an admirer of Charlie Macartney, who influenced my outlook on batting – I was not satisfied to score fewer than the maximum number of runs from any ball. So I decided to step across and hook it for four. You may wonder how Larwood's pace allowed time for this but the definitive speed of the brain is something wonderful.

'I hooked a fraction too soon and the ball struck me here' – with a wicketkeeper's gnarled fingers he touched the right side of his forehead, just below the hairline. 'How lucky I was! Had it struck me here' (fingering his temple a couple of inches lower) 'it would have been the end of me. By good fortune it hit the thickest part of my cranium. These are all afterthoughts, of course. The blow knocked me over and for a while I lay stunned.

Larwood was not bowling to a bodyline field-setting as all the recognised batsmen were out. But Oldfield was going along so well that, soon after taking a new ball at 200, he dropped one short to unsettle him. 'All hell broke loose when the ball hit Oldfield,' the bowler says. 'Critics and spectators had been prophesying that bodyline would kill someone sooner or later. It now seemed that dark moment had arrived. Bert dropped his bat, clutched his head in both hands, staggered away from the wicket and fell to his knees. As a low rumble of hooting and rage swelled from the crowd I ran to the crumpled figure and said "I'm sorry Bertie". "It's not your fault Harold" Oldfield mumbled as soon as he was able to speak. The scene that followed was one that had never erupted on any other cricket field and it is difficult to imagine it ever being repeated.'

Thousands of infuriated onlookers began counting Larwood and Jardine out. From the mound they beefed : 'One, two, three, four, five, six, seven, eight, nine, OUT, you b——!' Others bellowed : 'Go home, you Pommy b——s!' Barrackers untiringly repeated a noun that, in the cussword vocabulary of the time, had more offensive personal connotations than its surface asper-sion on the chastity of the recipient's mother. The word carried more sting than it does in today's permissive society or it did in William the Conqueror's day. Occasionally amid the hubbub a few coarser hecklers rang in other improper nouns, one of which Sir Alan Herbert has called a short and unattractive word. If Napoleon, who labelled the British a nation of shopkeepers, had been resurrected to watch this day he could have called South Australians a nation of bullock-drivers.

The blow made Adelaide Oval like one huge hornets' nest. As Allen brought a jug and towel to bathe Oldfield's head many in the crowd worked themselves into a frenzy. Maurice Tate, watching from in front of England's dressing-room, said in his low voice : 'I'm getting out of here,' and went inside. Larwood thought that if one man jumped the fence the whole mob would go for the English team. He and others moved toward the stumps, ready to grab them if a mob rushed the field (as hap-pened in 1879 when barrackers' invasions after a run-out dispute stopped play at Sydney and A. N. Hornby seized and marched off a larrikin who menaced Lord Harris with a stick).

The whole ground was in uproar for five minutes. It seemed longer. The next batsman, O'Reilly, took some time to get on to the field as he had to force his way down crowded steps between rows of incensed members standing on their seats as they gave vent to their indignation. The members were restrained by comparison with the outer crowd. On the mound near the scoreboard bar men were jumping in the air shaking their fists and even the mounted troopers' horses seemed restive.

Unwilling to bowl amid such din, Larwood lay on the grass, tossing the ball in his hand. The 32,500 present were making as much noise as almost 51,000 had on Saturday. When Oval officials appealed for police reinforcements constables were hurriedly mustered at Angas Street headquarters on the other side of town. When Hammond ended Australia's innings at 222, a deficit of 119, not a clap was heard as the Englishmen left the field, their faces set in resentment of the crowd's rancour. They could scarcely have expected three hearty British cheers! As they mounted the stairs, wrathful members stood enfilading them with insulting crossfire.

Whatever the merits and demerits of Jardine's captaincy, his courage, like his success, was beyond question. With the risk that some inflammatory incident might touch off a mob incursion, it might have seemed politic for him to bat later but between-innings rumblings, audible in the dressing-room, not only failed to deter him from again opening the innings but provoked him into putting away his true-blue England cap and hauling out his longest-peaked and loudest multi-coloured Harlequin cap – one that might almost make itself heard above the din. Amid hoots he pointedly took strike instead of Sutcliffe, but there were some counter-cheers from the stands. In the evening a mob waited to boo the Englishmen leaving the ground. Constables stood near them and one policeman walked close behind Larwood. More abuse was heard but no attempt was made to molest him.

As no arc of short-leg fielders had been associated with the two most damaging balls of the match pitching outside the off stump, neither could properly be called bodyline delivery. The demonstrators, indelicately ignoring that scrupulous distinction, read them into the general context of events which rendered the intimidated batsmen jittery. The Board of Control had failed to heed Bradman's suggestion for action while the series stood one-all in Melbourne but the impassioned Adelaide demonstrators forced the hand of Board members attending the match. Interviewing the MCC co-managers, they suggested that the controversial bowling be called off. Replying that they had no power to interfere with the captain's control on the field, the managers fobbed them off by hinting that a cablegram to the Marylebone C.C. might meet the case. Hence the pyramids, as the saying goes. It was not foreseen that a message drafted while Oldfield's wound was covered with plaster would have a tone that shocked

MCC committeemen, who had no evidence of what was really happening.*

The undiplomatic cable read : 'Bodyline bowling has assumed such proportions as to menace the best interests of the game, making protection of the body by the batsmen the main consideration. This is causing intensely bitter feeling between the players as well as injury. In our opinion it is unsportsmanlike. Unless stopped at once it is likely to upset the friendly relations existing between Australia and England.'

Though without foundation, reports of dissension in the England side were taken seriously enough for a night team meeting to be called to vote confidence in Jardine.

The match went on, with one eye fluttering between the wireless counter and the skipper's cap, flaunting bold quarters of deep crimson, indigo blue and a light yellow ochre. It made a showy contrast with the dark, glistening hair of Victor Richardson, keeping wicket because a lineal fracture of the frontal bone had put Oldfield out of the match (and the following Test).

Disdainful of barrackers' jibes – some exhorted Wall to give him a dose of his own medicine by knocking him over – the angular captain took no more notice of noises than if they had come from Adelaide Zoo. Picture Lawry in a Harlequin cap and cream choker, sternly guarding his wicket right-handed, and you have the nearest thing to Jardine that day: 6 foot 2 inches of fleshless concentration, but with a nose more like Julius Caesar's.

Jardine owned the straightest bat in captivity. Captivity is right; he kept it in close custody while 56 runs accrued to him at the rate of 13 an hour. No doubt his intention was to wear down the bowling but he wore the barrackers' tempers raw. When a shoulder of his bat broke and he sent for another bat hecklers advised him : 'You won't need it, you b——!'

Immobile periods made it easier for flies to settle on him. Once as he swished them off a voice called : 'Don't swat those flies, Jardine – they're the only friends you've got in Australia.' (Douglas himself thought that less funny than a remark from the Sydney Hill as he was being handed a drink on the field : 'Don't give the b—— a drink ! Let him die of thirst !')

* See *The World of Cricket*, pages 126 to 128, 307 to 311.

If anyone expected the stir about the Board's cable, on top of
the first-innings scenes, to cause Jardine to modify bodyline in
the last innings they underestimated the character and inflexibility
of purpose of England's captain, a Scot of unbending backbone.
Though the only time he left his team on tour was to go trout
fishing, the stork-like angler was not swayed by a Victorian's
contention that bouncers to batsmen hemmed in by leg-trap fieldsmen were tantamount to putting a rainbow trout in a pail of
water and fishing for him with a rod and line.

Jardine's 13-an-hour rate was the chief reason why England
averaged only 2.1 runs an eight-ball over. The side's stylemaster,
Hammond, was making the bowlers feel his wicket was little
larger than a postcard. Toward the day's end Woodfull tossed
the ball to Bradman, causing Hammond and Ames to confer,
as they had never seen him bowl. After Ames cracked a long-hop
for four and a full-flopper for a single, Hammond called to him :
'There are only two overs to go, so don't try to make a meal
of Braddles. We don't want to lose another wicket tonight.' Wally
played the next ball quietly but it was followed by another full-
pitch. It was too tempting for Hammond who tried to hit it
too far – by the look of it a mile, when 100 yards would have
done. His head came up, he missed the ball and it was straight
enough to bowl him for 85. Even a player of such emotional
mien as Hammond was upset by missing 100 with an out-of-
control shot at a ball that deserved anything except a wicket. His
swarthy face looked livid as he walked away. Perhaps such
untoward fate made Wally regret not having asserted himself a
little more in the last hour of his 221-minute innings.

Hobbling on an ankle wrenched in a fielding mishap, Paynter
tried to bat. He was left not out when England finished with
412 midway through the fifth day, unassailably ahead by 531.

On the fifth afternoon, as Larwood had Fingleton and Ponsford out with only 12 on the board, a Wednesday crowd of
24,500 cheered him in six sizzling overs to a slipfield. Cheers
turned to boos when he switched to bodyline. To make the most
of Larwood and Allen's rest period Bradman tore into the other
bowlers, racing past 50 in little more than an hour. After on-
driving Verity for six he was out next ball for 66 when the
Yorkshire left-hander held a hot drive intended to be Don's
eleventh four.

No partner could build on Woodfull's anchor-man foundations (he scarcely averaged one run an over). Watching his side crumple for 193, the Melbourne High School master looked ready to defend Australia to the last rabbit-burrow. When Allen's eighth wicket of the match brought England victory, Woodfull, 73 without a chance, carried his bat through a completed Test innings. He was the only man to do so a second time, the first having been for 30 of Australia's 66 at Brisbane in 1928 when two injured batsmen were absent.

England's Adelaide win was by 338 runs, the widest margin gained there since W. G. Grace was captain in 1892. Several larger crowds have since watched Tests at Melbourne, Sydney and some Indian grounds but the six-day total of 174,452 in 1933 still stands as an Adelaide record in which unprecedented publicity played a considerable part.

Before playing (and winning) the remaining Tests at Brisbane and Sydney, Jardine insisted on withdrawal of the imputation that his sort of leg-theory was unsportsmanlike. Several days of tension and much buzzing of wireless messages were needed to wring this reluctant retraction from the Board, put on the spot by MCC's offer to permit the rest of the tour to be cancelled.

It took 20 years for all parties to hammer out a workable rule to outlaw persistent and systematic intimidation. By then Larwood had migrated with his family to Sydney, where all his five daughters have married. On a business visit as a solicitor 21 years after the Battle of Adelaide, Jardine at 53 was able to say: 'Though they may not generally hail me as Uncle Doug, I am no longer the bogeyman – just an old so-and-so who got away with it.'

Adelaide, Jan. 13, 14, 16, 17, 18, 19, 1933. England won by 338 runs.

ENGLAND 1st innings, 437 minutes		2nd innings, 560 minutes	
H. Sutcliffe, c Wall b O'Reilly	9	c O'Brien (sub) b Wall ...	7
D. R. Jardine (c) b Wall... ...	3	lbw Ironmonger	56
W. R. Hammond, c Oldfield b Wall	2	b Bradman	85
L. E. G. Ames, b Ironmonger ...	3	b O'Reilly... ...	69
M. Leyland, b O'Reilly	83	c Wall b Ironmonger ...	42
R. E. S. Wyatt, c Richardson b Grimmett	78	c Wall b O'Reilly	49
E. Paynter, c Fingleton b Wall	77	not out	1
G. O. B. Allen, lbw Grimmett ...	15	lbw Grimmett	15
H. Verity, c Richardson b Wall... ...	45	lbw O'Reilly	40
W. Voce, b Wall	8	b O'Reilly... ...	8
H. Larwood, not out	3	c Bradman b Ironmonger	8
B 1, lb 7, nb 7	15	B 17, lb 11, nb 4	32
Total off 146.1 overs	341	Total off 191.3 overs ...	412

Fall—4, 16, 16, 30, 186, 196, 228, 324, 336, 341.
7, 91, 123, 154, 245, 296, 394, 395, 403, 412.

Bowling.	Balls	Runs	Wkts.			Balls	Runs	Wkts.	
Wall	205	72	5	...	...	174	75	1	Aust.
O'Reilly	300	82	2	...	...	303	79	4	122 balls
Ironmonger	120	50	1	...	...	342	87	3	an hour;
Grimmett	168	94	2	...	...	210	74	1	2.95 min.
McCabe	84	28	—	...	...	96	42	—	an over
		Bradman		...	...	24	23	1	

AUSTRALIA 1st innings, 322 minutes		2nd innings, 235 minutes	
J. H. Fingleton, c Ames b Allen	0	b Larwood	0
W. M. Woodfull (c.) b Allen ...	22	not out	73
D. G. Bradman, c Allen b Larwood	8	c & b Verity	66
S. J. McCabe, c Jardine b Larwood ...	8	c Leyland b Allen ...	7
W. H. Ponsford, b Voce... ...	85	c Jardine b Larwood ...	3
V. Y. Richardson, b Allen ...	28	c Allen b Larwood ...	21
W. A. Oldfield, retired hurt ...	41	absent injured	0
C. V. Grimmett, c Voce b Allen ...	10	b Allen	6
T. W. Wall, b Hammond ...	6	b Allen	0
W. J. O'Reilly, b Larwood ...	0	b Larwood	5
H. Ironmonger, not out... ...	0	b Allen	0
B 2, lb 11, nb 1	14	B 4, lb 2, w 1, nb 5 ...	12
Total off 94.4 overs	222	Total off 71.2 overs ...	193

Fall: 1, 18, 34, 51, 131, 194, 212, 222, 222.
3, 12, 100, 116, 171, 183, 183, 192, 193.

Bowling.	Balls	Runs	Wkts.			Balls	Runs	Wkts.	
Larwood	150	55	3	...	...	114	71	4	England
Allen	138	71	4	...	...	104	50	4	107 balls
Hammond	106	30	1	...	...	54	27	—	an hour
Voce	84	21	1	...	...	24	7	—	3.35 min.
Verity	96	31	—	...	...	120	26	1	an over.

Umpires: George A. Hele, George E. Borwick.

Chapter Five

FLYING BOTTLES

IN Guyana's capital, Georgetown, parasols are more in demand than pyjamas and less dispensable. Outside the Dutch-designed city's Bourda cricket ground a Guyanese girl cyclist in a leopard-pattern skirt held a yellow sunshade aloft at an angle that made me wonder how she could see where she was going.

Inside the world's most tropical Test ground some of the men, too, have parasols, gay splashes here and there on sun-scorched northern benches near the scoreboard. The score can be viewed more comfortably over an iced rum-and-soda in shaded bars in two pavilions built with their backs to the flaming west. Here you meet such men as Berkeley Gaskin, a public notary who became a successful Test team manager, chatting with famous veteran cricketers Lance Gibbs, Basil Butcher, Joe Solomon, now a solicitor, Clifford McWatt and George Camacho, father of opening batsman Stephen Camacho.

For players and watchers here cricket is a truly multi-racial game. Typified by Lloyd, Gibb and Butcher, one-third of the people, whose ancestors 150 years ago where woolly-topped slaves from Africa, are now outnumbered but not surpassed in keenness by the straight haired half of the population (Kanhai is one). Descended from estate labourers indented from India these East Indians grow most of Guyana's sugar and rice. Add a sprinkling of Portuguese and Amerindians and you still have segments of mixed races left over. To be teasingly called Mudlanders or Mudheads by islanders from Trinidad, Barbados and Jamaica scarcely ruffles the pride of the Guyanese. In a semi-open-air bar amid piers supporting the Woodbine Hotel, they tell you how, before W. G. Grace's father was born, the country was a Dutch colony, until captured by the British – with the sly addition : 'The Dutch did not put up much of a fight for it.'

If below-sea-level Georgetown has to wait for low tide before its sluice-gates open to empty the city's drains through the sea wall, I found Guyanese hospitality always at spillover level, with no perceptible wait between drinks. If we take medical scientists' word that a man can perspire up to two pints of sweat an hour this is the place to do it. For batsmen running in pads, bowlers toiling up to the crease and fieldsmen in vain chases on a small, fast field, I am tempted to call it the exhaust-pipe of the world.

A shop salesman or chauffeur trying to keep a family on the equivalent of £2.60 sterling a week, a labourer earning 31p a day (£1.50 in West Indian dollars) or a sugar plantation worker whose job was only seasonal, could afford only cheap seats in 1954 to see the strongest English team that had visited the West Indies. In the last days of February, they watched through an eight-foot high wire-mesh fence, designed to prevent over-excited fans intruding on the field.

It was a timely toss for captain Len Hutton to win, as the tour had been going badly. After wresting the Ashes from the Australians in England in 1953 it was disappointing for his side to lose the first and second Tests by 140 runs in Jamaica and 181 in Barbados. Adding sting to those honourable defeats an accumulation of misunderstandings and unpleasant incidents prevented the Englishmen from being as popular as most of the sides MCC had sent abroad. Among these were instances of pavilion attendants over-officiously turning back guests invited by England's captain and leading players. In two or three cases of a sort which Englishmen particularly dislike, fieldsmen had no doubt about low catches yet saw batsmen remain, necessitating appeals to umpires to confirm the dismissals.

Most of the friction came from dissatisfaction with the umpiring, a state of mind not eased after it became known that toughs had menaced Jamaica's top umpire Perry Burke. After rejection of an appeal for a catch behind the wicket an English cap was thrown on the ground. Manager Charles Palmer had to advise a couple of young players to eliminate gesticulations that might cause offence. Some senior players also set crowds buzzing. No doubt the Englishmen would have been able to bear all afflictions better had they been uplifted by the buoyancy success brings.

Conventional concern was felt in the islands about some of forthright Freddie Trueman's words and deeds on his first shake-

down tour. It's a long way from the snow-clad haunts of the
yeti to the sunny Caribbean yet for a while some West Indians
seemed to be thinking of Freddie as the Abominable Trueman!
Island newspapers were reprinting criticisms from eight touring
London pressmen who were dismayed to see their saltiest snippets
cabled back out of context. In his *West Indian Adventure* E. W.
Swanton of London *Daily Telegraph* says this just about completed the impression in the minds of many West Indians that
English fair play was a thing of the past.

Reading a less-known London pressman's opinion that England
had to play 13 men – implying that the umpires were on the
other side – West Indians assumed that this was echoing squeals
emanating from the team. Accompanied by Coleman's Calypso
Boys' steel band, Lord Kitchener sang plaintively:

De MCC proclaim dat dey are not pleased
About some unfair decisions in de West In-dies.
Well, in de cricket season dese things always happen,
So Ah'm askin you please
Don't put de blame on de West In-dies . . .
It happens in England and Australia.
De rules and regulations: no man condemn de umpire's decision.
Dat's why Ah'm askin you please
Don't put de blame on de West In-dies.

Incidents in a preceding colony game against Guyana (then
called British Guiana) left Hutton without faith in the two local
umpires appointed for the Georgetown Test so he asked either
that Burke and Tom Ewart be flown in from Jamaica (1,200
miles by Viking prop aircraft) or Harold Walcott and Cortez
Jordan from Barbados (400 miles) – the two who had no-balled
Tony Lock's elbowy fast ball three times earlier in the month.
Officials' fears of trouble if umpires were imported caused
England to agree to have E. S. Gillette, a Chinese customs agent
who had umpired when Hutton played in the 1948 Georgetown
Test, and Indian groundsman Badge Menzies, the Bourda
wicket-maker and coach to the Georgetown umpire's association.
If bi-lingual Gillette is addressed in English he answers to 'Errol',
if in Chinese to 'Wing'. As umpire he has the shortest coat and
the longest dismissal finger in South America. Menzies, short

but equally conscientious, finished the pitch sitting in a combined mower-and-roller, spinning it around like a dodgem-
car in a fun park. Both umpired the six-day Test without
pay.

Despite pre-match rumblings the start was peaceful – too
peaceful for most of the 15,000 Guyanese present, whether it
was the three-quarter pace opening bowling of all-rounders
Gerry Gomez and Frank Worrell or the half-pace scoring of
Hutton and Willie Watson. Once captain Jeffrey Stollmeyer,
leaping at second slip, had tried to catch Watson (4) off Gomez.
As if conserving their energies for lunch, the two Yorkshiremen
quietly picked up 33 runs before Sonny Ramadhin spun a ball
back inside the left-hander's defensive push. Agile fielding allowed
England only 40 runs in 90 minutes before the interval.

The crowd's noisy protests after lunch might have influenced
England's youngest batsman, 24-year-old Peter May, to hook too
adventurously at medium-paced Atkinson and fall leg-before-
wicket for 12. Loss of the second wicket at 76 brought in sun-
tanned Denis Compton, his rolling gait perhaps more evident
because of recent knee cartilage trouble. Here we had England's
two pre-eminent batsmen of the first post-war decade. Knowing
this, the crowd grumbled when neither batted up his reputation.
A new ball, taken after 65 overs before the total reached 100,
served no more purpose than to allow stock bowlers Ramadhin
and Atkinson a few overs' rest and the crowd a couple of
authentic strokes to applaud.

With 107 for two wickets by tea interval and two great batsmen well set, they had unobtrusively reached the sort of position
that consistently governs England's batting policy: a platform
from which to attack tiring bowlers. On this day it did not
work out that way. Each averaged only 16 runs an hour. At
practice early on the tour the skipper had nodded toward the
sun as he told his players: 'That fellow up there shining all
day is the best bowler out here.' Not much better than Ramadhin, though, or so it appeared. Stollmeyer had called on the
spinner when the total was only 16. On this plumb Bourda pitch
neither Ram nor Valentine could coax the ball to perform
unplayable tricks of the kind that, on softer surfaces, brought
them 59 wickets in five Tests in England in 1950 – and won

calypso immortality in the line : 'Hail to the bowling superfine of Ramadhin and Valentine.'

Compton felt he was labouring under a self-imposed jinx. Back in Jamaica earlier, as Graveney and Watson were hitting huge sixes off left-hand spinner Alf Valentine in a colony game, Compton had rested an arm on Ram's shoulder and jested: 'Take a look, Sonny – the shape of things to come !' The shape Denis had prophesied was a long time coming.

Though Hutton comes from the same country as Captain Cook, the navigator who for better or worse put Australia on the map, Sir Leonard concentrated his reign to a realm within a yard or metre of his blockhole; to him, explorations farther along the pitch would have meant venturing into unchartered seas. Unlike Harvey or Hassett, he was never a believer in skipping forward to turn Ram's length balls into half-volleys. Sonny had done a day's work by tea (25 six-ball overs, 16 of them scoreless). Yet, as the sun was their witness, the distinguished pair were still unable to find more than seven runs in the last half-hour. Hutton, though seldom beaten, batted all day for 84 off 106 overs in five hours (less ten minutes off for rain). England averaged not quite a run and a half an over. Besides Ram's 31 overs for 39 runs Atkinson bowled 28 overs of off-cutters for only 24. Swanton summed it up this way : 'Under the old order it was the bowlers who by now had become tired. According to the English system of the 1950s the bowlers remain fresh while the batsmen wear themselves remorselessly down.'

With only five regular batsmen in the England XI, Swanton sensed in every stroke of Hutton's, in every protective movement of his legs his apprehension for his side if he should get out. All four batsmen appeared to feel that, if runs did not come from them, they would not come at all (though this pessimistic approach was spurned next day by the last six – Wardle, Bailey, Evans, Laker, Lock and Statham – making 156, more than one-third of England's 435).

Those who came back to watch the second day – risking scoffing as gluttons for punishment – had their faith rewarded by seeing attractive strokes Hutton and Compton had mostly kept hidden on the woebegone Wednesday. Hutton, the finest cover-driver in the game, took command and Compton, the surest sweeper, helped carry their third-wicket stand to 150.

Hutton astonished everyone by dragging balls from Valentine, well outside the off stump, across to the leg side, guarded by only two men. Such daring strokes against the tide would once have courted disaster but Hutton's observant blue eyes noted that Val had unwittingly departed from the side-on action that helped give him more turn than any other left-hander since sheltered wickets came in. As the general tendency of Val's bowling had become inward with his arm, Hutton was actually hitting with the tide, though appearances suggested rank unorthodoxy. To strengthen the leg side Stollmeyer had to switch a man from the covers, and the crowd saw the usual procedure reversed when fieldsmen set deeper for Hutton came in closer for Compton.

The custom of cutting out shots before an interval contributed to the downfall of Compton (64). Five minutes before lunch he pushed Atkinson's off-cutter to Stollmeyer at forward short-leg. Graveney, on his way to becoming England's surest player of leg spin since Hammond, learned never to trust a spinner, not even one whose deceitful arm hid in a buttoned-down sleeve. After several balls from Ramadhin's flicking fingers had not turned, a leg-break spun almost the width of the stumps, leaving Tom standing.

Promotion of Johnny Wardle to invigorate England's lagging run-rate was an imaginative move that deserved success. Providence concurred, as Stollmeyer dropped a mishit. The miss denied Ram this wicket at six and he had to wait until the Yorkshire pair put on 79. Hutton allowed himself the liberty of on-driving the accurate Atkinson for four and six. This prompted the appearance of the third new ball before 300, but again the wicketless medium-pacers did no more than give Ram a rest. After 7¾ chanceless hours Hutton swept at the little spinner and was caught behind square-leg after adding 85 this day to reach 169.

Playing the right game for a tail-ender, England's fourth Yorkshire-born man, Jim Laker, swung Val for six and two in an over, only to be bowled by the left-hander for 27. Judging by joyful caperings around the boundary, this was the most stirring event of the match so far, indicating the crowd's awareness that it was the popular Jamaican's 100th wicket in Test cricket. Playing his 19th Test, Val was the first bowler to reach this milestone inside four years. He did so four months quicker than England's record-holder, Alec Bedser, and in one Test fewer than Bill O'Reilly. (First to reach 100 before turning 24 Valentine held this distinction for ten years until fast bowler Graham Mc-Kenzie captured his 100th wicket three months younger, in his 23rd Test for Australia).

A Benaud at Georgetown might have aimed to get the West Indians in for a half-a-dozen overs at the fag-end of two tiring days in the field but when the second day ended with the total 401 off 211 overs, England's rate was still short of two runs an over and two wickets had yet to fall.

One was that of Trevor Bailey who, although not fully recovered from a finger injury, made 49 as seventh man in a prospering innings. They took him $2\frac{1}{2}$ hours – breathless going for a man whose forward prod caused him to be regarded as the hangnail of Test cricket. Hitherto unrevealed shots which he played and attempted in this innings at last answered the jester at Lord's who, seeing Trevor heading for the nets, said : 'There's Bailey, going to practise his stroke.'

Considering the near-perfection of the pitch, I rank Rama-dhin's six wickets for 113 off 67 overs – a rate of $1\frac{3}{4}$ an over – ahead of more sensational figures on more helpful tracks. The round-cheeked little Indian with a toothbrush moustache and a toothpaste smile, who undid many a strong side with his either-way turn, stands only 5 ft. 4 in. but was entitled to feel 10 feet tall. Going on to a total of 158 victims in 43 Tests, Sonny was West Indies' heaviest wicket-taker until Wesley Hall fired out 192 men in 48 Tests and Lance Gibbs topped this with 209 in 51 Tests.

Ten and a half hours gone, more than one-third of the match time, before the West Indians, refreshed by a night's rest, were brought to the wicket to answer England's 435. As has become rather a pattern, England's bowlers had to make up for the time their batsmen had allowed to elapse.

In six overs on the fastest wicket of the series lithe Brian Statham, straightest of all fast bowlers, had three out for 12. Worrell, the most graceful and polished of the three Ws, snicked Statham's second ball to wicketkeeper Godfrey Evans. Sucking in his bottom lip, Frank departed scoreless. A dozen balls later an unplayable leg-cutter from Statham sent Stollmeyer's off stump cartwheeling two-thirds of the way toward the keeper. For powerful Walcott, Hutton brought two fielders insultingly close at silly mid-off and silly point. Trying to shift them, Clyde drove a four but inner-edged another ball into his stumps. This was one of 'George' Statham's characteristic in-cutters, after his first two victims had been surprised by balls that ran outward. Rating this the best opening burst by an English fast bowler since the war, his fellow-players had yet to see 'the Greyhound' in double harness with Frank Tyson in Australia later in the year. Rain denied England's bowlers opportunity to follow up Statham's Georgetown breakthrough in the afternoon.

An eventful 62 stand by Weekes and Robert Christiani, a local batsman, began the fourth day's excitements. Barbadian parents like to give a baptising parson something to roll his tongue around, hence the name Everton DeCourcy Weekes, which team-mates contracted to 'Shorty'. This nimble 5 ft. $7\frac{1}{2}$ in. strokesman was the only West Indian to exceed 4,000 runs in Tests until Sobers and Kanhai came along, and he made 15 of the three W's 39 Test hundreds. If Weekes ever heard of the injunctions against hooking early in an innings and cutting off-breaks he either knew they were meant for less voracious batsmen or suspected they were propaganda to put him off his game. Hooks as hard as Milburn's and square-cuts like Barrington's were among his many shots. The 'Barbados Butcher' – a bowler must have labelled him that – unexcelled in my time as a back-foot square-shot player, cut even Laker in a way nobody else dared.

If reducing a day's quota of overs was an unworthy part of Hutton's Test captaincy he deserved only praise in this match for realism in not placing outfields to dissuade the run-a-minute pair from attempting boundary hits. He was repaid when Christiani's uppish on-drive off Laker and Watson's forward dive from midwicket brought the fourth wicket at 78, though Willie's rolling catch was so low that the striker waited for the umpire's decision. As with Walcott a day earlier, Statham's breakback cannoned from Gomez's bat into his stumps. Half West Indies' wickets were down for 132 but, far from stalling for time, in-coming Denis Atkinson crossed the departing all-rounder midway to the wicket.

Loss of partners usually tautens a team's batting but Weekes was averaging two runs an over off his own omnivorous bat. At 94 Lock's best ball of the match turned past him and evidently clipped the off bail down, though Weekes' pads prevented the bowler and Umpire Gillette from seeing this. Unsure what had happened Everton waited while Gillette walked across to confirm from umpire Menzies that the ball had not rebounded from the wicketkeeper's pads. Who can tell what thoughts were set up in the crowd at the unusual sight of an appeal for bowled being necessary to dismiss a star batsman six runs short of 100? At the next interval Everton apologised for not having walked straight away and manager Palmer assured him that if he had been the batsman he would have waited for the decision. More than likely, betting contributed to the confused din – not only among those who had backed Weekes to make 100 but incidental bettors about which over would yield the 100th run, and which ball of which over! Atkinson's hard shoulder-high drive was heading for the unpopulated longfield when Lock bounded across to intercept it with one of the few left hands in the world that could have made a catch of it. Atkinson stayed on as substitute runner for John Holt, an opening batsman who had been kept back because of a pulled leg muscle. It limited him to prodding defence and waiting for short balls. England had a chance to get the eighth wicket at 141 when left-hander Clifford McWatt (5) edged Statham to second slip, where Compton did not sight the ball properly against the crowd. With the best stand of the innings McWatt and the crippled Holt revived hope that the West Indies might recover to 286 and so avoid the danger of having to follow on.

When their batsmen need one or two runs to reach 50 or 100 Guyanese clap gentle and rhythmic encouragement. They were doing so when the partners added 98. As McWatt, a local boy making good, tried to squeeze a second run for a leg hit the clapping rose in an excited crescendo. May's quick gather and throw above the bails at Evans' end ran out McWatt (54) by about two metres. Seeing Menzies signalling him out, as he must have expected, McWatt continued running on to the pavilion.

As Ramadhin joined Holt amid the noise of a row in a public stand behind square-leg, a bottle sailed over the wire-mesh on to the field. It was the forerunner of a barrage of bottles, followed by tins and boxes. Within seconds, hundreds of bottles lay in the outfield.

At Bourda cricket ground it is not far from the boundary wire to the square-leg position, as the bottle flies, so Menzies and the nearest fieldsman, May, lost no time in getting to safer terrain. As the pelting fever spread, isolated missiles fell on other parts of the field.

The Colony's Cricket Board secretary, Ken Wishart, who had been broadcasting with Crawford White, hurriedly handed the microphone to the Englishman, ran to the pavilion and telephoned police headquarters. HQ sent a helmeted riot squad with truncheons and teargas. A couple of dozen fans came inside the boundary, patrolled by a few mounted troopers, but only one ran to midfield. He spoke to Ramadhin then returned to the crowd.

In his book *Cricket Cauldron* Alex Bannister wrote. 'By now some boys, with highly-developed commercial instincts, had gone on the field to collect the bottles. Another missile narrowly missed the head of one of them. Immediately he picked up a bottle and returned it, with a strong left-arm action, right back into the thick of the stand from which most of them had been hurled. He followed up the attack strongly and then beat a gallant but hasty retreat. For ten minutes not a ball was bowled. Players and umpires stood there surveying the growing mess. Then Denis Compton tossed a bottle back to the edge of the boundary and Johnny Wardle raised a laugh, at least from part of the crowd by picking up another bottle, pretending to take a swig and feigning intoxication. This eased the situation but Mr W. S. Jones, president of the British Guiana Board of Control, acting on the advice of senior officials, then left the pavilion and went out to Hutton. 'This scene is becoming ugly,' he said, 'I think you and your team should come off the field.' To which Hutton made his magnificent reply: 'No, we'll stay. We want another wicket or two this evening because we want to win the match. These people are not going to get us off. That may be their idea but, if so, they are wrong.' 'The simple action of the dour, strong-minded England captain in turning his back on the mob and concentrating on the job in hand was a symbol of English character and, as such, more eloquent than a thousand speeches,

Six leg-trap fielders watch Woodfull duck under a Larwood bouncer, Brisbane, 1933. Bouncers hitting Woodfull and Oldfield, who was knocked out, infuriated an Adelaide crowd

Georgetown, 1954. Mounted police control the crowd after a shower of bottles and boxes halted play between England and West Indies. Left to right: Trevor Bailey, J. K. Holt, Tom Graveney, Umpire Badge Menzies, Brian Statham, and Denis Compton. Foreground: Umpire Wing Gillette and substitute runner Denis Atkinson

England's captain Len Hutton tells the Guyanese cricket president that the Englishmen want to stay on the field. 'We want more wickets,' said Hutton

A frightening fast bowler at peace; Chester Watson relaxes with a thriller that reminded passing batsmen of their peril

Surrounded by policemen, England's Ted Dexter is escorted off the bottle-strewn field, after a riot had ended the third day's play in the second test against the West Indies, Port of Spain, Trinidad, 1960

Rioting spectators invade the field amidst smoke and tear gas bombs thrown by the police, Calcutta, January, 1967. Police had charged hundreds forced on to the ground by overcrowding

more forceful than a volley of bullets. I have never felt prouder of "Our Len".'

In his *Island Cricketers* Walcott says Hutton's request for different umpires, however good his reasons may or may not have been, was obviously not calculated to please the Guyanese crowd which very quickly got wind of it . . . 'The run out decision cannot be said to have been responsible for the incident but, as it involved a local hero and came after ill-feeling had been mounting for some time, in a sense it pulled the trigger.'

Hutton could see a dozen men and boys inside the boundary picking up bottles and an attendant with a yardbroom sweeping debris away. As bottles, broken glass, fruit-juice cans, cigarette tins, cartons and wooden boxes littered the outfield when the game was resumed it could easily have been claimed that the ground was unfit for play but a much better purpose was served by getting the match going again. By bowling Ramadhin, Laker left only last man Valentine to be dismissed after the weekend.

When Saturday's play ceased at 5.30 p.m. more than 100 English residents and Guyanese friends hurried to line up in a protective avenue through which the players walked off. Thousands of the crowd swarmed on to other parts of the field but the police kept them at a distance. First off was Menzies, who ran to sanctuary in the pavilion and was joined from square-leg by Gillette, who had asked Godfrey Evans to bring in the ball and bails, so he could hurry off. The ever-indomitable Evans obliged and strolled off with Compton as if it were the placid end of a county game amid marquees at Canterbury. Threats from a group of drunken hooligans outside the ground caused police to guard Menzies' home on the Saturday and Sunday nights.

In horrified shame Georgetown's three daily newspapers deplored the disputing of a decision by a competent umpire whose fairness had never been questioned. The bottle-throwing interruption was castigated in such terms as 'unwarranted', 'a flagrant breach of good manners', 'indefensible', 'disgraceful', 'disgusting', 'mob rule', 'lawlessness and venom'; one even went as far as 'the jaws of hell'.

As a fire in the same weekend burned down a stand in Trinidad – scene of the next Test – relatives at home were alarmed about the safety of England's team. The depth of the anxiety largely depended on which of the eight versions they read. *The Cricketer's* correspondent, Philip Thomson, wrote: 'Disgusting as the outburst undoubtedly was, no missile was directed at any of the English players or the umpires, as readers of some of the English papers might have every excuse for believing.' It's the same the whole world over . . . Readers interested in getting the truth have to take the trouble to know where it is most likely to be found.

Extra police were assigned to the ground before the fifth day, when Hutton and Palmer assured the umpires that on their part every precaution would be taken to see that no harm would be done them. After Palmer discussed the situation with the Argyll and Sutherland Highlanders – who had been stationed in George-town because of a political crisis – they decided not to ask for troops to be posted at the ground because their presence would incite would-be demonstrators.

The wisdom of this decision was borne out by the trouble-free fifth and sixth days in which the West Indies, 251, followed on 184 behind and made 256 in the second innings. The riot squad remained outside in their trucks, not needed, and when England won by nine wickets Swanton said: 'The crowd greeted the English victory with admirable sportsmanship and good humour.'

An after-game talk between Hutton and Menzies brought out a point full of piquancy. With the advantage of hindsight from now knowing what players thought, the umpire concluded that he probably made one mistake in the match: on the day after the bottles flew he turned down an appeal against Holt in the second innings for a catch by Evans off Statham. As the West Indians doubted a leg-before-wicket ruling against Walcott at the other end, believing the ball was rising too high to have hit the stumps, Menzies felt the teams broke even in real umpiring errors. He waved aside imagined ones.

As, for two nights after the bottle outburst, Hutton scarcely slept it was rewarding to receive a message from Lord's: 'Best congratulations to you all on a well-deserved victory and to you on personal contribution and fine example in difficult circum-stances – MCC.' With that match as a turning point Hutton and his team fought back to square the rubber. (A year later he became the only England captain who has won series against Australia in both countries. The Queen honoured him with a knighthood.)

In Trinidad later West Indies Cricket Board president Sir Errol dos Santos told the Englishmen he had apologised in writing to MCC secretary Ronald Aird for the behaviour of some of the crowds. He regretted that cricket had come to resemble more a battle than friendly rivalry and hoped the authorities would act to ban bouncers before some terrible accident occurred.

Misgivings in Guyana caused the hope to be expressed that the bottle incident would not influence the Australians against playing a Test in Georgetown in the following year. When Ian Johnson's side arrived a state of emergency was still in force – it had begun four months before the Englishmen's Test, when alarmist reports made Whitehall so jumpy that two warships and a regiment had been sent there.

We found the Black Watch had taken over garrison duties, Parliament and the Constitution were suspended and an appointed Council was running the colony (Colin McDonald and I attended the opening of one session). The deposed Premier, Dr Cheddi Jagan, an Indian dentist, had been arrested for allegedly disobeying an order restricting his movements. His strawberry-blond Chicago-born wife Janet had been arrested for, it was said, holding an illegal procession in protest. Meetings were forbidden – even school speechnights – so our group's chatter over rum and iced cordials amid the Woodbine's foundation piers might well have been a breach of regulations.

Turning up reports of the bottle-throwing Senior Superintendent A. H. Jenkins, a Welshman in charge of uniformed police, said no offenders had been prosecuted because of the difficulty of detecting the throwers in the crowd. 'We think it was an instance of mob psychology,' he told me. 'One stupid man, probably drunk, threw the first bottle, followed by a lot of other stupid people. Some of these men have no fixed address and just as likely will be living at the other end of town with some other woman tomorrow. The political situation in the colony was then precarious but cricket proved stronger than politics.'

In bolstering up police at the grounds to 60 for the Australians'

Test, including 12 mounted troopers, Supt Jenkins said the increase was purely precautionary. His prophecy of no disturbance, provided no unfortunate incident occurred, was borne out, although difficult decisions against Weekes and Gary Sobers caused noisy confusion in the crowd. Johnson (eight wickets) and Benaud (three wickets in four balls) spun Australia to victory, backed by six wickets to wicketkeeper Gilbert Langley.

Guyanese applauded five centurymakers in Pakistan's Test at Georgetown in 1958 and three – Sobers 145, Subba Row 100 and Dexter 110 – in England's Test in 1960, but fresh politico-racial strife followed. When an 11-million-dollar fire destroyed the main shopping street in 1962 Georgetown's Test against India was switched to calmer Kingston. In an earlier sit-down in Governor Sir Ralph Grey's driveway, the People's National Congress chairwoman, Winnifred Gaskin, had been among those lifted bodily by police. Typifying ups-and-downs of life in an emerging country, this ebony Boadicea became a successful Education Minister by the time Australians and Englishmen played their next Tests in Georgetown in 1965 and 1968.

Despite turmoil inevitable in a land on the way to becoming a republic in 1970, cricket had again proved stronger than politics.

Georgetown. Feb. 24, 25, 26, 27, Mar. 1. 2, 1954. England won by 9 wickets.

ENGLAND 1st innings		2nd innings	
L. Hutton (c.) c Worrell b Ramadhin ...	169		
W. Watson b Ramadhin	12	not out	27
P. B. H. May lbw Atkinson...	12	b Atkinson	12
D. C. S. Compton c Stollmeyer b Atkinson	64		
T. W. Graveney b Ramadhin	0	not out	33
J. H. Wardle b Ramadhin	38		
T. E. Bailey c Weekes b Ramadhin ...	49		
T. G. Evans lbw Atkinson	19		
J. C. Laker b Valentine	27		
G. A. R. Lock b Ramadhin	13		
J. B. Statham not out	10		
B 20, nb 2	22	B 3	3
Total off 221 overs	435	One wicket (21.1 overs)	75

Fall: 33, 76, 226, 227, 306, 321, 350, 390, 412, 435.
18

Bowling.	Balls	Runs	Wkts.					Balls	Runs	Wkts.
Gomez	192	75	–	...	...	...	...	30	15	–
Worrell	96	33	–	...	...	...				
Ramadhin	402	113	6	...	...	...	...	24	7	–
Valentine	264	109	1	...						
Atkinson	348	78	3	...	...	...	...	42	34	1
Stollmeyer	12	3	–							
Walcott	12	2	–	...	...	...	...	12	6	–
Weekes								13	8	–
Christiani								6	2	–

WEST INDIES 1st innings		2nd innings	
F. M. Worrell c Evans b Statham	0	c Evans b Statham ...	2
J. B. Stollmeyer (c.) b Statham	2	c Compton b Laker ...	44
E. D. Weekes b Lock	94	c Graveney b Bailey ...	38
C. L. Walcott b Statham	4	lbw Laker	26
R. J. Christiani c Watson b Laker	25	b Bailey	11
G. E. Gomez b Statham	8	c Graveney b Wardle	35
D. Atkinson c & b Lock	0	b Wardle	18
C. A. McWatt run out, May to Evans ...	54	not out	9
J. K. Holt not out	48	b Lock...	64
S. Ramadhin b Laker	0	b Statham	1
A. L. Valentine run out	0	b Wardle	0
B 8, lb 7, w 1	16	B 2, lb 4, nb 2 ...	8
Total off 105.5 overs	251	Total, 117.3 overs ...	256

Fall: 1, 12, 16, 78, 132, 134, 139, 238, 240, 251
79, 96, 120, 168, 186, 200, 245, 246, 251, 256

Bowling.	Balls	Runs	Wkts.					Balls	Runs	Wkts.
Statham	162	65	4	...	...	...	...	132	86	2
Bailey	30	13	–	...	...	...	...	132	41	2
Laker	126	32	2	...	...	...	...	216	56	2
Wardle	132	59	–	...	...	...	...	75	24	3
Compton	18	6	–	...	...	...	...			
Lock	167	60	2	...	...	...	...	150	41	1

Runs per over: England 2.1. West Indies 2.27
Umpires: E. S. Gillette, B. Menzies

Chapter Six

TURMOIL IN TRINIDAD

HAD computers thought of taking over Test cricket a dozen years earlier their spools would have spun contentedly when fed with the names of the Englishmen playing the West Indies at Port of Spain, Trinidad, early in 1960. Admirers of British batsmanship have seldom been able to glory in a team so bedecked with talent. Many a captain before or since would have liked to write down a list containing Geoff Pullar, Colin Cowdrey, Ken Barrington and Peter May before coming to Ted Dexter and Mike Smith. Such a batting order virtually called for embossed notepaper.

Next came Ray Illingworth, though nobody knew then that a Test century was lurking in the bottom of his cricket bag. Illy was followed by little wicketkeeper Roy Swetman and three bowlers whose batting could not be despised, Freddie Trueman, David Allen and Brian Statham. For the formidable task of getting the West Indians out, after their declared innings of 563 in the Bridgetown Test, England had the most successful pair of fast bowlers international cricket has seen (Trueman 307 wickets, Statham 252) supported, by Allen and Illingworth's tactical off-spin and Barrington's leg-spin, so effectively that May had no need to call on Dexter's energetic medium-pace until the last afternoon.

West Indies' opening batsman Conrad Hunte would have been sure of No. 1 berth in the strongest World XI of the time. A crisis brought the best out of his partner, Joe Solomon, despite his habit of taking guard 12 inches inside the crease. I could never be sure whether the advantage of thus turning a yorker into a half-volley was not cancelled out by converting a full-toss into a yorker. Rohan Kanhai was showing it was possible to succeed in Tests with strokes of his own distinctive brand. They had started him along the road to 5,000 runs; only Gary Sobers

54

has scored more for West Indies. At 23 Sobers already held the world individual Test record, 365 not out, one more than Sir Leonard Hutton's highest and 31 past Sir Donald Bradman's record for Australia. The best bowlers were getting used to seeing their best balls go from the left-handed Barbadian's free-swung bat as if they were second-rate. Sobers had been shaping ominously like another triple century when Trueman bowled him for 226 at Bridgetown.

Fifth on the list was knight-to-be, Frank Worrell, a graceful strokeplayer whom any school coach would have liked his boys to watch. His innings, even short ones, were usually models of batting art. The sequence of appointment at the time was keeping Frankie waiting another half-year before he was given opportunity to prove himself one of the pre-eminent captains of Test history. Sixth batsman was Basil Butcher who at 25 had two Test centuries behind him, on his way toward becoming seventh man to top 3,000 runs for the West Indies. Captain Jerry Alexander, the Cambridge wicketkeeper of 1952–53, had topped West Indies' score in an innings at Kanpur and Destiny was lining him up for a Test century at Sydney.

By the time bowlers got this far (at Bridgetown the total was then 556) they were entitled to look for a quicker passage through tailenders Sonny Ramadhin, Charran Singh, Wesley Hall and Chester Watson, though before the year was out Hall was to flay Australian bowling for 50 at Brisbane.

In the theatrical world an equivalent bill of topline performers would cause box office queues to stretch around neighbouring blocks. So it was this day at Queen's Park Oval, the finest ground in the West Indies and the only one that can somehow enclose 30,000 people, give or take a few crushed shirts and trampled toes. Trinidad's shirts, the most dazzling in the Caribbean, are so varied that you count 20 or more passing without seeing a like pattern. Massed around the wire-mesh boundary barricade, they look more kaleidoscopic than Jamaica's – but Jamaicans, so proud of their beaches, their hotels and their rum, can't expect to have everything. With peaks advertising Carib beer, yellow caps blossom like buttercups amid the tropical profusion around the oval's crowded borders. Eyeshades, too, are scattered through the mass, perhaps to help their wearers read Ramadhin's spin while the Englishmen can't. Outside, those who can't pay but can climb, perch in the spreading branches of samans, the most commodious 'freedom stands' in the Indies. Behind them the verdant savanna leads to forested hills, like the three peaks spotted above the skyline by Columbus when he named the place Trinidad as his ship's company approached – forerunners of European oppressors come to disturb the realm of the savage Caribs.

Ethnically, Trinidad is the multi-racial capital of the world. A resident of French and Spanish extraction once introduced me in Port of Spain to a pharmacist of mixed parentage who said that, although he looked predominantly negroid, he had a half-sister who was pure Chinese. Trinidadians claim to have every strain of the human race except Eskimoes; after all, how long could an igloo last 10 degrees north of the Equator on an island where top day temperatures average 87 degrees? It is the only one of the Indies where I have heard some cricketers described as creoles. They are players of less definite hue than Trinidad's most-admired celebrity, the one and only Learie Constantine. A slave's grandson of undiluted African lineage, this cricketer-lawyer-diplomat won distinction as a governor of the BBC, a member of Britain's Race Relations Board and was honoured in the House of Lords as Baron Constantine before asthma ended his fruitful life at 69.

While thousands of Americans were serving at the U.S. Navy's leased Chaguaramas base on the island, Trinidad's open-ended bloodstream comfortably absorbed copious infusions which gave rise to the calypso Rum and Coca-Cola with its sociological chorus ending:

Both mother and daughter
Workin' for de Yankee doll-ar.

Trinidad is the true home of the calypso, imitated on other islands, as the Japanese do with Scotch whisky. All Trinidadians needed to invent steel-bands were a few old oildrums, whose tuneful by-products fill racks of discs in SaGomes's shop on Marine Square. The island's contributions to musical culture include a droll song about a free-living pixie who elusively gives her address as 29 Port of Spain.

On Trinidad you can see bamboo clumps as big as the Albert

Memorial or Melbourne's Shrine of Remembrance, and walk on the 150-acre Pitch Lake. This bitumenous freak is darker, duller and more yielding than the strip in the middle of Queen's Park Oval, rolled until it glistens in the sun, a surface almost as grassless and shiny as a ballroom floor. When sudden showers blow over, covers are rushed to the pitch by ground superintendent Man Borde's flying squad of 18, nicknamed Borde's hordes.

Nobody expected England's strong batting to run into trouble on a good wicket. There were two reasons, named Hall and Watson, both adequate to explain the concern in England's room. Batsmen were discovering that a minor role given Wesley Hall in Britain in 1957 had prevented them from recognising that the swiftest bowler of the jet age was arriving to make life more difficult than at any time since Frank Tyson burst his last bootlace.

Hall's fame is written on the wind. It has been so ever since that morning, at 22, the 6 feet 3 inch Barbadian came scudding along a runway he had stepped out with 33 giant paces. No other bowler in my time could sweep across the crease at such breakneck speed, a gold necklet cross bobbing on his ebony chest as he gave his 200 lb. body maximum momentum. (At Brisbane in the same year, a ball that hit the Reverend David Sheppard on the hip caused the flapping cross to strike Hall on the eye – unmistakably a sign of divine displeasure.)

Amid all the button-straining bustle, Hall's side-on action, over-the-top delivery and out-swing were classic. Besides the poetry of tempestuous motion his bowling had the poetry of emotion – his own and the batsmen's. Wes's personality has come across clearly – as outgoing as a batsman he'd just evicted. You'd forget he was a heavy man as he hurled himself after every ball, all bounds and leaps, as if his whalebone wrists were matched by rubber ankles and his boots had inner-spring soles. The batsmen's emotions all sprang from self-preservation being the first law of Nature.

As the great speedman's yokemate, Chester Watson, 20, was filling the vacancy left by the West Indies Board's exclusion of Roy Gilchrist. The untamable Gilchrist, 22nd child of a Jamaican factory worker, had been sent home from a tour of India after a clash with his captain, Alexander, who ordered him off the field for disobedience in bowling a turban-high beamer at Swaranjit Singh, a former Cambridge team-mate of Jerry's.

A stranger watching Watson in action could scarcely have guessed he was a shy clerk on leave from a desk job in Kingston who could be found in a quiet corner engrossed in a thriller, with almond eyes wider apart than his wickets. Though the 6 feet 1 inch Jamaican could not rival Hall in velocity he equalled his partner in stamina and outdid him in richness of plum-like complexion. Had they bowled late on an overcast afternoon it would have been enough to make us reporters appeal against the light! Once a team manager joked: 'We'll have to tie a light on Chester!'

Watson, too, had a side-on delivery stride, his arm was vertical at the zenith of its arc and his right shoulder chased after the ball in his animated follow-through. Yet the speed and rise Chester produced after an easy 11-stride run caused batsmen to suspect some illicit elbow-play that neither West Indian nor Australian umpires noticed. Every ball that hit England's batsmen added circumstantial evidence to confirm their thoughts about his quicker one. If they were right, not only caution was being thrown to the winds.

Opening England's innings Pullar, the tall Lancashire left-hander, looked as calm as the Mersey Canal, his hands as steady as if repairing a watch – their occupation before they took on batting gloves for a living. In opening with him Cowdrey was putting the side's needs first. Nothing visible in Colin's technique accounted for his preference for coming in fourth – in fact, I liked his batting better against seamers than spinners – yet such dissimilar bowlers as Alan Davidson and Neil Adcock welcomed his appearance before the ball lost any gloss. Pullar and Cowdrey owed their nicknames, Noddy and Kipper, to the ease with which they could take a doze. Bowlers could see little on-the-field significance in this: 12 runs off Hall's opening over, however, were a rate no opening pair could live up to.

Before the bare-looking pitch could take all the shine off the ball Hall and Watson took the shine off England's early batting. Alan Ross put it succinctly by saying they settled on a length, short and uppish. From Pullar's attempted glance off Watson the ball went almost straight through to Alexander's gloves at 37.

Barrington's arrival was a signal for a sharp increase in the proportion of bouncers, which led to the downfall of Cowdrey for 18. A batsman struck on the body and boot by Hall in four balls would need ice in his blood to play the next ball with precision. It streaked from the inner edge of Colin's bat to send a stump somersaulting and make two down for 42.

Finding short-pitched balls paying so well, the bowlers served more to May. One struck him on the shoulder. Except for an over by Worrell to enable the pair to switch ends the batsmen had no respite. With lunch a few balls away Watson followed a bumper with an outswinger that flicked from May's scoreless bat to be caught by Kanhai, second slip.

Bouncers were causing enough tension in Trinidad for umpire E. L. (Sandy) Lloyd to warn Hall not to exceed two short-pitched balls an over, and for Eric Lee Kow to admonish Watson similarly next morning. The cautioned couple were the most alarming West Indian pair post-war English batsmen faced until Charlie Griffith took over from Watson. At their deadliest, Hall and Griffith had as much kick as Smith and Wesson.

Noting that at least a dozen balls in Hall and Watson's 16 pre-lunch overs had kicked head or shoulder-high, E. W. Swanton reported that the proportion of bouncers was not as great as Freddie Trueman and Frank King had bowled at times on England's preceding visit in 1954.

To men under fire, of course, the quota of bumpers always seems higher. Describing the hammering he took, Barrington says in *Running into Hundreds* that they never seemed to let up. Clearly identifiable bouncers are not the only members of this terrorist tribe. For a non-hooking man who ducks, the worst peril comes from short-pitched balls that unaccountably fail to jump – blood relations, you might say, but far from identical twins. Batsmen are unable to tell which from which. To lessen impact against his ribs Cowdrey had padding sewn into the vest he wore under his shirt. (Later in the year McDonald, Simpson and Favell had similar problems with Hall and Watson who in Melbourne flung down 47 unmistakable bumpers spread over 43 overs in Australia's two innings.)

For a while, Englishmen looking on at Queen's Park Oval found it almost painful to watch Barrington. With three gone for 57, lunch brought relief for over-wrought nerves. Though

Ken tried to put a flippant face on it by doffing his cap to a bowler who had gone close to knocking it off and by pointing his bat at Hall like a rifle, his distress was too real to be concealed, especially from the potent young men who were causing it. Most batsmen find it better to show no reaction to bumpers, not even to rub the newly bruised spot – if they are stoics enough.

Who would be willing to attack such bowling? Ted Dexter for one. Entering with an aura of self-confidence and after-shave lotion, the one-time dinner-jacket cricketer (his early label) shows himself at ease in a flannel shirt. At this time it is 18 months since the handsome Cambridge ex-captain stepped down from the Upper Ten to pursue Test centuries and he already has two (with seven to come). His strokes are imperious, banishing the ball from his presence. Lord Edward they call him, soon to be clipped to Lord Ted. His bat has the power of a Daimler in overdrive. England's most vigorous gum-chewer is England's hardest driver, on cricket ground or golf course. He attacks bowling with socialite severity, hitting through the ball and making shins as hard to save as fours.

Neither mid-on nor cover could get a hand near two fence-bound shots in Hall's first over after lunch. With Dexter pegging the bowling back, Barrington found it more manageable. As if their 90-minute bowl before lunch had been little more than a warm-up, their captain kept Hall and Watson going for half an hour more, their shirts sticking to their willing backs. By some oversight, nobody phoned the R.S.P.C.A. Dexter's commanding use of his height and unsurpassed power off the back foot were never an encouraging sight for quick bowlers. Soon after Ted's right hand was split when he tried to hook Watson after tea, he drove at Singh, whose subtle change of pace was rewarded with a return catch. Dexter's 77 and a stand of 142 carried England to the threshold of 200 for four wickets.

The pair who rallied England came from the opposite ends of batsmanship, poles apart. Heir to an insurance chieftain, the 6 feet Cambridge Blue exemplified the unburdened outlook of men classed as amateurs until that distinction was abolished. Playing for his living, Barrington exemplified the approach of men aware that club committees engaging professionals judge more on end-of-season totals than over-by-over strokes or day-to day scoring times. Hence percentage batsmen. Ken was the undisputed prudent prince of percentage players who set aside shots he rated as unprofitable and awaited balls suitable for riskless strokes with his reduced repertoire. For all his self-imposed restrictions, I thought him his country's surest cutter and sweeper and a good hooker – until Hall and Watson had him flopping on his back. A complex character, Barrington is a clever mimic with a Higgins-like ear for local accents, who became known as the 'The Colonel' for his ramrod send-up of brasshat batsmanship. Yet he often lay awake or paced the corridors worrying about his next Test innings and took tablets to quieten his jangled nerves. He was stood down for boring an Edgbaston crowd with an over-ripe 100 against New Zealand, yet delighted Melbourne with a peach of a century off 122 balls in less than half the time. His Melbourne 100 was one of five Test tons which the so-called one-gear machine completed by driving spectacular sixes. Nobody else thought of this way of making onlookers forget the worst of what they (and he) might have endured when he was held tight in patience's grip.

Battling his way toward 93 that day in Trinidad Barrington under-estimated Hall's speed with the second new ball, taken for the last half-hour. Ducking late, Ken was laid low for a while by a blow on the side of the head but resolutely rose to his feet. No more bumpers came his way, and few runs, as he and Mike Smith concentrated on seeing out the day, with England 220 for four wickets off 78 overs bowled at the low rate of 86 balls an hour. It was the second time Barrington had been knocked down and the seventh time he had been hit between fingers and head. Even a fakir tires of a bed of nails after a few hours. The habitual fun-maker re-entered the room with a lump above the ear and a bitter outburst, including coarsely emphatic words not usually heard from him. They began with: 'This a fine - - - - - - - way to play cricket. If these bowlers don't watch out they'll - - - - - - - well kill someone!'

After some calming philosophy from manager Walter Robins next morning and a wry joke about the need for crash helmets, Ken faced the music again. Watson's downbeats for two bumpers in four balls caused him to go to ground but after Lee Kow's admonition to the bowler the music became noticeably less martial. The umpire, slim as Chou En-lai, wore a red puggaree around his light panama hat. Reaching 100 was a salve for

Barrington. Besides being dogged, it was a century dog-eared from wear and tear. His 121 occupied 5¾ hours before he edged Hall's outswinger after lunch and Alexander plunged to catch him. It was Barrington's second step on the long trail that leads to 20 Test hundreds. Only five others have trodden it : Bradman 29, Sobers, 25, Hammond and Cowdrey 22, Harvey 21.

Through spectacles glinting in the sun Smith saw Sonny Ramadhin bowl Illingworth at 307. From that point Mike used his carefully laid 50 as a launching-pad to chase after 100 and help England nearer 400. Concentration showed in his baring his teeth as he played each ball. Another unconscious habit – straddling wider as the bowler approached – tended to anchor his footwork and cause his bat to go across the line. His answer to most balls spun along by Ramadhin and left-hander Charran Singh was the forward smother. Yet it was off the spinners that Smith hit two sixes and his ability to drive wide of mid-on repeatedly found gaps. Trueman stayed an hour for two scoring strokes, prompting a theory that he must have mistakenly brought in a bat belonging to a quieter character. Freddie saw Smith to 80 and the tenth man, Allen, competently kept an end intact while Mike ran to 108 in 4½ hours before Worrell nonchalantly caught a hard drive at short mid-on. Half the 1956 Oxford captain's runs came while the ninth and tenth men were his partners. England's 382 had come at slightly better than 2½ runs an over.

At this stage in their unappeasable careers Trueman and Statham, both in the high twenties, could not rival the speed of their dusky counterparts but Trueman's five overs before the second day ended contained enough bouncers to remind the swaying Hunte that there were still some nasty shots in the older Englishmen's lockers.

On the third day bumpers were kept to a less conspicuous role – Trueman averaging about one in 12 balls and Statham bouncing one only occasionally. The Yorkshireman's swing and his Lancashire partner's exceptional cut from the pitch brought a breakthrough that owed much to the activities of U-formation fieldsmen, all in catching positions except cover.

In the third over Hunte snicked Statham's breakback down to his boot and the rebound was smartly intercepted by True-

man's left hand at leg gully. Hunte stayed, apparently thinking
the ball had touched the floor too. When umpire Lloyd upheld
the fielding side's appeal a hoot of dissent came from a section
of the crowd. A Yorkshire-born instrument engineer, Lloyd was
a South Trinidad umpire while employed at Texaco's Point-a-
Pierre plant.

Soon Kanhai suffered the triple mortification of missing a
swinging full-toss from Trueman, being out lbw and hobbling
away on a bruised foot.

Sobers, who had plundered most of these bowlers for 226
in the preceding Test, sliced a forcing shot at Trueman's third
ball to him, outside the off stump. Flying over third slip, the ball
smacked May's upflung hand, whence it curved slowly upward
and descended into Barrington's waiting hands at first slip, half
a dozen paces away.

In every way it was enough to make Trinidadians mutter
about 'a touch of the Obeah'. Obeah (West Indians pronounce
it obee-air) is a form of superstition which slaves brought from
West Africa, as they did the voodoo to Haiti. Laughingly discounting it, friends say it is taking longer to die out than Anglo-
Saxons' medieval belief in witchcraft and the Evil Eye. With
a touch of the Obeah an ill-wisher can doom a batsman to a bad
trot or cast a blight over a whole team, as seemed to be happening this day. The victim may be unaware of the evil spell, otherwise he could try to offset it by carrying three grains of rice in
his wallet or an unripe lime in his cricket bag. Some who deride
it as necromantic nonsense see nothing odd in other people paying
fortune-tellers' fees, thinking a four-leaf clover well worth finding,
regard a broken mirror as ominous and notice gratefully that
some airlines have no seat numbered 13. The Obeah had been
singularly ineffective as the Englishmen's ally against Sobers until
this day brought mounting evidence that occult influences were
at work. How else could England get for o in three balls the
greatest batsman of the time, holder of the Test individual
record and a growing list of other unprecedented feats? How
else could that ball, hurriedly intercepted, be guided gently to
where another fieldsman stood with cupped hands?

To see Allen's bang-on throw from cover run out Solomon for
23 was bad enough. When the partner who sent Joe back was a
man of Frank Worrell's unsurpassed cricket knowledge the mis-

understanding seemed to call for a more eerie explanation than
that Statham's seaming had upset the judgment of Solomon,
goading him into a desperate attempt to get to the other end.
Upset, Worrell edged Trueman's outswinger and when Swetman
darted to get gloved fingers under it five West Indians had gone
for a paltry 45.

Anxiety not to lose another wicket squeezed even the back-
foot strokes out of Butcher's batting and Alexander allowed himself only shots of which he was doubly sure. Seven overs for
eight runs were no novelty for economical Illingworth but Barrington's 16 overs for 15 may make posterity wonder why this
handy leg-spinner was so often neglected in subsequent Test
series – a fate that later befell Robin Hobbs. No smile gave a
glimpse of Butcher's gold tooth as he laboured more than 100
minutes for nine runs before Statham trapped him lbw inside the
crease.

For some the influence of the Obeah was confirmed beyond
doubt when Alexander, mistaking Trueman's line, offered no
shot and was ruled lbw. The captain's uncharacteristic 28 were
strung out over two hours, with hardly a sign of his natural firm
drive – Jerry was seemingly saving it up for Benaud in the tied
Brisbane Test, later in the year.

At 98 betting quickened on whether 100 would be raised by
Ramadhin or Singh, both Indians, like most of the port's taxi-
drivers. In the unaccustomed role of head man in a partnership
Ram called for a sharp single off the last ball of an over, so
he could keep the strike. Dexter's throw from cover into Swetman's gloves was too swift for them. Run out by what most
people estimated was a yard, Singh did not pause to absorb Lee
Kow's decision but ran on toward the pavilion.

A storm of protest and hoots rose from the thickest crush on
a grassy bank to the right of the pavilion, though the objectors
were not square-on with the end where Lee Kow signalled
Singh out. Except for the incontrovertible two-men catching
of Sobers, all the eight wickets West Indies lost for 98 had
been by decisions on appeals, including three leg-before-wicket,
one low snick and two run out. From their first booing of Lloyd
when he gave Hunte out the rowdiest complainants had
reviled the umpires for every decision and raved at them as
they walked off for lunch.

An element in the demonstrators' mood was probably a carry-over from earlier agitation to induce the Board to lift its ban on Gilchrist. A group from Port of Spain's tough east-side district had urged a boycott of the Test as a protest against his exclusion. Though intractable *Nut* Gilchrist was a Jamaican, Trinidadians had seen him take seven Pakistani wickets as opening bowler on Queen's Park Oval two years earlier and knew all about his 57 wickets in 13 Tests before he was sent home from India and docked $150 for having flouted tour chiefs. The Board was considering whether to reinstate Gilchrist for the tour of Australia, as Worrell believed he could handle him, but the ban was to be re-affirmed a month later.

To rum-primed demonstrators, overheated, overcrowded and overwhelmed by West Indies' batting disasters, the second run out (a local hero) put the last straw on an unbearable load of exasperation. Amid the yelling and hooting a bottle, glinting in the sunshine, sailed over the wire grid. It was like the first germ in a epidemic. It had scarcely finished rolling when more followed. Two men clambered over the wire and picked up bottles, not to tidy up the outfield but to hurl them back into the crowd, among the innocent as well as the guilty. This turned disturbance into riot. Bottles flew everywhere, some smashing and splintering when they landed on others. Some were already broken before they were thrown. Among the bottles were beercans and fruit refuse as an increasing hail spread to most parts of the ground. Never had so many bottles littered a sportsfield. It made the scene at Georgetown six years earlier seem a minor incident in crowd unruliness.

Next people began surging on to the ground, like sheep escaping over a collapsed panel of an overcrowded pen. Beginning from the opposite side it became an invasion. Many were pushed on by pressure from behind. When the next batsman, Hall, stopped on his way, Alexander said: 'Go on, Wes, you're in.' Hall said he took one more look at the flying bottles and bolted for the safety of the dressing-room, exclaiming: 'I'm not going out there for anybody's money, man!'

May's demeanour amid all the uproar was impeccable. Every Englishman present had reason to be proud of him. Peter and Ramadhin quietly ushered people away to preserve the pitch from trampling. Soon the players were marooned amid a turbulent sea of excited intruders. Fights broke out here and there but no attempt was made to molest players. It was clear that the disturbance was not aimed at the Englishmen. The umpires had more cause for anxiety, not knowing whether fist-waving toughs in the crowd might follow up foul abuse with violence. The 15 police on duty had no hope of controlling the invaders. Appeals by the Governor, Sir Edward Beetham, the Premier, Dr Eric Williams (known as little Eric) and the Works Minister, Learie Constantine, had no effect and Learie almost caught one bottle sailing in their direction.

The players stayed in midfield until Alexander came through the intruders to talk to England's captain. A Jamaican veterinarian from 1,000 miles across the Caribbean, Jerry advised Peter to bring his men off, as mob mysteria might take a worse turn. As policemen escorted players and umpires through the throng Trueman and Statham carried a stump each but the only harm came from a ricocheting stone striking Pullar's elbow.

A fire hose was brought out to clear the field but failed because only a trickle got as far as the nozzle – water escaping from the punctured hose had more force and one jet drenched the fireman from behind. Resentful rioters renewed throwing bottles and other missiles. This time a broadcaster's use of the term hooliganism brought Radio Trinidad's lofty box under fire in an exposed position above the wide slope where the riot began. Ex-captain Jeffrey Stollmeyer and the BBC's Rex Alston were among those besieged when missiles smash its glass front.

When a dozen mounted troopers galloped into the field and reinforcements of riot squadmen in tin hats marched on, the uproar ended after 45 minutes. Pelting ceased and brawls gave way to peaceful co-existence. Thirty casualties were driven to hospital and 60 given first-aid were taken home. One squadman suffered a shocking gash from a spike and flying scraps of bottles cut the police chief's legs.

Alan Ross estimated that out of 30,000 (the biggest crowd ever to witness a sporting event in the West Indies) some 500 had actually fought or thrown, though several thousand had invaded the field. The instigators might have been a mere couple of dozen. In his *Through the Caribbean* Ross says irritation at West Indian failure boiled up in packed stands that were

as hot as pressure cookers, with sun, rum and whisky playing
their part (dozens of bottles of spirits were discovered later
among the piles of Coca-Cola and Seven-Up).

The riot appalled and saddened Constantine and other skilful
players who had brought Trinidad fame in the cricket world,
such men as ex-captains Stollmeyer and Gerry Gomez, fast
bowlers Prior Jones and Lance Pierre, and century-maker Andy
Ganteaume. Their home crowd's reputation had been among
the best, notable for appreciation of visiting teams' qualities,
though through misunderstanding they had blamed the fielding
Australians for a long delay caused by rain getting through the
wicket-covers in 1955. To his cabled apology to the MCC Dr
Williams added the reassurance that not the slightest hostility
had been directed against the English team or any player. Every-
body knew that in this the Premier intended no belittlement of
the opening bowlers' belligerence.

As soon as he heard rumours that the Englishmen would
discontinue the match and go home, manager Robins announced
that the tour would go on and his team would return to Trinidad
for the fifth Test unless the West Indies Board decided otherwise.
He added: 'Our sympathies are entirely with the good people
of Trinidad who have been let down by a few hooligans.' Robins
and May agreed that the 75 minutes lost be made up by starting
half an hour earlier on three remaining days.

Before the umpires took their positions again, outwardly
as calm as if there had been no riot, Dr Williams, Constantine
and Robins walked around the ground and were good-
humouredly received when they paused by the mound where
Saturday's troubles had begun. Its Monday occupants had
breathing space and betting room. Borde's hordes had cleared
away the broken glass but nobody was left to pick up the pieces
of West Indies' innings which ended for 112, 270 behind. Had
it been in England's untrustworthy weather May would have
had good reason to think a follow-on the surest route to a win
but with a prospect of 16 hours' play in sunshine he decided
to set a target beyond West Indies' probable reach and still have
time for his bowlers to get them out again.

The West Indian skipper's response was a defensive field, yet
wickets fell. Two were out for 79 when the crowd welcomed

May with heartiness that compensated for the concern Saturday's outbreak had caused him. Peter was not stroking the ball with the certainty well-known to the world's best bowlers. For the second time Singh's held-back ball yielded a prized wicket, caught-and-bowled 28. Another month had to pass before the truth came out that May was troubled by a re-opened wound from a bowel abscess operation and he had to return to Britain before the last two Tests.

Though hasty evasive action under bumpers landed Barrington on his back a couple of times, Ken had the temperament to pick up again where he had left off when rudely interrupted. On 49, however, he waited so long for a suitable ball to complete 50 that Alexander caught him off Hall's outswinger – the same combination as before. What mattered more was that Barrington had the satisfaction of topping England's score in both innings, yet the quick bowlers continued to go after him in the following Tests. I think it was as a result of this series that Barrington's defence developed a hurried hop on the back foot, prompting a mischievous wit to describe him as the world's best batsman six inches above the ground. Watching Ken playing McKenzie later, this motion reminded me of a farmer's stump-jump plough.

When the sixth wicket fell at 133 England's lead of 403 was probably enough before Trueman slammed 18 off an over from Singh, including two sixes. Two Yorkshiremen's 68 was the quickest partnership of the match. Illingworth finished 41 not out, giving advance notice of a time when, as England's captain, he would make six fifties in a series and join the skipper century-makers. Ex-players praised the fielding as the best ever by a West Indian side. It gave pleasure to Constantine, the most spectacular fieldsman cricket has known, and reflected credit on the skipper. Alexander was making himself the first West Indian 'keeper to take 23 wickets in one series, equalling John Waite's record (which the great South African hoisted to 26 two years later).

A closure with a lead of 500 on the fifth morning left West Indies 10 hours to last out to escape defeat. For a batsman of Hunte's standard to be repeatedly beaten was clear evidence of the difficulties Statham's seaming presented. Yet Conrad survived long enough to make 47 out of 107 for two wickets.

Kanhai, a man subject to explosive moments, used to play too many bold-looking shots to be everyone's nomination for a stayput role, yet he proved his versatility by holding fast as sheet-anchor of this innings. Though he uses the lightest bat in international cricket, only 2 lb 2 oz, the angle of Rohan's cap-peak is the most defiant in the game, challenging those who say he is too venturesome in slashing off balls either side of point or slamming straight ones over mid-wicket. The individua-lity of this compact Guyanese Indian, a pocket powerhouse, is epitomised for me in the way he finishes his sweep as a hip-in-the-blockhole shot. It is the most down-to-earth stroke played before mixed company in a permissive age since Keith Miller's forward lunge occasionally became over-extended and let him down. Many a cautious record-seeker can envy Kanhai's 13 Test hun-dreds and 24 half-centuries in 66 matches, this man the team affectionately call Lallie.

Kanhai's moods vary like his attire. One day he will have an English-style choker at his throat, shirtsleeves down to his wrists, unbuttoned. Batting in similar weather in the same match, he wears no choker, folds his sleeves to the elbow. Some superstition, no doubt, but he smilingly says it's his secret. Suffering from 'flu one bleak day in Melbourne he came in encased in so many sweaters and wrappings that he was the nearest Test cricket has seen to a mummy, sorry to leave its cosy sarcophagus. At Queen's Park Oval he batted chokerless, sleeves folded enough to show stretches of chocolate forearm above his white gloves. The man who once swung Derek Underwood's first ball for six has usually shown flighted spin more respect than other bowling. He pushed the handle of a sloping bat well forward to Barring-ton's wrist-spin and the off-spin of Allen and Illingworth, not caring whether the ball only dribbled to silly mid-off so long as the blade put it straight down to earth. Despite loss of his third fingernail in attempting to catch Sobers, Illingworth bowled seven more overs for 10 runs.

By having the opening pair and Alexander caught off his bowling David Allen spun out the first three of his 122 wickets in 39 Tests. At that stage the Gloucestershire off-spinner took so few steps that he could almost have bowled off a window-ledge. The theory was that a brief shuffle led to more effort in his follow-through. No other English off-spinner turned the ball so much on hard-rolled turf overseas. Nicknamed Pinnochio from a supposed resemblance to Walt Disney's puppet, Allen had the perseverance and humour to see out the hottest days in four countries. When a sympathetic Melbourne ringsider offered him a drink of beer, David looked imploring at his skipper for permission and for emphasis wiped the back of his hand across his scorched lips.

No need for any touch of the Obeah this time to get rid of Sobers for 31; bowlers' bootscrapes outside the left-hander's off stump attended to that. Going around the wicket to land the ball on them Trueman got one to keep low for an lbw decision. With another squatter Statham sent Worrell back for 0 and the innings went into a quick decline. To make sure of 100 while partners lasted Kanhai suddenly struck 16 off a Trueman over with strokes in five different directions.

A full-pitch from Dexter invited Kanhai, 110, to hit a 20th four but the ball wobbled enough to be misdirected for a catch at midwicket. After six chanceless hours of throttling down to fewer than 20 runs an hour, seeing his side into the last afternoon, such an end caused Rohan to beat the ground with his bat in self-reproach. (When he did that on his dismissal lbw for 115, second of his twin Test centuries at Adelaide a year later, some mistook his action for anger about the decision, but umpire Egar knew better.)

On a pitch where bowlers seamed the ball right into the last afternoon – Statham most of all – each side's pace pair shared 11 wickets. By dismissing West Indies for 244 England won by 256 runs an hour and three-quarters before time. Ram was the fourth lbw victim of the last innings and the seventh West Indian of the match. As four Englishmen had also gone that way Law 39 had been given a thorough workover by bowlers and umpires – a contrast with the effect of the 1970 experimental rule on England's series in Australia, where only five lbw appeals were upheld in more than 17,000 balls.

The last-day attendance carried the match total close to 100,000 who paid the equivalent of £20,000 sterling in dollars, both records for the West Indies. The crowd's applause for the victorious English team was ungrudging, yet onlookers at the remaining three Tests were losers in two senses after England became one-up so early in the series. The surest way to shut out any risk of an equaliser or worse was to make a finish in six five-hour days unlikely. Those were the prevailing tactics, disregarding the paying customers and imposing a strain on the loyalty of English correspondents. They could hardly pretend not to notice the number of overs bowled in a full day once sank to 68. Just 408 balls in a day! What a sad comedown in five years since West Indians had seen Test bowlers deliver 500 to 600 balls in a day! At 408 balls a day, only 82 an hour, onlookers were given no more than three-quarters of the cricket they paid to see. If a team containing three fast bowlers, Lindwall, Miller and Archer, could bowl 92 thirsty overs in a five-hour day under this sun can a drop of 140 balls a day be explained by other than inattentive consciences? Unless 87 degrees have grown hotter than 87 degrees were in 1955!

Port of Spain, Jan. 28, 29, 30, Feb. 1, 2, 3, 1960. England won by 256 runs.

ENGLAND 1st innings		2nd innings	
G. Pullar c Alexander b Watson ...	17	c Worrell b Ramadhin ...	28
M. C. Cowdrey b Hall...	18	c Alexander b Watson ...	5
K. F. Barrington c Alexander b Hall...	121	c Alexander b Hall ...	49
P. B. H. May (c.) c Kanhai b Watson	0	c & b Singh	28
E. R. Dexter c & b Singh ...	77	b Hall	0
M. J. K. Smith c Worrell b Ramadhin	108	lbw Watson	12
R. Illingworth b Ramadhin ...	10	not out	41
R. Swetman lbw Watson	1	lbw Singh	0
F. S. Trueman lbw Ramadhin ...	7	c Alexander b Watson ...	37
D. A. Allen not out	10	c Alexander b Hall ...	16
J. B. Statham b Worrell	1		
Lb 3, w 1, nb 8	12	B 6, lb 2, w 4, nb 2 ...	14
Total off 143.5 overs...	382	9 wkts. (90.4 overs) ...	230

Fall: 37, 42, 57, 199, 276, 307, 308, 343, 378, 382
18, 79, 97, 101, 122, 133, 133, 201, 230

Bowling.	Balls	Runs	Wkts.				Balls	Runs	Wkts.
Hall	198	92	2 ...	...	...	...	142	50	3
Watson	186	100	3 ...	...	...	...	114	57	3
Worrell	71	23	1 ...	...	...	...	72	27	–
Singh	138	59	1 ...	...	...	...	48	38	2
Ramadhin	210	61	3 ...	...	...	...	168	54	1
Sobers	18	16	–						
Solomon	42	19	–						

WEST INDIES 1st innings		2nd innings	
C. C. Hunte c Trueman b Statham ...	8	c Swetman b Allen ...	47
J. S. Solomon run out by Allen ...	23	c Swetman b Allen ...	9
R. B. Kanhai lbw Trueman	5	c Smith b Dexter... ...	110
G. S. Sobers c Barrington b Trueman...	0	lbw Trueman	31
F. M. Worrell c Swetman b Trueman...	9	lbw Statham	0
B. F. Butcher lbw Statham	9	lbw Statham	9
F. C. M. Alexander (c.) lbw Trueman ...	28	c Trueman b Allen ...	7
S. Ramadhin b Trueman ...	23	lbw Dexter	0
C. K. Singh run out, Dexter to Swetman	0	c & b Barrington... ...	11
W. W. Hall b Statham	4	not out	0
C. Watson not out	0	c Allen b Barrington ...	0
Lb 2, w 1	3	B 11, lb 6, w 2, nb 1 ...	20
Total off 68.3 overs	112	Total off 134.5 overs ...	244

Fall: 22, 31, 31, 45, 45, 73, 94, 98, 108, 112
29, 107, 158, 159, 188, 222, 222, 244, 244, 244

Bowling.	Balls.	Runs	Wkts.				Balls	Balls	Wkts.
Trueman	126	35	5 ...	...	...	...	114	44	1
Statham	117	42	3 ...	...	...	...	150	44	2
Allen	30	9	– ...	...	...	...	186	57	3
Barrington	96	15	– ...	...	...	...	155	34	2
Illingworth	42	8	– ...	...	...	...	168	38	–
Dexter				...	...	...	...	36	7	2

Runs per over: England 2.6. West Indies 1.75
Umpires: E. Lee Kow, E. L. Lloyd

Chapter Seven

UP IN FLAMES

NO wonder thousands more people than the Eden Gardens ground could hold wanted to see the West Indies play India as 1967 began. Never had such clear-cut world champions as the West Indians come to Calcutta. After a clean-sweep 5–0 against India in their home islands they had triumphed 6–2 on English soil in two visits – under Sir Frank Worrell, 1963, and his chosen successor, Garfield Sobers in 1966. In between they had crushed the Australians touring the Caribbean, though the Aussies had retained the Ashes in England after a squared rubber against the South Africans.

Bombay crowds set a five-day record for the Brabourne Stadium at the first of the champions' three Tests in India, a match of many gripping incidents. Left-handers Lloyd and Sobers steered West Indies to a win by six wickets, yet the outstanding performance was by Bhagwat Chandrasekhar for the losers. In capturing 11 of the 14 wickets lost by West Indies he attacked unflaggingly through 93 overs, more than one-third of his team's bowling.

This lean googly bowler, who had been a Mysore University student in his first Test at 18 against Mike Smith's English side, is a wonder of post-war cricket. With a right arm withered by boyhood poliomyelitis, Chandrasekhar hurries his sleeves-down wrong'uns and topspinners through, giving them the kind of bounce that keeps three short-legs in business. To throw from the field he uses his stronger left arm. A leg injury in Australia when aged 22 caused his disappearance from Test cricket for four years, but he crowned his comeback in 1971 as the main matchwinner in India's first triumph in England. His six for 38 off 109 faultless balls at the Oval spun the Englishmen out for 101.

Calcutta's cricket enthusiasm needs no stoking to develop a

73

full head of steam. An old Indian proverb, related to me by William Walker, says that if a Bengali and a cobra confront you on a road, you kill the more dangerous one first – the Bengali. Though not qualified to uphold this as an axiom or dispute it as a slander, ever since I witnessed their fervour at a Test match in 1956 I have placed Bengalis first among the world's most volatile cricket-watchers. From a swelling chorus of yells as the opening bowler delivers until their last homeward surge, the Eden Gardens know no peace.

More onlookers had swarmed in than the ground could accommodate, so thousands were pressed forward over the boundary fence. They sat on the outfield grass, seven to ten deep. This added to the displeasure felt by many because a pace bowler they favoured for a place, Subrata Guha, was squeezed out of India's side by the selectors' late call to a left-hand spinner, Bishan Singh Bedi.

Sobers' pleasure at winning the toss would have been even greater had he imagined what would happen to the pitch later. Reliable Conrad Hunte, a Moral Re-armament adherent, had Robin Bynoe as opening partner against the medium-pace bowling of left-hander Rusi Surti and Venkatraman Subramanya, a Bangalore bank officer. For the first time, Bengalis saw both partners in a Test opening pair run out – an excitement until then savoured only by citizens of four other cities in 90 years of international cricket. Deafening roars accompanied every desperate stride that failed to save Bynoe (19) and Hunte (43). Conrad the consistent, who wears shoes 12 inches long – not easily led into temptation – would have needed the mythical three-league boots for salvation this time from Jai's throw.

Half a dozen overs from each end showed that the track held no more for pacemen than the usual Indian strip, so the Nawab of Pataudi turned to spin from Chandrasekhar and a new partner, Bedi, both bank officers. Fulfilling promise he had revealed at 17 for North Zone against the Englishmen, Bedi was being hailed up there as another Vinoo Mankad. The bearded light-stepping Sikh looks a picture of innocence as the ball gently curves from his hand. Yet, on this day, three months past 20, he bowled as if an older brain were scheming inside his powder-blue turban.

Never having seen a Test until he played in this one, Bishan concealed his nervousness when called on to tackle such renowned international stars as Rohan Kanhai and Basil Butcher, both centurymakers on their previous visit to Calcutta. With Chandrasekhar's dug-in spin bouncing and Bedi's waftmanship forming a teasing contrast, the pair allowed the West Indians' batting none of its traditional effervescence. One of Pataudi's most spectacular catches made Butcher (35) Bedi's first victim (the young left-hander confessed later: 'Taming a batsman of whom I had read so much gave me more confidence'). Playing for turn that wasn't there, Clive Lloyd (5) tickled a catch into Kunderan's gloves – fourth out at 154. Though Kanhai had rosy memories of this ground, scene of his West Indies – India Test record 256, the spinners, over after over, prevented him from reproducing typically insolent touches in reaching 78. Twice fieldsmen were unable to get under skied shots off Bedi which fell into the spillover spectators sitting in the outfield. Accurate bowling kept the West Indians to about $2\frac{1}{4}$ runs an over on a day of 92 overs for 212 runs, four wickets and two dropped chances.

Overcrowding far beyond the ground's capacity, 57,000, led to a riot before the players could begin the second day, Sunday. People with tickets were still squeezing in. Holding two tickets under the Indian skipper's nose, one spectator demanded to know: 'Why is my seat already filled by a man with a ticket bearing the same number?' A rumour spread that thousands of forged tickets had been sold, indistinguishable from the genuine issue. Surti stood ready to bowl the day's first ball as soon as the umpire lowered a restraining arm.

Forced forward by the crush, hundreds began clambering over the railings on to the strip of grass outside the boundary line. Police and Home Guards lathi-charged them in an attempt to drive them back. Police beat up a man, Shri Sitesh Roy, who tried to remonstrate with them for throwing teargas grenades into a packed stand, causing women and children to panic.

Seeing incensed spectators stone police, the players retreated to their rooms. A brickbat struck an officer on the head and he was carried away on a stretcher. The infuriated mob tore out bamboo struts for hand-to-hand fighting with the outnumbered police. Others set fire to hessian awnings and the flames spread around the stands. P. N. Sundaresan wrote in *Indian Cricket:*

'What followed was like hell being let loose and the whole Eden Gardens was swallowed up in flames.'

Enraged by clashes with the police, men seized benches and carted them to make a fire in midfield. Grabbing stumps, some tried madly to gouge holes in the pitch.

Smoke penetrated into the dressing-rooms. As the riot became more destructive, prudence dictated that the teams should get away. Hunte, patriotic as well as religious, clambered up to save the West Indian flag. Eyes streaming from the irritation of teargas, some players did not wait to see whether cars would take them. With their skipper, several West Indians broke through the fence by the pavilion and ran across the Maidan park past the memorial to Queen Victoria, a white marble anachronism. Heedless of people's calls to them, they were unaware that some of the callers were trying to direct them to their hotel half a mile away. Amid the confusion Griffith and Lloyd lost their way and the big fast bowler was so upset when he stormed into the hotel that bystanders wondered were all the tears in his eyes from gas.

A few Indian players ran to the hotel but cars evacuated most of them. Terrified Bengal cricket officials hid under cars' seats, fearful of mob vengeance. A selector was among them.

All the timber scaffolding supporting the roofs of the stands was burning. So were some trams, buses and police cars outside after the riot. Army guards were posted around the smoking ground and the teams' hotel.

Next to the ground staff labouring to clear up the mess the busiest people on Monday were cricket officials and parliamentarians using all their wits to persuade the teams to resume the match. Aware that Calcutta's future as a Test city was at stake, West Bengal Government leaders tried to overcome fears of both sides that resumption would expose them to unpredictable dangers if renewal of the riot trapped them in no-man's-land between furious mobs and the police. Another reason for the players' refusal was a report that damage had left the pitch in no state for play of Test standard. The Chief Minister summoned his Security head to a meeting at his residence, with Pataudi among those present.

Calling a team meeting, the Nawab told his players that the Chief Minister had assured full security, but some remained

76

reluctant; Sunday's alarm was too fresh in their minds. In talks to individual Indian players, officials assured them that everything would be all right. They emphasised the need to continue the match to preserve their country's prestige as a Test nation.

Managing the world champions, Prior Jones, an ex-player who had nine Tests as a fast bowler, was so worried about their safety that even assurances of adequate protection failed to sway him. At a meeting his players were solidly against attempting to resume the match. Two former Indian Cricket Board presidents, the Maharaja of Baroda and M. A. Chidambaram, persuaded Jones to put the matter to his team again. Reluctant, he stipulated that the Indian Board be responsible for supervising safe conduct of the match.

Not until assurances were coupled with a bonus for each player – the equivalent of danger money in workers' pay packets – could a decision to play next day be announced. A bonus of 100 rupees lifted the Indian players' usual Test fee to 600 rupees each (about £45). In addition to this inducement players heard via the grapevine that if they continued to refuse they would have to face whatever action the Indian Board would take. They sensed that this could possibly mean being black-listed from future selection.

Against a backdrop of burnt-out stands, charred poles and gaps where benches had stood, another big crowd gathered on Tuesday. The teams found the dressing-rooms undamaged. Kit-bags forsaken in the escape were intact. The playing area had patches of charred grass but the groundsmen, with skill akin to plastic surgery, had repaired the wicket's surface. Holes dug with stumps had been filled with soft mud and rolled – a form of pancake make-up which made the pitch presentable, if no more. Most of the repairs were about the area where length balls would land at the end nearest the All-India Radio box.

If the surroundings were blackened the batting was gay with colour, after Pataudi caught Kanhai (90) off Surti. The spacious Melbourne-type scoreboard at the pagoda end was still working. Though most batsmen think a slow track, responding to spin, unfavourable for stroke-play, Nurse and Sobers acted otherwise. Two members of the nobility of West Indian batsmanship, a black knight and the brown prince, delighted the crowd.

77

Should a portrait painter ask me the finest representative specimen of the Negroid race I have seen in the West Indies or Africa I would name Seymour Nurse, with his rich prune-like colouring, sunny expression and generously moulded lips ready to smile or to part as he sings like a second Nat King Cole. Put alongside Seymour, a handsome white man looks thin-lipped, sharp-nosed and anaemic, with lank hair. The quick-eyed Barbadian's batting, too, could be put alongside that of Anglo-Saxon right-handers for timing and almost every quality except front-foot driving. Besides good bowling, it took injuries and assorted misfortunes to keep Nurse's international average below 50 – happenings such as an outfielder catching a 40-yard ricochet off short-leg Eric Freeman's head at Melbourne.

Seymour made 56 at Calcutta before Jaisimha caused an uppish stroke to Surti. Goodnight Nurse! but his play had charmed all watchers (though less dazzling than his Weekes-like part in 40 off four overs in an Adelaide Test two years later – the swiftest punishment I ever saw dealt a new ball in the hands of such front-rank pacemen as McKenzie and Connolly).

Admiration rose to the highest level as Sobers regaled the crowd with 70 in an hour and a quarter of the most exhilarating batting Bengalis have had the fortune to see in 14 years, although Harvey and Dexter each played there in that period. In sparing the scoreboard from the flames, omniscient Providence must have foreseen that it would have a treasure of the batting art to enshrine. So easy, Gary makes it look: a sure step here or there, the back foot busiest, a grateful sway and a full-swung, disrespectful bat. Writing from a Test century-maker's standpoint, Rusi Modi hailed his innings as superb, revealing Sobers' class and versatility in adjusting his game to suit the occasion. Modi thought some of Gary's strokes off his toes were out of this world.

Seventh in the batting order, cricket's brown prince and his mainly tail-end retinue so gingered up the scoring that off 51 overs they piled on 178. Next time anyone, repeating old catch-phrases, tries to justify two runs an over by saying it's a Test match, remind him of this average of $3\frac{1}{2}$ runs an over, a rate of 57 runs per 100 balls. Remind him, too that the runs were struck up in an atmosphere of tension and uneasiness following the most savage riot any cricket field has known. They had to be made on a patched-up pitch whereon wicket-ridden batsmen's self-torture can be left to painful imagination. Yet in this setting Sobers could lift his game to unroll the kind of innings that enchants onlookers into forgetting that it is fast putting their own country's team into a losing position.

Though facing 390, Kunderan and Jaisimha kept India's alive by raising 60 for the first wicket. Kunderan was the player who set the pattern for India to send a bold-stroking wicket-keeper in first (a role which Farokh Engineer carried on with equal spirit). Kunderan's thrashing bat obviously came from a different willow tree from that of Jai, whose upright correctness was to bring him 101 a year later at Brisbane, the only Test century of the Indians' tour of Australia.

Sobers and Griffith could not make the new ball hurry from the lethargic Calcutta track. Nor could Wesley Hall, who had spent energy making 35 runs in the preceding hour or so. Yet it was Hall who got one through Kunderan (39).

After Sobers changed to spin, with Lance Gibbs as partner, the pair treated India's innings like a mango tree laden with fruit ripe for plucking. Most successful of international off-spinners – first of the tribe to take 200 Test wickets – Gibbs comes at batsmen with a short, stamping approach, looking as hostile as a slow bowler can. Facing the lean Guyanese – by nickname 'Toothpick' – batsmen get not a single ball's respite from the strain of detecting a range of variations, especially the ball that starts life as a potential half-volley and changes in flight to a length off-break. Sobers made himself the perfect foil by turning the opposite way, going around the wicket with orthodox left-hand spin, as on his Test debut at 17. In India's 167 and follow-on 178 on a worsening strip, the pair shared 14 wickets, one fewer than their tally of Australian victims at Brisbane nearly two years later. Though in appearance and manner they could scarcely look less like Laker and Lock they work on somewhat similar principles – perhaps near enough to justify substituting their names in a jingle written about Surrey's irresistible pair in the 1950s:

> *Ashes to ashes, dust to dust,*
> *If Gibbs don't get you, Sobers must*

Only Jaisimha reached the thirties twice, though Modi rated Hanumant Singh's 37 the best innings because he hit all half-volleys and short balls, besides blocking the good ones with a dead bat. Called on as third spinner to rest the ubiquitous Sobers at last, a novice leg-twister of 22, Clive Lloyd, undid two of the best, Pataudi and Chandu Borde, on a surface deteriorating nearly as quickly as the batsmen's averages. To bowl Borde, Clive landed a leg-break just outside the leg stump and tilted back the off peg. That was nine inches of screw by anyone's calculation until translation into 22 centimetres made it sound less playable still. The three spinners curled along four-fifths of the balls needed to bring victory by an innings and 45 runs.

Feeling about the riot continued so strongly that 181 witnesses made statements to a commission of inquiry by Mr Justice Kamalesh Chandra Sen. On the evidence of more than 4,000 typed pages of depositions the judge set the blame squarely on the Cricket Association of Bengal and the police: official mismanagement caused the overcrowding and the police were guilty of gross provocation of the spectators by the lathi charge, use of teargas and merciless beating of Sitesh Roy. No proof was produced of malpractice in printing extra tickets but faulty numbering led to figures on duplicate tickets being mistaken. In addition to issuing tickets without due regard to actual accommodation, the association issued volunteers' badges and an inordinate number of passes.

Mr Justice Sen recommended that the cricket association might be left responsible for organising Test matches at the ground if the State Government imposed certain conditions. First, the Government should nominate at least six representatives, including veteran cricketers, to a broad-based tour sub-committee with cricket officials. The committee should prevent issue of tickets in excess of the stadium's accommodation. Complimentary tickets and V.I.P. cards should be abolished except, if at all, for Board of Control officials, ex-international cricketers and international and Ranji Trophy umpires. Not less than 50 per cent of season tickets should be reserved for affiliated clubs and sports bodies. The remaining season and daily tickets should be sold in advance to the public at counters at Eden Gardens and adjoining enclosed football grounds.

I append one passage from the judge's finding: 'We people in

Cricket's most savage riot – Calcutta, 1967. Rioters try to damage the pitch after the Indian and West Indian players had run off

Infuriated by a police lathi charge, Bengali rioters tore up bamboo stakes and retaliated in kind

Furious onlookers hurl chairs and benches on to a midfield blaze

Wes Hall airborne while playing for Queensland in Australia. The only people to complain about his menace were batsmen

Cowdrey and Sobers try to calm the crowd at Sabina Park, Kingston, Jamaica, during a lull in the 'battle of the bottles', West Indies *v* England, 1968

All style and grace – Tom Graveney drives . . .

. . . but at Karachi, 1969, he and Colin Milburn found themselves surrounded by milling spectators, some intent on congratulating Milburn on scoring a century, scored off 163 balls; this 100 won the annual prize

Carrying banners, student demonstrators swarm on to the playing area in the Karachi National Cricket Stadium during the test between Pakistan and England, March, 1969

Led by their captain, Saeed, the Pakistan team head for the safety of the dressing room, while behind them the demonstrators gather and cause play between England and Pakistan to be abandoned

Calcutta are passing through severe stresses and strains in various walks of life. To quote some instances, when compelled to travel in trams, buses and trains like hordes of cattle and goats we have taken it as part of our independent national existence . . . In taking advantage of this the Cricket Association of Bengal forgets that discomfort experienced by the spectators might erupt in a disaster . . ."

The judge's words may have significance to residents of other cities than Calcutta.

Calcutta, Dec. 1966, Jan. 1, 3, 4, 5, W. Indies won by innings and 45 runs.

WEST INDIES 1st innings

C. C. Hunte run out by Jaisimha	... ...	43
M. R. Bynoe run out by Surti ...	... ...	19
R. B. Kanhai c Pataudi b Surti	... ...	90
B. F. Butcher c Pataudi b Bedi...	... ...	35
C. H. Lloyd c Kunderan b Bedi	... ...	5
S. M. Nurse c Surti b Jaisimha...	... ...	56
G. S. Sobers (c) c Jaisimha b Chandrasekhar		70
J. L. Hendriks b Surti ...	... ...	5
W. W. Hall c Subramanya b Chandrasekhar...		35
L. R. Gibbs lbw Chandrasekhar	... ...	1
C. C. Griffith not out ...	... ...	9
B 7, lb 11, nb 4	... ...	22

Total off 137 overs (8 hrs. 35 mins.) ... 390

Fall: 43, 76, 133, 154 259, 272, 190, 362, 371, 390.

Bowling.	Balls	Runs	Wkts.
Surti	180	106	2
Subramanya	36	9	–
Chandrasekhar	276	107	3
Bedi	216	92	2
Venkataraghavan	78	43	–
Jaisimha	36	11	1

INDIA 1st Innings   2nd innings

	1st		2nd
B. K. Kunderan b Hall	39	lbw Hall	4
M. L. Jaisimha	37	c & b Gibbs...	31
R. F. Surti lbw Sobers	16	c Griffith b Sobers	31
C. G. Borde run out by Lloyd ...	11	b Lloyd	28
Pataudi (c.) c Griffith b Gibbs ...	1	c Griffith b Lloyd	2
Hanumant Singh c Bynoe b Gibbs	4	b Sobers	37
V. Subramanya c Hendriks b Gibbs	12	run out by Gibbs' deflection ...	17
S. Venkataraghava b Sobers ...	18	c Hendriks b Sobers	2
A. A. Baig b Gibbs	4	b Gibbs	6
B. S. Bedi st Hendriks b Sobers ...	5	c Bynoe b Sobers	0
B. S. Chandrasekhar not out ...	3	not out	1
B 12, lb 1, nb 4...	17	B 14, lb 2, nb 3	19
Total off 84.5 overs (4 hrs. 25 mins.)	167	Total off 77.4 overs (4 hrs. 15 mins.)	178

Fall: 60, 98, 100, 117, 119, 128, 139, 161, 161, 167.
4, 38, 89, 105 ,108, 155. 170, 176, 176, 178.

Bowling.	Balls	Runs	Wkts.			Balls	Runs	Wkts.
Sobers	173	42	3	...	...	120	56	4
Griffith	36	14	–	...	...	30	4	
Gibbs	222	52	5	...	...	184	36	2
Hall	30	32	1	...	...	42	35	1
Lloyd	24	4	–	...	...	84	23	2
Nurse	24	7	–	...	...			
Hunte				...	...	6	5	–

Runs per 100 balls: West Indies 47, India 35.
Runs per over: West Indies 2.9, India 2.1.
Balls per hour: West Indies 111, India 96

Umpires: Dr. I. Gopalakrishnan and S. Pan.

Chapter Eight

TEARGAS PANIC

HEARTIEST of the people in the West Indies – and this is saying a lot – are the Jamaicans. Undertones have little or no place in their speech. An opinion worth holding is worth expressing emphatically. If a convivial Jamaican slaps you on the shoulder, getting your arm into your shirtsleeve is likely to be uncomfortable for a day or two.

Kingston's Test ground, Sabina Park, is an area subject to recurring outbreaks of Test fever. A vaccine to moderate its severity has yet to be developed. In its absence many turn to bottles of Red Stripe ale. On this beautiful island photographic memories may be no more common than elsewhere but Jamaicans watching cricket in Sabina Park react to incidents so rapidly that I can only liken it to flash-bulb speed.

Diligent rolling usually polishes the brown, clay-like soil in the pitch until it shines like the boots of an Army officer who has a five-star batman. As he picks up fallen bails a stooping wicketkeeper sees a reflection of his face. Looking from the shuttered pressbox you see on the strip's mirror-like surface streaks of different shades stretching from the striker – the cream of his flannels, the white of his pads and the lard-like blade of his bat. On such a wicket Gary Sobers batted 10 hours for 365 not out against Pakistan in 1958 to lift the world Test record from Sir Leonard Hutton. Here Neil Harvey batted seven hours against West Indies and was caught for 204 after planter Douglas Vaughan offered a dollar a run if he could beat Sir Donald Bradman's 334, the record for Australia.

After a sneak thunderstorm two nights before England's Test here in 1968 caused intensified rolling, the pitch looked uninviting. Yet Colin Cowdrey's decision to bat first gave England use of it for nine hours before it utterly turned from torpor to outright treachery. Adverse fortune had brought out qualities unsuspected by those who had classed the urbane Kent leader as too good-humouredly unassertive for the demands of Test captaincy. Some try to make out that manners and mastery don't mix, implying that other ingredients in an international skipper matter little, so long as he has the remorseless toughness not only to beat the opposition but to grind them face-down into the dirt, not caring whether mean gamesmanship lowers the game nearer street-fighting level. They were not amused when a big enemy partnership moved slipfielder Cowdrey to mop his face with his handkerchief then hold it to flutter like a white flag, when he should have been grinding his teeth. Then there was his remark when a well-wisher advised more forward play to long-dragger Gordon Rorke. 'Thank you, sir,' said Colin, 'but I'm afraid that if I play forward more he'll tread on my foot.'

After Brian Close's Edgbaston misadventures, involving a distressed onlooker and time-wasting overs, had cost the indomitable Yorkshireman the post of honour, the captaincy was offered back to an earlier displaced incumbent, Mike Smith, before Cowdrey was asked to lead the side in the West Indies. Wounded by this vote of reduced confidence, Colin said he felt 'like a schoolboy who ran third in an egg-and-spoon race and had been awarded the prize because the first two had been disqualified.'

I should never describe the marked change this caused in Colin as iron entering his soul – no receptacle for that kind of element – but the Cowdrey who led England in the West Indies was clearly determined to show himself a masterful leader, a skipper with armour all over and no soft spots – none that anybody could get at, anyway.

To me, some had gone rather far in presenting the magnanimous Cowdrey as all courtesy and no crust. Bowlers and fieldsment had never found him all soft under-belly. The graceful perfection of his cover-drive never deceived them into thinking there was anything gentle about a stroke that could bruise a wrist or dislocate a finger. To spin bowlers he had for years been Cowdrey the brainy batsman who solved the problem of saving his stumps with his pads without being given out leg-before-wicket. As director of England's batting in 23 Tests so far he was no believer in allowing the hands of the clock to distract his attention from the basic plan of a first innings large enough to preclude defeat and long enough for wear on the pitch to encourage hope of ordering a follow-on.

This was again his hope at Kingston. John Edrich, a left-hander Australia's bowlers have never been able to rattle, reached 96 in $4\frac{1}{4}$ hours before Sobers' spin tricked him into being caught by Kanhai near mid-off. Before lunch on the second day Cowdrey completed 100, his third hundred in five innings on Sabina Park. It had taken $5\frac{1}{4}$ hours but what scope exists for a glowing innings when one fast ball kicks shoulder high and the next scoots along like a rat mistaking the block-hole for a bolt-hole? The pitch had begun to behave in a manner matching its ill-favoured appearance. Its flawed surface could no longer be likened to a mirror – except perhaps one for use by a witch long past caring.

The captain was the only Englishman to make a century in the match. When the main bowler, Gibbs, was rewarded with the wicket of the best batsman, Cowdrey 101, whose attempted cut nicked a catch to Derryck Murray's gloves, England had 279 with seven wickets left. They were all gone 93 runs later, after leg-spinner David Holford, leaping wide to catch Barrington, 63, with his left hand, began a breakthrough of three for nine.

By dismissing four men Wesley Hall moved a step nearer his target of 200 Test wickets. Despite a knee injury in a road accident, the unquenchable Barbadian was still trying to live up to the rank of swiftest bowler on earth. No one had been able to wrest the title from him between 1958 and 1967, when he swerved his car to avoid running over a stray dog. Berkeley Gaskin put in words what everyone recognised in this magnificent cricketer: 'Wherever you touch Wes, he's heart all over.' I believe that within a year of this Kingston match only more injuries suffered through wry fortune in Australia prevented the big fellow from rounding off his career with 200 Test wickets. If ever we see another bowler storm up to the wicket like Hall it will be great for cricket – for everyone except batsmen, that is.

Thirteen overs by three English pacemen in the last hour of the second day made their side's 376 look too far beyond any team's reach for the distance to be calculated without calling in the National Aeronautical Space Administration. When David Brown had Murray caught in the first over and John Snow sent a lizard-like shooter scuttling under Stephen Camacho's bat both openers had been fired out for five. For freshness' sake as well as fearsomeness, Cowdrey used Snow, Brown and Welsh left-hander Jeff Jones in short bursts. An unsortable mixture of bumpers and shooters turned the game into some outdoor cousin of Russian roulette. The angle at which Jones' bowling kicked from widening cracks made his fliers the most difficult to avoid.

Discussing this diabolical pitch with the players years later, I noticed Rohan Kanhai's first reactions were to roll his eyes and gently caress his left ribs, as if they were still tender. Clive Lloyd's habitually happy expression turned into a grimace. Struck on the shoulders and chest, the 6 feet 3 inch Guyanese left-hander had twice thrown his bat away in pain. Height and heart helped Lloyd to carry his bat for the top score, 34, in a meagre total of 143. The three pacemen took just 48 overs to dispose of the whole West Indian side. No other bowlers were required. While not lagging behind Jones and Brown as a source of physical danger, Snow outdid both in picking on cracks from which balls skidded through low. Brian Close called it one of the most terrifying and best attacking spells of fast bowling he had seen, reminding him of Hall and Griffith at the height of their powers in England in 1963. After a kicking out-cutter to Kanhai, one of Snow's shooters trapped Sobers on one leg in front of the stumps. John is the only bowler who has taken this eminent wicket first ball twice in Tests (the other instance having been a hook which Close caught at the Oval in 1966). To get Kanhai and Sobers with two balls would make any bowler's day but Snow wrapped these prizes up in a bundle of seven for 49 in 126 balls. It was the Sussex poet-bowler's most reward-ing day in international cricket until his bowling tore divots out of the Sydney track as he took seven for 40 with 15 more balls in January, 1971.

The way the Sabina Park wicket was misbehaving, averting an innings defeat would call for extraordinary batting in the follow-on. Nurse began this with high cricketing intelligence, impelled by the state of the pitch to make the most of two hours against tired bowlers before they had a Sunday's rest.

With his new authoritative front, Cowdrey imposed a curfew on his team. After fixing an hour for them to be in on Saturday night he forbade golf, fishing or sight-seeing jaunts on Sunday – outlets which the Duke of Norfolk had defended when someone said England's players in Australia were having too much golf. On the Sunday in Kingston, all had to rest at their hotel. They loafed around the swimming pool and Jack Jennings' hands loosened the quick bowlers' muscles for Monday.

The wicket looked like a jigsaw, and not a first-quality product of the jigsaw industry at that. More like the first attempt by an apprentice who had nothing like the hang of it. Keith Miller could put his fingers down the cracks. Nurse said to slim Lance Gibbs : 'You'd better not tread on the wicket, Toothpick, or you might slip out of sight.'

Resuming his stirring counter-attack, Nurse made 73 of the first 100 opening stand of the series before chopping a low in-cutter into his stumps, as had happened in the first innings. After three hours of supporting defence for 25 Camacho lost his off peg to a grubber from D'Oliveira and one from Brown deviated abruptly off a crack, like a fast leg-break, to shatter Lloyd's wicket. By contrast with those two shooters, Brown's first ball to Sobers kicked from a crevice and popped from the captain's bat just above Titmus' reach at close forward leg. So Gary narrowly escaped the ignominy of a king pair – out first ball in each innings. Two awkward out-cutters found his bat's edge. One sent Graveney off from second slip for repairs to a damaged finger. Replacing him there D'Oliveira turfed a low chance when Sobers was seven.

Keeping wickets up at the stumps was almost as difficult as batting, so Jim Parks was standing back to Dolly's medium-pace bowling. When Butcher 21 glanced fine, the Sussex 'keeper lunged low to get his left glove between ball and earth. When umpire Douglas Sang Hue signalled Basil out, half West Indies' wickets were down for 204 – still 29 short of the total needed to make England bat again. The decision was a formality, because Butcher, turning with the shot, saw the ball settle in Parks' red-palmed glove and walked without looking to see how Sang Hue was answering the Englishmen's appeal. As he turned away, however, some of the crowd took a shake of his head for disagreement with the decision rather than a sign of his feelings about having to bat in a Test on so execrable a pitch. As Holford came in cries of dissent came from open benches and standing room in the cheapest sector of the ground.

Before Holford could face D'Oliveira's next ball a bottle

sailed over the wire-mesh fence. Of all the sights that tempt men and boys to mischievous mimicry few can rival a flung object, whether it be pennies into a boxing ring, orange peel, an empty bottle or a beercan. Herd instinct takes over and a crowd becomes a mob out of control. As at Georgetown and Port of Spain, it required only one to start a hail of bottles from the open slope. Police swinging batons as they ran to this boundary to uphold law and order had the reverse effect, doubling the crowd's anger.

Gamely taking the risk that random or malicious bottles might hit him, a substantial target, Cowdrey walked to the wire. Sobers joined him in appealing to the demonstrators to quieten down, so that the game could go on. Back came yells of 'We want Butcher!', 'Sang Hue no more!' Protests turned to insult when some shouted: 'Sang Hue ras umpire!' (a Jamaican slang term), 'What de hell a Chinee know about cricket?', 'How much you pay dat Chinee, Cowdrey?' and worse.

Through the tumult, both captains tried to assure the protesters that Butcher had been fairly caught. (In his readably enlightening book on the West Indies, *In the Main*, J. S. Barker says Professor John Figueroa, of the University of the West Indies, told him that in the back-streets and backyards of Kingston a local custom makes a batsman not out if the catcher's hand touches the ground. The striker challenges the catcher to show the back of his hand; if there is dirt on it the batsman stays in.)

The captains' pleas had a sufficiently calming effect for Jones and Brown to begin clearing the long-on sector of bottles, using their sun-hats to collect chunks of broken glass. A simmering near-calm was broken when a crash-helmeted riot squad with mesh shields ran across the ground to positions near the wire barrier. Hoots and catcalls greeted them and a fresh rain of bottles began. As more squadmen marched across to the trouble-spot the players left the field.

The riot squad flung canisters of teargas into the seething mass behind the wire. This caused a frantic stampede. As the wind blew clouds of gas back across the field panic-stricken people rushed toward the other end, desperately trying to escape the choking fumes. Men, women, children, ground attendants and police (except the riot squadmen in gasmasks) ran pell-mell towards two narrow exits at the pavilion end. Distressed women's

"Didn't mind withdrawing east of Suez – but this is ridiculous."

screams and frightened children's cries added to the tumult. The rush knocked benches over and people were trampled underfoot. On his way from the evacuated pressbox Close picked up two women and carried them clear. Nobody knows how the stampede did not result in a death-roll, as occurred at Calcutta later.

Players were gasping for breath in the English room, in the front of the pavilion. Whiffs of teargas even drifted to the West Indians' room at the back of the building. Tea interval was taken in the 90 minutes before the players re-entered the field. Even then, resumption was delayed by a few bottles sailing into the outfield, long-range parting shots from implacable throwers beyond the outer wall of the ground. England's bowlers were unable to reassert their dominance and probably were apprehensive of another outbreak. Sobers and Holford put the West Indies 25 ahead, with one day to go, plus 75 minutes which England requested be made up on a sixth morning.

On the fifth day cracks made the pitch look like the dried-out floor of a desert saltpan, so Englishmen who were sure the stoppage reprieved West Indies from imminent defeat still felt that postponed victory was only hours away.

The challenge of this desperate situation seemed, if anything, to quicken Sobers' reflexes, always close to electronic in swiftness. Evolution's ultimate specimen in cricketers overcame the surface's falsities with batting that held watching players incredulous, marvelling at the range of his genius. If Gary's 132 in the tied Brisbane Test at almost 50 runs an hour was high among dazzling virtuoso performances against international bowling since McCabe and Bradman's day, his 113 not out on the splenetic track at Sabina Park was the most absorbing of post-war innings. Keith Miller recalls it as Gary's greatest. How does Sobers rank it? 'I was lucky,' he told me. 'To bat on that wicket you needed luck – and I had it.' Close says it was unbelievable in its excellence of shot production, defensive probing and mature thinking.

It completed for Sobers the dual distinction of having played such memorable Test centuries on one of the best and by far the worst of wickets. With unplayable balls to be kept out, reaching 50 required two hours (five minutes short of his Brisbane 100). Getting through the nineties, single by hard-won single, took almost an hour, his second 50 about four hours.

Withstanding whatever came, Sobers' willow bat seemed to acquire the toughness of greenheart, timber through which the strongest man cannot drive a nail; yet the bowlers were trying to get a ball through it.

In making 35 Holford stayed long enough for their sixth-wicket stand to add 110, recalling how these cousins rallied West Indies from 95 to 369 at Lord's in 1966. Some thought Cowdrey erred tactically by sticking so long to pace bowling. Long afterward Sobers revealed that was his own opinion – he thought use of spin would have increased his difficulties. Though no ball shoots as disconcertingly as a fast one, spinners' greater accuracy carries the risk of a well-pitched grubber sneaking through to the base of the stumps. No sign of concern was visible when, toward the end of his innings, he hit 16 off an over from off-spinner Fred Titmus, beginning with a six over a sightboard. Murray and Griffith stuck with him while the seventh and eighth wickets added 74. In this innings 38 byes swelled the total toward 70 byes in the match, an index to the wicket's spite.

In the same Test that brought his first-ball duck he raised the 18th of his 25 Test centuries and passed 5,000 runs (on his way to 7,000 and who knows what?)

With the suddenness of one of his flashing hooks, Sobers dramatically changed the tone of the match. Coming after more than two days' struggle to ward off defeat, his closure at 391 for nine wickets deserves to stand as one of the most mercurial strokes of captaincy. It was like a boxer long pinned to the ropes surprisingly launching a telling jab to snap his opponent's wind. It left England, 158 behind, 155 minutes to bat on a satanic track.

Ten minutes after his six-hour innings Sobers began bowling on a cloudy evening and made himself the only Test century-maker who has taken two wickets in the next over. After flattening Boycott's leg stump, he rapped Cowdrey's pads with the next two balls and succeeded with his second appeal. Cowdrey's attitude, a rare lapse in so good a sportsman, indicated disagreement with the umpire's ruling. If the ball grazed the bat first, the touch was too slight for the umpire to detect. Slow-motion television playbacks did nothing to weaken Englishmen's opinion that Cowdrey and Barrington (13) were an unfortunate pair among the eight men out lbw in the match – four of each side. A light appeal saved 40 minutes – or lost them, according to whether you were hoping for a draw or a win.

The only man who passed 20, Graveney, swept Gibbs firmly and saw the ball bounce from Camacho's hip at short-leg to be caught by Griffith. (Following the same pattern, Nurse's shot in a Melbourne Test bounced from the side of Freeman's head to be caught deeper on the leg side by Stackpole. As he ran to the prostrate fieldsman, Lawry saw the catch taken and called: 'He's out!' Freeman, shaking his ringing head, sat up saying: 'No fear, I'm not.')

During the carried-over 75 minutes on the sixth morning gamesmanship to reduce the number of balls faced did the Englishmen no credit. Seeing such tactics must have induced wry thoughts in the mind of Close, as time-wasting had been a much-mentioned ground for his loss of the captaincy. Were consciences at ease a month later at Port of Spain when the West Indians did not retard their over rate while the Englishmen chased runs against the clock and won?

In a determined effort to win the Sabina Park Test against shrinking time Gibbs took three wickets for five in one burst and two slip-chances by D'Oliveira off him were spilt. The escapes did not disturb Basil's calm. When he saw Brown eighth out at 68, yorked by Sobers after two bouncers, Dolly walked off with the outgoing batsman. As England had two wickets left with only one ball to go, to have completed the over could not have altered the result of the match, one of four draws in the 1968 series.

With the sweet smell of victory titillating their nostrils, until teargas took over, nothing could sway members of the English camp from their conviction that the bottle-throwing let the West Indies off the hook when the game was running strongly against them and the innings was nearing the point of collapse. They certainly had a case. The list of dramatic recoveries, helping make cricket the game it is, is to long for this to be taken for granted. Some West Indians have contended that, with Sobers and Holford against tiring bowlers, the 75 minutes lost prevented the cousins from taking earlier steps toward victory. While the last surviving witnesses have breath it is a subject for argument beyond the powers of arbitration to settle.

TEARGAS PANIC

Kingston, Feb. 8, 9, 10, 12, 13, 1968. England won toss. Drawn.

ENGLAND 1st innings		2nd innings	
G. Boycott b Hall	17	b Sobers	0
J. H. Edrich c Kanhai b Sobers	96	b Hall	6
M. C. Cowdrey (c.) c Murray b Gibbs	101	lbw b Sobers	0
K. F. Barrington c & b Holford ...	63	lbw Griffith	13
T. W. Graveney b Hall	30	c Griffith b Gibbs	71
J. M. Parks c Sobers b Holford ...	3	lbw Gibbs...	3
B. L. D'Oliveira st Murray b Holford	0	not out	13
F. J. Titmus lbw Hall	19	c Camacho b Gibbs	4
D. J. Brown c Murray b Hall ...	14	b Sobers	0
J. A. Snow b Griffith	10		
I. J. Jones not out	0		
B 12, lb 7, nb 4	23	B 8	8

Total off 169.2 overs (9 hrs. 51 mins.) 376   8 wkts. off 38.5 overs (1 hr. 55 mins.) 68

Fall: 49, 178. 279, 310, 318, 318, 351, 352, 376, 376.
      0, 0, 19, 19, 38, 51, 61, 68.

Bowling.	Balls	Runs	Wkts.			Balls	Runs	Wkts.
Hall	162	63	4	...	...	18	3	1
Griffith	188	72	1	...	...	30	13	1
Sobers	186	56	1	...	...	186	56	3
Gibbs	282	91	1	...	...	278	11	3
Holford	198	71	3					

WEST INDIES 1st innings		Follow-on	
S. Camacho b Snow	5	b D'Oliveira	25
D. L. Murray c D'Oliveira b Brown	0	lbw Brown	41
R. B. Kanhai c Graveney b Snow	26	c Edrich b Jones	36
S. M. Nurse b Jones	22	b Snow	73
C. Lloyd not out	34	b Brown	0
G. S. Sobers lbw Snow... ...	0	not out	113
B. F. Butcher c Parks b Snow...	21	c Parks b D'Oliveira	25
D. Holford c Parks b Snow ...	6	lbw Titmus	35
C. C. Griffith c D'Oliveira b Snow	8	lbw Jones	14
W. W. Hall b Snow	0	c Parks b Jones	0
L. R. Gibbs c Parks b Jones ...	0	not out	1
B 12, lb 5, w 1, nb 3.	21	B 33, lb 10, nb 5	48

Total off 48 overs (2 hrs. 23 mins.) 143   9 wkts. dec. off 135 overs (6 hrs. 18 mins.) 391

Fall: 5,   5, 51, 80, 120, 126 142 142 ,,143
     102, 122, 164, 174, 204, 314, 388, 388,

Bowling.	Balls	Runs	Wkts.			Balls	Runs	Wkts.
Brown	78	34	1	...	...	198	65	2
Snow	126	49	7	...	...	162	91	1
Jones	84	39	2	...	...	180	90	3
D'Oliveira						192	51	2
Titmus						42	32	4
Barrington						36	14	–

Runs per 100 balls: England 36, West Indies 48.
Balls per hour: England 87, West Indies 106.

Umpires: Douglas Sang Hue, Cortez Jordan

93

Chapter Nine

BE ENGLAND WHAT SHE WILL ...

SCHOOLBOYS reading of what the Crusaders did in Palestine and what Henry the Fifth said to his troops before Harfleur and how Edward the First earned the title of Hammer of the Scots must be curious when they turn to cricket history. After noting the Duke of Wellington's inside opinion that the Battle of Waterloo was won on the playing fields of Eton they are entitled to wonder what has happened to the combative spirit of the English, as evidenced in those who go to cricket matches.

Can the weather's coolness, if that is the word, be the reason why onlookers endure passively upsets of a sort that in warmer climes have brought bottles and objects of mineral and vegetable nature over the boundary fences, sometimes followed by the irate throwers in person.

To time of writing, not one of more than 230 Test matches on seven grounds in Britain has been halted by an invasion of Englishmen. Though no English ground figures among the place-getters in the riot stakes the citizens of Manchester deserve mention for a good try, in which a crowd did hold up a Test at Old Trafford.

It was after a riot abroad that a British fan wrote to *Playfair* editor Gordon Ross suggesting that, if a disturbance prevented a team winning, the International Cricket Conference should award the Test to the deprived side. He thought inclusion of such a provision in the laws might be a deterrent to potential rioters; if framed so that hooliganism could cause disqualification of the demonstrators' national team such incidents might cease.

The time lost in the 1921 Test at Old Trafford, about half an hour, was to England's disadvantage. It balked a move by the Hon. Lionel Tennyson, the poet's grandson, to press on from the first good start England had made after three losses to the most powerful Australian side England had seen. About 6,000 people waited through Saturday while recurring showers kept the wet wicket too soft for play to begin. Several times small groups of people walked out to the pitch to test the turf with fingers, feet or prod its edges with umbrellas. Each time police quietly escorted them off. About 4.30 p.m. captains Tennyson and Armstrong gave up hope of play. Abandonment of the day without a ball bowled annoyed some of the crowd and hundreds invaded the field. They were tactfully ushered off by Manchester police and placated by the issue of rain-passes for Monday, suggested by Australian manager Sydney Smith although a notice outside had warned people that they entered at their own risk.

That blank day reduced the Test to a two-day match in which the pitch rolled out so placidly on Monday that batsmen could face the dreaded fast pair, Gregory and McDonald, without alarm. Essex right-hander A. C. ('Jack') Russell, 101 with two chances in four hours, and Kent left-hander Frank Woolley, 41, tried to score at the rapid rate England needed, but Hampshire left-hander Philip Mead's 47 took $2\frac{1}{4}$ hours. With dash like that Dexter showed here 40 years later, Lancashire right-hander Ernest Tyldesley, 78 not out, and hard-hitting Surrey captain Percy Fender, 44, did their best to make up for that slow rate by rattling runs on to the board at almost three a minute.

The fifth-wicket pair had made 81 and the total was 260 when Tennyson entered the field at 5.40 p.m. and waved the batsmen off. His closure was designed to get the Australians in for the last 40 minutes of the day. Primed by a word from Australia's Halifax-born wicketkeeper, Hanson Carter (the only Yorkshireman in the match) Armstrong challenged the legality of the closure. Reference to the laws proved that the attempted declaration was 50 minutes too late for the first day of a two-day match – a point overlooked by several ex-captains in the pavilion who had been advising Tennyson. Meanwhile players and umpires left the field and the Australians enjoyed 20 minutes' rest from bowling and fielding.

Mystified, the crowd greeted the Australians' reappearance with a storm of hooting from all around the ground. No doubt most of the hooters were not sure why they came back but felt that 20 unexplained minutes off the field when England might at last have a chance deserved censure. Hooting as Armstrong took the ball to bowl caused him to sit down until it eased. As he had bowled the last over before the stoppage it was illegal for him to deliver the next but amid the din neither the players nor the umpires noticed.

Ever-sportsmanlike, the debonair Tennyson went around the boundary to explain the position and clear the Australians from blame. Umpire Street also spoke to the noisiest section of the crowd. Play was resumed and Tyldesley and Fender carried their partnership to 102 in a total of 362 for the day (5 hours 33 minutes). This tally and the Australians' average of 130 balls an hour (21½ overs) illustrate how much more cricket crowds used to get for their money. There were two fast bowlers, medium-pacer Hunter Hendry, leg-spinner Armstrong and left-hand spinner Charlie Macartney.

After overnight rain the prospect that England might bowl the Australians out twice in a day on a drying wicket attracted 25,000 to Old Trafford on Tuesday. One man stood in the way, vice-captain Herbert Collins. His was not the sort of batting the crowd had come to see, all defence with strokes a secondary consideration. Few except players on the field or watching could fully appreciate his care and concentration on a pitch responding to the spin of Cecil Parkin, left-handers Woolley and Charles Parker and leg-spinner Fender. Collins saw six partners come and go for low scores before he was joined at 125 by all-rounder Jack Gregory. With almost three hours to go the game could still be lost. By the time Collins fell leg-before-wicket to Parkin only 90 minutes were left and England's chance had been smothered. While holding out for four hours 49 minutes he had inconspicuously put together 40 runs.

This innings was brought to life, so to say, two years before Trevor Bailey was born. Though most of the crowd had long tired of the sight of Collins, 14 fellow Australians in the dressing-room applauded heartily enough for double their number, well aware that his patient bat had averted a real danger of defeat. In keeping the bowlers out for five hours 18 minutes, the Australians made only 141 off the bat from 117 overs. England's four spinners and one medium-pace swinger, Johnny Douglas, had made them play an average of 132 balls an hour. Six of the 10 batsmen had their stumps hit, and the pitch was awkward enough for 22 byes to get past George Brown and swell the extras to 34. The Australians were 187 behind but, as there was time for only 13 overs, Tennyson did not order them to follow on.

For an English crowd's invasion halting a touring team's play we have to go back to a lesser match than a Test in Queen Victoria's reign, the 1884 visit by W. L. Murdoch's Australians. In a game at the Oval, where scarcity of runs gives clues to the state of the wicket, F. R. Spofforth took eight for 62 and six for 34 in dismissing Players of England for 107 and 71. As they had made 151 the Australians needed fewer than 30 to win, but a complication arose when Edmund Peate (who had taken five for 50 in the first innings) bowled giant batsman George Bonnor. I am grateful to historian Irving Rosenwater for unearthing this gem from *Cricket,* 1884 :

'The Australians were left with only 28 to win, and just as two o'clock arrived Bonnor was bowled with the score at 17. It was generally thought that, as there were only 11 left to win, the game would be completed before lunch. The bell rang, though, and this gave rise to a very disorderly scene. The Players remained in the field but, Emmett's application to the Australian captain for the continuance of the game being met with a negative, there was no other course for them but to retire.

'For some time a certain section of the crowd remained in front of the pavilion, behaving in a very disorderly manner. When the bell rang for a renewal at half-past two their attitude became still more hostile, and the middle of the ground was not only occupied but the stumps were sent flying.

'Seeing the mob pull up the stumps, some of the Australians went out to explain that they left the field not to get more gate-money from people coming in after lunch but to save the caterers heavy loss. No charge would be made after lunch.

'A Surrey official asked some of the Players to join in trying to persuade the invaders to leave. Tufty-haired Edmund Peate, the skilful slow left-hander from Leeds, replied : "Naw, sir. Ah didn't coomere t'quell riot, Ah coom to play crickit."

At last, after the arrival of a reinforcement of police, and on Murdoch and McDonnell proceeding to the wickets, the crowd gradually cleared away from the centre and the game was resumed at half-past three. The 11 runs wanted were quickly got and the match ended in favour of the Australians by nine wickets. The two batsmen were loudly cheered at the finish and there was no sign of renewal of the disturbance.'

Old Trafford, Manchester, July 23, 25, 26, 1921. Drawn.

Hon. L. H. Tennyson won toss from W. W. Armstrong.

ENGLAND 1st innings 5 hours 33 minutes   2nd innings 29 minutes

A. C. Russell b Gregory	 101	
G. Brown c Gregory b Armstrong	... 31	
F. E. Woolley c Pellew b Armstrong	... 41	
C. P. Mead c Andrews b Hendry	... 47	
E. Tyldesley not out 78		
P. G. H. Fender not out 44		
C. Hallows	not out 16	
L. H. Tennyson (c.)		
J. W. H. T. Douglas		
C. Parkin	c Collins b Andrews ... 23	
C. W. L. Parker	not out 3	
B 12, lb 5, nb 3... 20	lb 2 2	
4 wickets dec. off 120 overs) 362	1 wicket off 13 overs ... 44	

Fall: 65, 145, 217, 260   Fall: 23

Bowling.	Balls	Runs	Wkts.		Balls	Runs	Wkts.
Gregory	138	79	1	Andrews	30	23	1
McDonald	186	112	–	Pellew	18	6	–
Macartney	48	20	–	Taylor	6	1	–
Hendry	150	74	1	Hendry	24	12	–
Armstrong	198	57	2				

AUSTRALIA 1st innings 5 hours 18 minutes

W. Bardsley b Parkin	3
H. L. Collins lbw Parkin	40
C. G. Macartney b Parker...	13
T. J. Andrews c Tennyson b Fender ...	6
J. M. Taylor b Fender	4
C. E. Pellow c Tyldesley b Parker ...	17
W. W. Armstrong (c.) b Douglas... ...	17
J. M. Gregory b Parkin	29
H. Carter b Parkin...	0
H. L. Hendry c Russell b Parkin	4
E. A. McDonald not out	8
B 22, lb 5, nb 7	34
Total off 116.4 overs	175

Fall: 9, 33, 44, 48, 78, 125, 161, 161, 166, 175

Bowling.	Balls	Runs	Wkts.
Parkin	178	38	5
Woolley	234	38	–
Parker	168	32	2
Fender	90	30	2
Douglas	30	3	1

Runs per 100 balls: England 50, Australia 25.
Balls per hour: England 132, Australia, 130.
Minutes per over: England 2.7, Australia 2.7.

Umpires: J. Moss, A. E. Street.

Chapter Ten

DON'T SPARE THE HORSES

SIGHTS unknown in Oxford Street meet the eye on the way to the National Cricket Stadium outside Karachi. If you are not John Lennon and you wish to smarten up, you may squat by the edge of the footpath while a Pakistani street barber shaves or trims you in the shade of a tree. As the sun burns on westward, this pavement tonsorial artist gradually shifts east to keep in the tree's moving shade.

A south-westerly blowing off the Arabian Sea makes the clear, dry heat in the stadium bearable, even at 92 degrees. Should the Sind desert exhale a north-easter from its gritty throat two words would be used locally to describe the day: stinking hot. Wide mats held aloft by bamboo poles shade the most privileged parts of the concrete terraces ringing the stadium's field.

When the Englishmen began their last Test match here in March, 1969, weather was the least of their worries. It seemed mild by comparison with political crises at fever-pitch in the Islamic Republic of Pakistan. Like the falcon kites hovering above the ground, political curses had hung over the tour from the start. The visit was arranged at short notice to plug a gap created by the South African Government's objection to an MCC team containing Basil D'Oliveira, the former Cape Coloured all-rounder who had carved out a cricket career in England. Before Cowdrey's team flew from Ceylon into West Pakistan riots in denser-populated East Pakistan (as it then was) caused a state of emergency and cancellation of that section of the tour. The decision was resented in the already-aggrieved eastern division of the two-part nation, where farm labourers' pay was half that paid in the western wing.

The first Test at Lahore revealed a pattern of political and economic upheaval: railway and dock strikes for wage rises, power blackouts, students' protests against academic stagnation and financial rigidity, processions, mass demonstrations flaring into violence, fanatical assassinations, all aimed against the authoritarian regime of President Ayub Khan. General Ayub, who had first taken power as Army chief under martial law in 1958, was harder to get out than John Edrich. The disturbances contained no hostility to the Englishmen but spread to cricket fields as a sure way into headlines around the globe. It was unsettling to the players to be locked in the Continental Hotel for a day before the Lahore Test, then to see chairs thrown on to the field and hear mobs chanting 'Ayub is a dog!' As personal adviser to the general, Pakistan's Cricket Board president Fida Hassan was himself a target for vituperation.

Cowdrey's innings, containing two let-offs, lacked the touch that made the best of his 22 Test centuries look as if he could make a hundred with a barbecue fork. But no other captain has put together 100 in such uneasy circumstances, demanding exceptional concentration. A noisy crowd threw rubbish at policemen, Army guards patrolled with rifles at the ready and nobody knew what would happen next. Pakistan's team included a little law student of the rebel Students' Action Committee, Aftab Gul, whose name means flower of the sun. Aftab opens innings with Favell-like strokes. 'He bats like he talks,' they say. His presence was said to be a sort of insurance that riots would not stop the match. Once he went into the crowd, urging restraint. As Cowdrey, caught for 100, walked off, quarrelsome groups of youths were throwing chairs at each other. Colin waved to D'Oliveira to follow him off but Aftab laid a pleading hand on Dolly's arm, persuading him to stay, as the chair fight was subsiding into a ceasefire. When the Pakistanis were battling to avoid defeat in the last session of the fourth day, sections of the Lahore crowd bombarded police stationed around the boundary with fruit and pieces of wood from smashed chairs. A chunk of ice narrowly missed Roger Prideaux. An hour before the end the police retaliated by throwing debris back into the crowd. The resultant uproar caused troops to intervene and acting captain Graveney led the Englishmen off to have drinks in their room instead of on the field, before Mushtaq and Hanif Mohammad played out the last 50 minutes. Among the Englishmen a feeling grew that, as the atmosphere was so unsuitable for international cricket, they should not be there.

When pressure for a Test in riot-torn East Pakistan brought the Englishmen to its capital, Dacca, despite the state of emergency, manager Leslie Ames said they refused to play without police protection. University students who led the best-organised political demonstrators thereupon threatened to block any attempt to leave without playing the match. Wisely Ames did not allow the incongruity of the situation to prevent him from treating with the All-Party Students' Action Committee, who took over control from police and troops. He induced them to have the boundary line painted 15 yards inside the eight feet barbed-wire fence. They posted 30 students with megaphones around the field, making them responsible for different sections of the crowd.

In the country's worst trouble-spot the students kept their part of the bargain. The best crowds of the tour watched the Test without riotous interruption. Not an orange or a mango, much less a chair, was thrown by the 20,000 on the first day, though their patience was sorely tried by tactical attrition on an under-prepared pitch of dried mud. In response to Pakistan's sole toss win of the series England bowled only 14 overs an hour. Accurate bowling and deep fields restricted even Majid Jehangir Khan and Mushtaq mainly to singles. One correspondent called the over rate unforgivable, even in oven-like heat. Majid's 27 contained no reminder that in scoring the fastest 100 in 1967 (61 minutes at Swansea) he smote 13 sixes, the most ever hit in an innings in Britain. After tea the Dacca crowd jeered, hooted, whistled and blew bugles. In one section exasperated fans lit a few fires on terraces without alarming sari-clad women next door. Only 176 runs struggled on to the board in a day; Pakistan averaged $2\frac{1}{4}$ runs an over. Drinks taken twice each session swallowed 27 minutes. One drink-break stretched to eight minutes when a television interviewer hauled a microphone out to chat with Mushtaq and Cowdrey as Colin swigged a bottle of soft drink. Throughout this drawn game Cowdrey showed by several gestures his appreciation of the student leaders' part in enabling the Test to be played. From the crowd's angle a more substantial gesture would have been choice of Milburn who had flown in after breaking records for Western Australia.

Soon after the MCC team flew on to Karachi mobs rampaging through Dacca's red-light district burned down a brothel and three cinemas.

Winning the toss gave England first use of a pitch that Hanif thought capable of lasting eight days. Milburn batted as if he felt England ought to win in five-eighths of that time (the Government having sanctioned an extra day). Never one to wait for opportunity to knock, the Northumbrian heavyweight began his first Test innings on an overseas wicket with four boundary hits in Asif Masood's first four overs – a glance, two square-cuts and a hooked bouncer. No sign of concern about dew's effect in a 10 o'clock start. No need for the crowd to spit red betel juice and call 'Maro!' (Urdu for hit out) as this full-blown strokes-man made 24 in half an hour and Edrich twice reached the off boundary with back-foot shots off Majid, a Cambridge captain in the making.

The medium-paced accuracy of 20-year-old Sarfraz Nawaz (who signed for Northants) and Intikhab Alam's leg spin steadied the scoring a while. In scarcely an hour – next to no time for such an adjustment – Milburn had skilfully adapted his timing and technique to the balls' slower and lower arrival than the come-on-to-you bounce he had mastered in Perth. Greeting Saeed's off-spin with a cover-driven four, Milburn scored at a variety of angles, mainly in the square sectors. A straight bat, kept in check, respected balls he could not feel sure of treating forcefully yet safely. Complications so easily beset so many international batsmen that John Thicknesse commented in the *Evening Standard* on the economy and simplicity of Milburn's game. In the best opening stand of the series Colin overshadowed Edrich, though having hardly one-third of the compact left-hander's Test experience. Bothered by Intikhab's spin, John was dropped off a sweep in making 32 of the first 78 before Saeed held him at short-leg off the spinner who was to become a Surrey team-mate.

Off his own uninhibited bat Milburn made 52 before lunch, showing up the lethargic scoring rate of the two preceding Tests. After lunch Saeed alternated pacemen at the opposite end from Intikhab, setting deep, hard-to-penetrate fields. It is a stamp of quality for anyone to bat with Graveney and not look inferior yet in 75 minutes after lunch Colin outscored England's master craftsman by 42 to 13. Not a man to fidget about the nervous nineties, Milburn lifted Intikhab over square-leg for six and twice dragged short balls from Mushtaq to the fence to raise a faultless 100 of England's first 153. No fieldsman had a hope of overtaking any of the 13 boundaries in his 3¼-hour century (42 minutes shorter than Cowdrey's Lahore 100 and over an hour quicker than D'Oliveira's at Dacca on a pock-marked pitch where most batsmen trod as suspiciously as astronauts stepping amid moon craters).

This prize-winning 100 off 163 balls sparked the first of two invasions. About 300 young fans rushed to congratulate the beefy centurymaker. The shoulder-high wire fence's eight-inch-wide mesh made climbing easy. There was no risk of a Pakistani posse abducting the batsman who was so quickly putting England in command of the game (admirers of Milburn's 126 not out against West Indies at Lord's in 1966 had been unable to lift their 260 lb hero) but Graveney went to Ollie's end with protective intent. Knowing that some enthusiastic back-slaps get uncomfortably close to kidney-punches, Tom circled around his partner (no mean circumference) flourishing his bat, which connected with a few rumps. 'They weren't very hard but I think they were my only decent strokes up to then,' he said later. Milburn's own comment: 'I was never frightened, because the mobs weren't against us. They just wanted to shake hands'.

As they were cleared, more than 50 Karachi cricketers started around the ground bearing banners, some in Urdu, a few in English. Other issues besides politics were rankling with West Pakistanis in Karachi, home town of the incomparable Mohammad family (four brothers have played Tests). The nation's main seaport had been the capital until Ayub's Government in 1960 moved administration to cooler Rawalpindi, in the hills up toward the Khyber Pass. Most of the banners called for the resignation of Pakistan's selectors, of whom three of the four came from Lahore. One placard named them and said 'Killers of cricket – go out.' Others demanded reinstatement of Hanif Mohammad as captain instead of Saeed. (Six months earlier Hanif had captained The Rest of the World at Lord's after an injury sent Pataudi off. Hanif impressed as Asia's most gifted batsman while making 104 and 93 against Australia at first acquaintance with the Melbourne wicket in 1964; Saeed, as his free-stroking vice-captain, scored 105 in his first Sydney innings).

Some placards called for the return of the Cricket Board from Rawalpindi to Karachi. The procession gathered fence-scaling recruits as it circled, so Saeed led his players off and tea was taken early. After 20 minutes the Pakistan team began returning to the field but a throng still fumed around the dressing-rooms where a group of youths tried to make a new issue of Graveney's use of the bat against their friends. It was the first time MCC had been subjected to any hostility on the tour. Asked would he try to have the time wastage made up (as at Port of Spain in 1960) Cowdrey replied: 'Let's just get through today first. I am happy to continue the match, so long as the crowds let us, but we'll have to think again if this sort of thing recurs.'

Fifty minutes were lost before the 12,000 crowd settled to watch Graveney and Milburn carry their second-wicket stand past 100. In calmer times Pakistanis had seldom, if ever, seen better batting, though the ball's sluggishness from this pitch did not favour free forward shots of gap-finding speed. At one end Graveney, a tall player of handsome strokes that wear well, and owner of the best footwork of any Englishman since Hammond. At the other, 260 lb of Milburn, an eye-filling, wide-screen player gripping the handle with generous hands and demanding admittance to the upper echelon of international batsmen. In the grasp of these two, a bat looks as different as a Toledo sword from a butcher's chopper. No short ball had a hope of escaping Ollie's back-foot blows to the off boundary or being punched through or over midwicket. The only bowler who found that Milburn's bat was not all middle was Intikhab, who occasionally spun a ball to the outer edge, yet never sharply enough to cause a chance. Though five minutes were lost by intruders acclaiming Graveney's 50 the pair made 73 off the last 23 overs. They enabled England to reach 226 for one wicket off 75 overs in a shortened day on which Pakistan bowled 97 balls an hour. It was the only time in the series that a team attained three runs an over – an agreeable change from two an over at Dacca and $2\frac{1}{2}$ at Lahore.

After adding two on the second morning Milburn was dropped

at second slip off Asif Masood. Cutting at the next ball, a wider one, he was well caught by Wasim Bari, a fine wicketkeeper. Colin's 139, his highest Test score, took his international average to 46 an innings – food for reflection by those who miscast him as a slogger too impetuous to succeed often enough. The second-wicket 156 lifted England to 234. After helping Graveney add 52 for the third wicket Cowdrey (14) edged a slipcatch off a leg-break which Intikhab persuaded to bounce higher.

Off-driving as few can, Graveney raised his 100, his eleventh in Tests and the 119th of his first-class career. Excitement over this brought another rush on to the field 20 minutes before lunch to proffer boisterous congratulations and again trample on the once-sacrosanct pitch. His patience at low ebb, Tom fended them off with his bat. Police helped clear the field, but the way one of them belaboured the last recalcitrant intruder started a fresh outbreak. Over the fence came a shower of chairs and a dustbin, followed by thousands of incensed demonstrators, brushing police aside. His usually good-humoured face clouded with annoyance, Graveney advanced to meet them, urging them back. Bowing to the invasion, Saeed again led his team away and a shouting, jostling mob escorted Graveney (102) off. Lunch was taken early with England 306 for three wickets.

The churning mob demanded removal of most of the police protection on which manager Ames had insisted. Except for a few near the dressing-rooms, they were marched away – to other urgent duties. In the city people were being shot, amid outbreaks of arson and looting.

When play was resumed after an hour Graveney tried to press on but Asif Iqbal held a high drive at mid-off. Tom, who had entered at 78 was fourth out at 309. His 105 in 275 minutes, though rather gradual for him – even at 41 – was aptly described by Crawford White in the *Daily Express* as a character study of the highest quality.

He was the third victim of Intikhab, a bowler who has manfully tried to live up to a demanding name. Intikhab Alam literally means 'Chosen one of the world.' On his debut on the same ground in 1959, a few weeks before he turned 18, the chosen one's first ball in Test cricket had bowled Australian opening batsman Colin McDonald. In ten years burly Intikhab won recognition as the first of his race and faith to become the world's best leg-spinner, and he went on to confirm this as Sobers' vice-captain on the World XI's tour of Australia in 1972.

In the theocratic republic, the sons of the Prophet often name boys after the 101 qualities of God. Saeed's name stands for something celebrated, such as a significant holiday, and Ahmed was one of ten followers blessed by Mahomet. Hanif was called after a distinguished Islamic theologist who wrote a commentary on the Koran. Brother Mushtaq is one who is openly deserving. Asif Masood is one who has many good qualities, as well as a moustache that strayed into cricket from melodrama. The wicketkeeper's first name, Wasim, means 'very useful' (an under-statement) and Bari is 'a quality of God who grants blessing.'

Concentration was difficult. Although Keith Fletcher produced some pleasant shots, his 38 occupied more than two hours and D'Oliveira stayed 80 mistiming minutes for 16. Both fell to Mushtaq's leg spin, Dolly caught at midwicket and Fletcher hitting over a drive just before tea.

As Pakistan's players pushed their way out after tea popular Majid Jehangir Khan ('beneficial in his dealings with the whole world') went ahead to clear a passage for Saeed, butt of Karachi fans' disaffection. Ames would not allow Alan Knott and John Snow to go out until an escort was provided, then accompanied them through the crowd. Hundreds of the 10,000 carried chairs forward from the terraces and sat out around the boundary line.

Snow's stick-in ways in the last hour, besides making bar-rackers implore Allah to 'senda wickie', provoked disapproval from the women's reserve – much bobbing of dopattas (head scarves), fluttering of matrons' colourful saris and stirring of unmarried girls' shalwars and pyjama-legged gear. Some on-lookers wondered whether England's policy was to bat as long as possible, to have only two players on the field instead of 11. Yet Knott swung full-tosses from Mushtaq for two fours and a six to brighten the end of a trying day in which students had pelted police, sometimes with stones, and invaded the field six times, losing half an hour's playing time. In the last interrupted $3\frac{1}{2}$ hours since Graveney's century only 106 had been added off 52 overs making England's two-day total 412 for six wickets.

Riff-raff threw dust in the faces of some of Pakistan's players as they left the field and stoned the coach taking them from the stadium.

Sad news for Cowdrey caused the captain to fly off that night to attend the funeral of his father-in-law Stuart Chieseman, the former Kent C.C.C. president, leaving vice-captain Graveney to handle whatever the weekend brought forth.

When told that, if a general strike was on, the Englishmen would have to march to the stadium behind a students' black flag for protection, Ames replied: 'We will not carry any flag, black or white. If anybody tries to prevent us getting there that will be it – we just won't be there.'

They got there, and 15 runs were added on Saturday before a long-awaited event, Asif Masood's disarrangement of the stumps behind Snow, 9, at 427. Pakistan's expectation of getting England out by mid-morning for about 450 was rudely upset by Knott and tall David Brown pummelling the bowling in an unfinished eighth-wicket partnership of 75. Michael Melford described this in *The Cricketer* as the most exhilarating stand of the match. The total converged on 500. As the Kent wicket-keeper careered through the nineties Melford wondered would posting of a well-deserved 100 beside Knott's name be the spark to kindle the final explosion.

Fifteen minutes before lunch about 600 youths from outside stormed into the stadium, some with red banners. Yelling for the match to be stopped, they swarmed over railings. Knott was taking up his stance, hoping for four more runs for his first Test 100, when Brown, 25, saw the youths advancing toward mid-field. Running from his end David called: 'Come on Knotty. Let's get out of here – quick!' Alan ran off with him, though he said later: 'I didn't think there was anything to worry about. In fact, I didn't really know there was a riot on.'

Pulling up stumps, some of the invaders tried optimistically to dig up the unmarked pitch with them. Others wrecked the V.I.P. reserve, throwing chairs and 6-feet-long benches into it.

Police in red berets and khaki shorts charged, brandishing 4 feet lathis. As women fled from the guest area some of the spectators turned on banner-waving students and chair fights broke out on the terraces. Police arrested one student leader whose face and hands were spattered with blood from a wound in his forehead.

The players locked themselves in the dressing-rooms where frightened women had taken refuge. Graveney and Saeed agreed to abandon play, a decision confirmed by president Fida Hassan, who said: 'I'm sorry but we have no alternative after these crowd scenes today.' As the English players were leaving the stadium, watching crowds were told they were going out for lunch. It was a ruse to enable the players to get away before 8,000 paying customers who wanted play to resume reacted to news of the abandonment.

The Test that never finished, and had been fortunate even to start, had a duel distinction: the first match in 650 Tests in seven countries – and England's 452nd – to have been abandoned because of riots, and (as at Calcultta in 1967) no action by umpires or players could be blamed.

Twenty minutes after Ames announced cancellation of the rest of the tour the Englishmen were packing to catch the first available flight home at midnight. He said the Pakistanis were reluctant to call the tour off as they had paid a lot for it. 'One was always fearing the worst,' he said, 'and when it eventually came there was almost a sense of relief. MCC might have been in trouble if WE had called it off – in the end it was Fida Hassan who made the decision.' The strike had closed Karachi's banks so Ames was handed a £10,000 sterling cheque, the balance of Pakistan's guarantee (about 225,000 rupees). An appropriate slogan would have been: Home Ames, and don't spare the horses!

E. M. Wellings wrote in the *Evening News*: 'Words spoken by William Pitt in 1805 may be precisely applied to cricket today: "Roll up that map. It will not be wanted these ten years." Pitt was referring to Europe after Napoleon's victory at Austerlitz. We are now referring to Pakistan after the victory of the hooligans at Karachi.' That seemed to call for background sound-effects, such as cranking up a vintage phonograph to play the 1812 Overture.

From a different angle the students thought it wrong that a game should be going on while hunger-striking teachers in Karachi were risking their health, perhaps lives, in protest about national issues which were causing a death-roll of 150 and affecting the welfare of 120 millions.

Against the strains and frustrations of the ill-starred tour could be set pleasure given nearly 90,000 onlookers by almost 16 days of cricket, including centuries by Cowdrey, D'Oliveira, Milburn and Graveney – probably the two best innings Englishmen ever played in that troubled land.

Seventeen days after the English team flew to London the political storm blew Ayub out of office. The Army commander-in-chief, General Yahya Khan, a soldier to his eyebrows, proclaimed martial law. Yahya, whose name means Jehovah, promised the first one-man-one-vote election in the nation's 23 years of tempestuous history, aiming to give East Pakistan a share in a National Assembly proportionate to its greater population, about 75 millions.

Within nine months the map was unrolled. Karachi had Test cricket again, four uninterrupted days against New Zealand. In the only finish in this three-match series Graham Dowling's Kiwis won by five wickets at Lahore against a rebuilt team led by a new skipper, Intikhab, who was to bring the next Pakistani side to England. Except for a section of Dacca's 50,000 in the last hour of the last Test the crowds kept to their allotted side of the fences.

The pattern was similar when three of Ames' 1969 team, Robin Hobbs, John Murray and Bob Cottam, went back to Pakistan in 1971. They were among 10 Englishmen in a Commonwealth side captained by Mickey Stewart and containing Surrey's Pakistani left-hander Younis Ahmed, Australian bowler Neil Hawke and Jamaican batsman Ron Headley, of Worcestershire. Matches at Karachi, Lahore and Dacca proceeded smoothly until the fourth afternoon at Dacca when Pakistan's last two men were batting, only 125 ahead with $2\frac{1}{2}$ hours to go. Demonstrators spilling from a crowd of 30,000 East Pakistanis caused the teams to quit the field and abandon the match.

Existence levels in the eastern division had been lowered by the worst cyclone and tidal wave disaster of the century, leaving more than 160,000 dead and two millions destitute near the mouths of the Ganges and aggravating the province's grievance against the dominant western division. In the elections Sheik

Mujibur Rehman's Awami League candidates won an overall majority but the Assembly meeting was postponed because of a boycott called by West Pakistan's chief politician Zulfikar Ali Bhutto. Bhutto feared that the Sheik's home-rule proposals were a secessionist demand that would break the Islamic nation in two.

Flashpoint was close as Stewart's team flew out of the region in March, 1971. Eleven days later the world was shocked by reports of Army garrisons opening fire in sudden crackdowns through East Pakistan in civil warfare against a movement to make the province Bangladesh (Bengali homeland). Against backgrounds of smoke rising from blown-up buildings and razed villages terrified families trudged pitiably from a man-made holocaust into neighbouring India. The exodus caused the worst refugee crisis the world has known, estimated at nine millions, tormented by malnutrition, exposure, disease and death by the roadside.

Pakistan's all-west national team carried through their tour of Britain and played a well-contested three-Test series.

While Pakistani and Indian Test men were taking part in a World XI tour of Australia their countries' forces fought a 14-day war in which cities bombed included Karachi, Intikhab's home town, and Dacca.

The militarist attempt to solve political differences added another to history's stark examples of the nemesis of force : millions uprooted, countless civic officials dead, farming and trade disrupted, ports blocked, bridges wrecked – plus the embittering casualty lists of war. Cricket's problems shrank to insignificance at a time when satiated vultures were too well fed to fly.

At National Stadium, Karachi, March 6, 7, 8, 1969. Abandoned as a draw after riots.
Cowdrey (England) won toss from Saeed Ahmad (Pakistan)

ENGLAND

C. Milburn c Wasim b Asif Masood ...	...	139
J. H. Edrich c Saeed b Intikhab	...	32
T. W. Graveney c Asif Iqbal b Intikhab	...	105
M. C. Cowdrey c Hanif b Intikhab ...	...	14
K. W. R. Fletcher b Mushtaq Mohammad ...		38
B. L. d'Oliveira c Aftab b Mushtaq ...	...	16
A. P. Knott not out	...	96
J. A. Snow b Asif Masood	...	9
D. J. Brown not out	...	25
B 5, l-b 12, nb 11	...	28

7 wickets off 175.1 overs (11 hrs. 40 mins.) ... 502

Fall of wickets: 1–78, 2–234, 3–286, 4–309, 5–360, 6–372, 7–427.
D. L. Underwood and R. N. S. Hobbs did not bat.

Bowling.	Balls	Runs	Wkt.
Asif Masood	168	94	2
Majid	120	51	–
Sarfraz	204	78	–
Intikhab	288	129	3
Saeed	132	53	–
Mushtaq	139	69	2

PAKISTAN XI

Saeed Ahmad, Hanif Mohammad, Mushtaq Mohammad,
Aftab Gul, Intikhab Alam, Asif Iqbal, Majid Jehangir,
Shafqat Rana, Wasim Bari, Asif Masood, Sarfraz Nawaz

Runs per 100 balls: England 48.

Umpires: Shu'a-ud-Din, Daud Khan.

Demonstrators at Brabourne Stadium, Bombay, light fires in the stands during a riot following an umpire's decision against an Indian batsman. Falling bottles drove the fielder, McKenzie, from the outfield

Crowds the world over never complained when these players were in top form – maybe there's a lesson to be learnt! *Right:* Australia's 'Garth' McKenzie. *Below:* West Indian stars, Clive Lloyd (*left*) and Gary Sobers

Australia *v* India, Calcutta, 1969. Upstairs spectators in the stand pelted the crowd below, causing them to run on to the field and halt play. Lawry and Stackpole stayed at the wicket and fieldsmen waited uneasily until police ushered the crowd around the edges of the ground

A photographer watches Keith Stackpole (bat in arms) and Lawry as they wait for police to clear the playing area so they can score the winning runs, Calcutta, 1969

Minutes later another photographer fell as Lawry hunted him off the pitch. He accused Lawry (picking up bat) of striking him

Chapter Eleven

CAPTAIN BESIEGED

A CAPTAIN who follows up winning the toss by figuring in a century opening partnership can feel that it is a day worth remembering, even if he does get run out. 15th October was such a day for Graham Dowling, captaining the New Zealanders in India on their way back from the 1969 tour of England.

The New Zealanders came to Hyderabad after a loss by 60 runs at Bombay and victory by 167 at Nagpur. In the second Test Dowling and two or three others answered criticism that the Kiwis' batting lacked the footwork to cope with the spins of that troublesome trio Prasanna, Bedi and Venkataraghavan. The reward for overcoming them at Nagpur was New Zealand's first win on three tours of India.

Carrying on from that, Dowling and 6 feet 6 inch Bruce Murray led off in Hyderabad with 106 for the first wicket. Like nearly all Indian wickets of the period, the Lal Bahadur Shastri Stadium pitch gave no encouragement to the opening bowlers, medium-pacers Abid Ali and Jaisimha, and the batsmen shaped with a fair degree of confidence against Venkat and Bedi. The only time Dowling was troubled was by the fifth bowler, Eknath Solkar, a lissom Bombay left-hander playing his first Test at 21. Solkar leapt as he saw his first ball go from the N.Z. captain's bat to leg-gully but the chance was grassed. The young left-hander deserved to join the list of bowlers whose first ball in a Test has taken a wicket, as Intikhab Alam and left-hand spinner Dick Howorth have done since the war, and four pre-war bowlers did – Maurice Tate and George Macaulay for England, Tyrrell Johnson for West Indies and Arthur Coningham for Australia.

In the Hyderabad crowd of 25,000 many wondered why Pataudi did not call on Prasanna earlier than four overs before lunch. By making 106, Dowling and Murray put up the highest

113

partnership by either side for any wicket in the three-Test series. They kept India's bowlers waiting longer for their first wicket than Lawry and Stackpole were to do in Australia's five Tests against much the same bowling soon afterward. The New Zealanders' Tests were so dominated by bowlers that no batsman could make 100 and more often than not whole sides could not raise 200. This time it took Prasanna's fielding, not bowling, to separate the pair. Playing Bedi square to the off, Dowling dashed off, was sent back by his partner but could not beat Prasanna's throw to wicketkeeper Indrajitsinh. An in-drifter from Bedi across Glenn Turner's defensive bat gave the 'keeper a legside catch.

Almost an hour after lunch Pataudi coupled Prasanna with the Sikh left-hander. The Mysore off-spinner's curving flight and varied turn halted Murray on 80. Tied down by Prasanna's wiles, the tall batsman tried to burst the bounds by swinging one to leg but it landed in Jai's hands at deep square. By passing 120 before the second wicket fell, the Kiwis had been riding high but the spinners soon tipped them out of the saddle. Prasanna had Bevan Congdon, Brian Hastings, Dayle Hadlee and Bruce Taylor caught. Ashok Gandotra, playing his first Test at 20, brought off the most spectacular catch by dashing in from mid-on diving forward to send back Taylor (16) the first man to reach double figures since the opening pair. A second run out robbed the bowlers of Ken Wadsworth's wicket but Prasanna was bowling his thirtieth over when he finished with five for 51.

All his victims were caught on the densely populated leg side, from behind square-leg to long on. India's tactics were for the spinners to bowl mainly on the middle and leg pegs, with leg-trap fielders waiting expectantly. Usually Pataudi placed only three fieldsmen on the off side for Prasanna and six on the leg side (one more than the limit permitted in Australian cricket).

As a wet day and a rest day followed, the match was not resumed until the fourth day by the calendar, involving a dispute about mowing the wicket.

Until 1947 the Laws of Cricket gave the captain of the batting side, once a match had begun, absolute say whether the grounds-man should give the pitch its morning spruce-up with mower, broom and roller. It made no difference if this captain had only a few wickets left and the opposing team would soon become the batting side for most of the day. When Australia's first innings in the Brisbane Test, 1946, extended into the third morning Bradman had directed the groundsman to leave the pitch untouched. On the Monday it had not been mown since before the start on Friday. The captain of the batting side may still keep broom and roller off but he can no longer waive the mowing, which Law 10 hands over to the umpires:

'... In a match of three or more days duration the pitch shall be mown under the supervision of the umpires before play begins on alternate days after the start of a match, but should the pitch not be so mown on any day on account of play not taking place, it shall be mown on the first day on which the match is resumed and thereafter on alternate days. (For the purpose of this law a rest day counts as a day.) Under no circumstances shall the pitch be watered during a match.'

Of such stuff are barristers' daydreams made; by such wording do law-framers create a wide avenue for appeals – to the Privy Council, if need be.

New Zealand's team contained four schoolteachers, an orchardist, a fish merchant, an advertising manager, two salesmen and an insurance representative. No lawyer. The captain, a Christchurch accountant, had no difficulty working out that alternate days meant the third and fifth days. As it happened, the third day was a rest day. Some quoted part of the law's wording to contend that the question of mowing on a rest day did not arise, as the pitch had to be mown 'before play begins'. Weren't the umpires meant to have a rest day as well as the players, they asked, and how could the pitch be mown 'under the supervision of the umpires' if they were somewhere else with their feet up, sipping cool drinks?

Living in quarters in the stadium, the New Zealanders noticed midfield activity suggesting that the umpires were going to have the pitch mown at 5 a.m. on the fourth day to make up for missing the third. Without waiting to shave, the captain and manager Gordon Burgess went out to object to this. Pointing to the specification that a rest day counted as a day, Dowling contended that it would be a breach of the law to mow the wicket on the fourth morning and that the next alternate day would be the fifth, Sunday. The strongest argument against his stand was the law's apparent intention that the pitch should not go more than two days unmown.

Umpires M. V. Nagendra and Bhattacharya reported to the Indian Board of Control that when they ordered mowing of the pitch on Saturday they could not carry it out because Dowling protested and said if it were done he would not bring his players on to the field. To allow play to go on Pataudi reluctantly agreed to resume with the pitch as it was although it was to his side's disadvantage. The umpires complained to the Indian Board that Dowling was interfering in the discharge of their duties.

Six minutes' play on the untended pitch ended New Zealand's innings at 181, without another run. Solkar's low leg-slip catch dismissing Cunis off Abid Ali gave notice of the value his infielding was going to be as his career unfolded.

Unmown since before the start on Wednesday the pitch's surface looked rather like Ray Milland's chin after *The Lost Weekend*. Amid its whiskers, the wicket was crossed by a damp strip from which the ball jumped. Trying to land the ball on this, the bowlers succeeded only about once an over, but the unsettled batsmen expected the worst all the time, as batsmen do on such occasions. Two of the schoolteachers, Hadlee and Cunis, toppled four wickets in 11 balls while the score stood at 21, barely come of age. After trapping opening batsman Indrajitsinh lbw, Cunis made one kick from the damp patch and go from Jaisimha's glove for a catch in the gully. A wicked out-cutter from Hadlee shot from Pataudi's bat to second slip, where Murray held it with a second clutch.

When Wadsworth caught left-hander Ambar Roy off Hadlee the board showed the uncommon and unflattering sight of three ducks in succession. The score-posters were in danger of running out of 0 plates when this fate also befell Solkar in his first Test innings. Never mind, Eknath, it happened to Sir Leonard Hutton, too, in his first Test innings at 21, against a N.Z. team that included Hadlee's father, Wal.

Fair-haired Bob Cunis, an Auckland schoolteacher, is one of the marvels of international sport. He represented his country at cricket and his province at football, a stocky inside centre. In a club match Cunis tore the ligaments of his right knee so severely that his lower leg wobbled around out of control. A skilful surgeon operated, experimenting with a new method. After six months with the leg in plaster Bob had to learn to walk again. Eighteen months passed before he could resume playing. Yet here he was in Hyderabad, bowling for an hour and three-quarters after lunch in humid heat which would have made a fairer stretch three overs at a time. Bob's unconventional run to the wicket is enough to make a coach stare. He comes around a curve as if powered by a sputtering motor needing a change of sparkplugs before he settles into full strides. Then he makes a hop before delivering outswingers that pass groping bats, varied with in-cutters. A few weeks after his jaw was broken at Perth when a rearing ball from McKenzie glanced up to his chin this resilient sportsman captured nine wickets against England at Auckland in 1971, taking his tally to 45 wickets in 15 Tests. Next he represented New Zealand in the World XI touring Australia, before joining his country's first team to visit the West Indies. Cunis has continued exercising with weights each day to keep the muscles of the repaired leg toned up.

As six wickets tumbled for 27 Lala Amarnath said the Kiwi medium-pacers ripped through the Indian batting with length and direction that forced the batsmen into hurried shots: 'They were facing the seamers like monkeys on hot bricks, not playing the natural game but believing only in push and prod.' Gandotra was the only one of the first seven to reach double figures, 18, and the first to fall to spin. The wicketkeeper caught him off Hedley Howarth, an Auckland fish merchant whose left-hand bowling impressed England earlier in the year and who, R. T. Brittenden tells us, became a spinner because fast bowling made his back ache, a good and sufficient reason.

Joining Venkataraghavan, Bedi was the first tailender for 11 years to come in as last man with the total short of 50. This has been the depressing experience of last men in five Tests since World War II. In New Zealand's first post-war Test against a powerful Australian side at Wellington Donald Cleverley came in at 40 in the first innings of 42 and at 42 in the second innings of 54. Each time he was left not out one. For England against Australia at the Oval in 1948 Eric Hollies entered at 47 and was left scoreless when Don Tallon dived for a spectacular left-glove catch from Hutton, who made 30 of England's 52. When Hutton's team routed N.Z. for 26 at Auckland in 1955 John Hayes came in last at 26. At Lord's in 1958 Hayes appeared at 46 and Cowdrey caught him off Lock at 47.

Despite such lugubrious precedents, Bedi's heart was in the right place and his bat, too – often enough for him to stay more than an hour. Most of the last pair's runs came in singles but Bedi twice turned balls off his toes for fours and Venkat's last shot, a cover-drive to the boundary, was cheered as the best stroke of the innings. By making 20 Bedi probably set an all-time high for a last man of a side in such a predicament. He helped Venkat make the best stand of the innings, 40, hoisting India to 89, a total that took four hours to crawl on to the board. Venkat had held on more than half that time scoring 25 not out.

As the players were leaving the field a boy ran out to shake hands with the two top-scorers. As he was returning a guard chased him. Outpaced, the guard threw his lathi at him. The youth, confident of his superior speed, doubled back to pick up the stick, perhaps as a trophy of the chase. He did not notice another guard, who aimed a blow at his legs with a lathi. At that instant the boy rose and the stick struck his face between one eye and the cheekbone. The sight of blood staining his white shirt caused a thunderous roar of protest from the crowd.

Some ran on the field. They gathered near the pavilion, shouting protests and demanding punishment of the guard who injured the boy. A few threw stones. Others exploded crackers in parts of the stands. A thatched shed near the scoreboard was set on fire but the flames were soon under control. Demonstrators began throwing soda-water bottles, sticks, stones, shoes and chairs.

Central Reserve Police were sent into the stands to clear the disturbed areas, using lathis. Infuriated by this, chased-out spectators vented their resentment on the first official premises they saw, a State Public Works branch office in a shopping arcade forming the periphery of the stadium. Surging out on the Kothi road they pelted eight government buses, damaging the windows. Police took the boy to Sarojini Eye Hospital for treatment. In the affrays almost a dozen policemen, including a deputy commissioner, were injured.

The potty history of crowd control contains no simpler instance of unthinking actions by one or two law-enforcers starting a chain of events that involve their comrades in violent clashes by fanning a trivial prank into a destructive riot. As the boy who shook his heroes' hands was returning to the stand there was no need for a show of authority that could only antagonise the crowd. An ounce of the good-humoured firmness that has won London bobbies an enviable reputation would have saved tons of violence and heavy repair bills. The police commissioner at Hyderabad issued a statement that night regretting the unfortunate incident in the stadium and saying that the guard responsible was being dealt with severely.

Meanwhile the umpires had gone to the wicket at 4.55 p.m. for the last 10 minutes of the day but because of the disturbance New Zealand's batsmen did not attempt to begin their second innings. The umpires waited until 5.05 p.m. then lifted the bails.

Loss of six hours 40 minutes through rain and uproar greatly reduced time for N.Z. to convert a 92-run lead into a win before Monday evening. The position called for quick scoring on Sunday. India's bowlers, so sadly let down by their batsmen, set out to prevent this, making the most of a new-mown but deteriorating wicket.

Chunky little Abid Ali, an all-rounder of inexhaustible zest, bowled for four of the 5½ hours of the Sunday. Tried at both ends, he was most helped by balls from the north and keeping low. Shooters bowled Mark Burgess and Hadlee. Attempting to shake up the scoring, Dowling was dropped at 14 off Prasanna and 16 off Venkat. If he intended a closure to make India bat near the end of the day, runs came too slowly for him. Backed by tight-set fields, Abid Ali allowed only 47 runs off 27 overs and with Venkat, Jai and Prasanna restricted N.Z. to little more than two runs an over.

Only three scores exceeding 26 were made in the match – two of them by Dowling. He hit six fours in his second innings 60 but it took 250 minutes. Fair-haired Glenn Turner, who has rare sticking qualities in adverse going, was 15 not out when the day ended with N.Z. 175 for eight wickets. That put them 267 ahead, probably twice as many as the Indians would be likely to get on a wicket so mean.

Wickets fell to Hadlee, Cunis and Taylor almost as quickly as in the first innings. A close-in diving catch by Taylor inflicted a second o on Jaisimha, the Hyderabad captain, to the deep dismay of his home crowd. A fine batsman in classic mould, Jai had been a century-making hero at Brisbane in 1968, the only hundred for India in that series in Australia. To see a batsman bowled offering no stroke has long ceased to be a novelty but Cunis swung one so late and so far that it hit Gandotra's leg peg. Seven men had tumbled for 76, a leeway of 191, when a 20-minute downpour at 2.30 p.m. ended play. Hyderabad's wicket-covering methods did not get the tarpaulins in place quickly enough to prevent some rain getting into the pitch. When the downpour ceased before 3 p.m. the umpires inspected the ground and said they would look again at 3.30.

A bucket brigade took until 4.35 p.m. to drain water lying on covers. The New Zealanders watched with growing impatience. Breaking into the big league of international cricket usually means a long struggle, full of discouragements. Success has to be earned the hard way. Granted Test status in 1930, N.Z. had to wait 44 matches for the joy of a first win (against West Indies at Auckland in 1956). Their first success abroad was gained six years later by John Reid's team at Cape Town by 22 runs. Now they were within arm's length of a win at Hyderabad that would mean taking their first rubber in 29 series.

The players were fuming when removal of surface water seemed to be left to a handful of women squeezing cloths into bowls. Dowling said he understood that Indian officials and groundsmen might have been unfamiliar with wet conditions interfering with games but he urged that proper measures be taken. In other places the first thing had always been to haul the covers away and spill the surface water in the outfield, to enable the pitch to be got ready.

He told me later: 'About two dozen groundsmen and women were on the job at the start but the number dwindled to nine. I went around with a stump, pushing it into puddles, trying to hasten drainage into the subsoil. The umpires said I had no right on the field and ordered me off. I was loth to go, as it seemed to us not enough effort was being made to get the ground fit for play. Pataudi agreed that was so. It was frustrating to see our team's first chance to win a series go down the drain without some attempt to get play going.'

He accepted that he might have been in the wrong when he went about trying to hurry up the mopping-up process, but he contended that the groundsmen should have been doing such things to make play possible. He did not call on his team-mates to help remove the covers. Seeing what he was doing, they had come to help, and so did a number of spectators. 'All this might not have been in accordance with the conventions of the game but it was not against the laws, either, although the umpires objected,' he added.

Hyderabad Cricket Association secretary Ghulam Ahmed said that as the wicket had become wet the umpires were the sole judges to decide when play could resume. 'They were hampered by the hectic activity of the visiting captain who was bullying them and asking for resumption of play at once,' he said. 'Regarding the complaint that the ground authorities should have engaged more men to make the ground fit for play earlier, 40 others are employed each match day in addition to the permanent ground staff of 10. If having sufficient labour to deal with the situation means 1,000 strong I am surely to blame.' The Indian Board decided to take the matter up with the N.Z. Cricket Council.

When the pitch was at last visible the umpires reported that seepage across it made it unfit for resumption. Inspecting it again they reported to the captains at 4.45 that no further play was possible. As is the pattern for batting captains when rain gets into a pitch, Pataudi had no wish to see India's last wickets exposed to disaster on it. 'Rain helped New Zealand in our first innings, now it has helped us,' he remarked philosophically.

Soured by the abandonment, spectators started fires in stands. Others hurled stones and chairs at police on the field, their favourite target. Riot and teargas squads took up positions.

The Nawab walked to the dressing-room amid cries of 'Shame, shame, Pataudi!' Hoots spread around parts of the ground. A mass of demonstrators surrounded him until police came to the rescue and escorted him away. Some of the demonstrators broke into the dressing-room and police were called to raise the siege.

Enraged crowds overturned one bus and damaged others. They stoned vehicles and shops in the Abids Road business area. Several policemen were hit.

As a precaution, the New Zealanders were locked in their room for three hours, though none of the hostility was directed against them. One player said: 'It was clear to us that Indian crowds like to see good cricket whether it is played for or against their team. Apart from their disgust at their batsmen's failures in this match they obviously felt that events robbed us of a win. They loudly disapproved of this.' Some even shouted: 'Long live New Zealand – down with the Indian team!'

Ex-captain Vijay Merchant, selection chairman, said: 'Except for the record books, New Zealand won the series. They outplayed us at Hyderabad and taught us a lesson in first-class fielding.'

By one of the strange somersaults of mob psychology that make public opinion fickle, the demonstrators' rancour was directed against their country's captain. After his 1968 team in New Zealand won their first rubber abroad Pataudi had been voted India's Sportsman of the Year but his fall for 0 and 9 at Hyderabad dismayed them. Nobody sensed it at the time, but the following series against the Australians that season was to wind up his reign as national skipper at 28.

Suddenly made the youngest Test captain at 21, when Nari Contractor's skull was fractured in the West Indies, 'Tiger' led his country in 36 Tests, 21 more than Amarnath. For his valiant fightback in the Leeds Test, 1967, and his seven wins as skipper, cricket history will treat him more fairly.

Within a year of the Hyderabad Test the Nawab was one of 278 former Indian princes and other rulers whom the Government decided to strip of tax-free income and other privileges. Under a covenant as India achieved independence in 1947 the rulers handed over their States to the Indian Union and were given privy purses, tax-free imports, exemption from wealth tax and shooting rights on their old estates. The Nawab said he would henceforth be known by his Muslim family name, Mansur Ali Khan. Voters sided against him when he stood for Parliament, opposing one of Prime Minister Indira Gandhi's supporters.

Yet it was in this adverse period that 'Tiger' carried off a choice prize, Sharmila Tagore, the beautiful and talented Bengali actress, grand-daughter of the poet-philosopher, in a marriage that overran boundaries that religions try to set.

Hyderabad, Oct. 15, 16, 18, 19, 20, 1969. Drawn.
G. T. Dowling won toss from the Nawab of Pataudi.

NEW ZEALAND, 1st innings 336 minutes		2nd innings 330 minutes	
G. T. Dowling (c.) run out Prasanna ...	42	lbw Abid Ali	60
B. A. G. Murray c Jaisimha b Prasanna...	80	lbw Prasanna	26
G. M. Turner c Indrajitsinh b Bedi ...	2	not out	15
B. E. Congdon c Pataudi b Prasanna ...	3	c Prasanna b Venkat. ...	18
B. F. Hastings c Venkat. b Prasanna ...	2	c Venkat. b Prasanna ...	21
M. G. Burgess lbw Bedi	2	b Abid Ali	3
B. R. Taylor c Gandotra b Prasanna ...	16	b Venkataraghaven ...	18
D. R. Hadlee c Pataudi b Prasanna ...	1	b Abid Ali	0
K. J. Wadsworth run out	14	lbw Prasanna	5
R. S. Cunis c Solkar b Abid Ali	7	not out	0
H. J. Howarth not out	5		
Lb 7	7	B 6, lb 3	9
Total off 99.3 overs	181	8 wkts. dec (82 overs)	175

Fall: 106, 122, 128, 132, 133, 135, 136, 158, 166, 181
45, 86, 127, 133, 141, 141, 144, 175

Bowling.	Balls	Runs	Wkts.		Balls	Runs	Wkts.
Jaisimha	24	13	–	...	24	2	–
Abid Ali	73	17	1	...	162	47	3
Venkataraghavan	102	33	–	...	96	40	2
Bedi	204	52	2	...	54	19	–
Solkar	18	8	–				
Prasanna	177	51	5	...	156	58	3

INDIA 1st innings 235 minutes		2nd innings 192 minutes	
S. Abid Ali b Taylor	4	c Howarth b Taylor ...	5
K. S. Indrajitsinh lbw Cunis	7	c Dowling b Cunis ...	12
A. L. Wadekar c Congdon b Hadlee ...	9	c Wadsworth b Hadlee...	14
M. L. Jaisimha c Hastings b Cunis ...	0	c Taylor b Hadlee ...	0
Pataudi (c.) c Hurray b Hadlee	0	lbw Cunis	9
A. Roy c Wadsworth b Hadlee	0	c Wadsworth b Hadlee...	4
A. Gandotra c Wadsworth b Howarth ...	18	c Cunis	15
E. D. Solkar c Murray b Cunis	0	not out	13
S. Venkataraghavan not out	25	not out	2
E. A. S. Prasanna b Hadlee	2		
B. S. Bedi c Dowling b Congdon	20		
B 1, lb 3	4	Lb 2	2
Total off 54.2 overs	89	7 wickets (46.3 overs)	76

Fall: 5. 21, 21, 21, 21, 27, 28, 46, 49, 89   Fall: 10, 20, 21, 34, 44, 50, 66

Bowling.	Balls	Runs	Wkts.		Balls	Runs	Wkts.
Hadlee	102	30	4	...	60	31	3
Taylor	60	20	1	...	48	18	1
Cunis	84	12	3	...	72	12	3
Congdon	20	7	1	...	30	4	–
Howarth	54	12	1	...	30	4	–
Burgess	6	4	–	...	36	5	–

Balls per hour: India 99, New Zealand 85.
Minutes per over: India 3.6, New Zealand 4.1.

Umpires: M. V. Nagendra, Bhattacharya.

Chapter Twelve

AUSSIES, GO HOME!

CRICKET'S most substantial stronghold in Asia, the Brabourne Stadium, Bombay, is one of the few grounds where Test teams can sleep on the premises. From quarters in the Cricket Club of India's white clubhouse a sleepless player may look out over a moonlit field where a pitch of reddish soil slumbers over a base of truly laid bricks. Be he a batsman, nothing he sees from his window can lessen confidence for the morrow. Be he a pace bowler, better not to look out through the moonlight.

The other three sides of the stadium are enclosed by steep concrete stands, their roofs held aloft by steel uprights so tall that they look attenuated. The stands are backless to allow air to pass through, if it will, to the captive audience sweltering within.

The fattest man I ever saw watching cricket, the Thatur Saheb of Drohl, a racehorse owner, had his $2\frac{1}{4}$ hundredweight spread over two seats (or was it three?) in the Patiala pavilion with three women in saris dutifully at his side and rear.

Crowd noises inseparable from a Test at Bombay make it hard for a visiting batsman to concentrate while the bowler runs toward him. Players from England and New Zealand are most conscious of this rowdy contrast with the cloistral hush as a bowler runs up in their homelands. Top N.Z. runmakers, John Reid and Bert Sutcliffe, had difficulty playing normally and Indian ex-captain Vijay Merchant recalls a dialogue with Keith Carmody, opening the Australian Services innings on the way back from Britain after the war. When Carmody stepped back from the wicket, Merchant said: 'I'm sorry about all those noises, but what can be done?' Keith: 'How can I concentrate on the bowling?' Vijay: 'If you show you are taking notice of the crowd they will carry on. Best to disregard the noise if you can.'

Yet more visitors than Indians are among 24 men whose concentration has seen them through centuries in Bombay Tests.

Since Everton Weekes' 194 proved that a stranger could bat five hours amid such distractions as exploding bangers, Australia's Norman O'Neill has stayed six hours for 163 and Pakistan's master batsman Hanif Mohammad 6¼ hours for 160 run out. England's Ken Barrington stretched this to seven hours for 151 not out. Tom Graveney 8¼ hours for 175 and Australian opener Jim Burke almost 8½ hours for 161, batting into the 155th over. Transistor radios in the crowd have worsened the problem in the last dozen years, yet in this period hundreds have been made by O'Neill, Hanif, Saeed Ahmed, Harvey, Barrington, Hunte, Dowling and Stackpole, in addition to Dilip Sardesai's 200 not out for India against N.Z., two centuries by Chandu Borde and Nari Contractor's 108 against Benaud's Australians. Scalpers were asking as much as 260 rupees (about £20 sterling) for match tickets when the Australians played there in 1969.

An eight-foot wire fence erected to keep non-players off the field has failed to stop boyish fans running out to loop garlands around centurymakers' necks. Police hunting them off unfailingly come under a hail of fruit refuse and coconut husks across a boundary line stained red with betel juice.

In any nightmare disturbing the Nawab of Pataudi's sleep the figure of Graham McKenzie would be bound to loom with muscular menace. It was one thing for the powerful paceman known as Garth to unsettle India's batting on livelier Australian wickets but when the Nawab tossed too well for Lawry at Bombay in 1969 the stadium's placid strip offered the Indians an opportunity to get some of their own back. Seven boundary hits in the first half-hour, mainly drives, showed how Sardesai and Farokh Engineer appraised the situation against McKenzie and Alan Connolly.

With a great bowler's faculty for overcoming conditions as well as opponents, the rhythmic West Australian struck three times in his fifth and sixth overs. He swung one late through Sardesai's forward defence to send the off stump dancing. When he compelled Engineer and Borde to spar at his stock out-goer, Redpath's lean arm reached a gully catch and Ian Chappell held an edge to first slip with Simpson-like certainty. In seven balls which yielded two runs McKenzie dramatically changed the crowd's jubilant chatter to shocked mutterings. Six overs for 33 runs and three wickets earned Graham a rest with the total 42.

Two sons of famous fathers strove to prevent the cracks in India's innings going deeper. An habitual rescuer of his country's batting, Pataudi joined 19-year-old Ashok Mankad, playing his third Test and facing Australia's bowling for the first time. Batting in contact lenses, Ashok, taller and fleshier than his sire, proved himself a worthy son of renowned all-rounder Vinoo Mankad. Pressure on the young Bombay batsman's nerve increased when his captain, unable to sort out Johnny Gleeson's folded-finger spin, took 25 minutes' pad-pushing and dead-bat tactics before his first run and at five gave a midwicket chance which a fielder of Ashley Mallett's ability would normally have held. India struggled to 100 from 50 overs, whereupon Mankad (26) had a life off a Mallett off-break, a low chance at silly-leg too sharp even for Redpath.

Gradually the pair found confidence and opportunities to play firm shots. In making 74 (seven fours) in $4\frac{1}{4}$ hours of uninherited orthodoxy, Ashok at no time ventured into methods like those which an Australian critic once warned his father could never succeed – unsolicited advice that Vinoo cheerfully ignored in making himself the only all-rounder with 2,000 runs and 150 wickets in fewer Tests (40) than Sobers, Benaud and Miller.

Soon after Ashok and Pataudi passed India's fourth-wicket record against Australia, 128, which the skipper shared with Surti at Brisbane in 1968, Lawry called for a new ball at 163. With it, McKenzie ended a 146 stand by bowling Mankad. That brought Ajit Wadekar in for a last careful half-hour of a $5\frac{1}{2}$ hour day in which India made 202 for four wickets off 98 overs.

A Wednesday crowd exceeding 40,000 saw Pataudi carry on from his overnight 73, hoping for a seventh Test century. Though the ball was 18 overs old only five runs came from 36 balls by McKenzie before a double change brought Gleeson's spin with the breeze and Connolly's fast-medium swing and cut into it. Connolly's dismissal of Wadekar 9, leg-before-wicket, playing back, started a rattle of wickets that dismayed a crowd wanting a 400 total.

Pataudi's boundary shots were not only well placed but well spaced; he hit 14 yet the bowlers' accuracy kept him to 16 runs an hour. Six hours for 95 called for patience all around but, after all, Shajahan took 22 years to build the Taj Mahal. The captain was seeking another four when Gleeson trapped him into a mishit over the bowler's head. Racing from mid-on, Lawry needed all his length of arm to reach a catch just above ground. During the Nawab's stay India's total rose from 42 to 245. None of the last six batsmen reached 10 and the innings folded ten minutes after lunch on the second day for 271 off 814 balls. Australia's bowlers averaged 106 balls an hour and McKenzie's 29 overs yielded five for 69.

For good measure Garth caught Bedi to bring Gleeson's fiftieth wicket in 15 Tests. The lightweight countryman's sinewy fingers sprout from a sun-tanned right hand insured for 10,000 dollars. This may not rival the box-office value of Liberace's plumper paw, but no piece of pianoforte music has been harder to read than Gleeson's reverse fingering motions and wristplay. Since severe bowel surgery in 1967 saved his life Johnny has been as aware that human existence is fraught with perils as batsmen have been unaware which ball is his leg-break and which his wrong'un.

Although accustomed to much more hostile new-ball bowling, Lawry did not treat Abid Ali and Rusi Surti's medium-pace cheaply. He let his right-hand partner, Keith Stackpole, play the bulk of the shots and do the bulk of the scoring – a bulky batsman in every respect, alongside his skipper's spare figure. If asked to sit on the bowling, Keith is in good shape to do so with crushing effect, but it suits him better to shake the stuffing out of it. Nicknamed Humphrey Bear from a supposed resemblance to an entertaining television figure, Stackpole is a batsman with a vistavision stance and cinerama strokes. An eager hooker and willing square-cutter, he is Australia's nearest to a Milburn. Before promotion to open the innings Keith peeled off 100 in two hours between lunch and tea at Cape Town in 1967 – the only Australian to whip up 100 in a Test session since Richie Benaud's tempestuous 121 in 96 minutes at Kingston in 1955.

I have always believed Stackpole's batting answers pace better than spin but 48 of the 57 overs this day were spun along by Bedi, Prasanna and Venkataraghavan. The 200 lb Victorian often drove forcefully off the back foot but three factors prevented his getting anywhere near his Cape Town gallop. Spectacular interceptions by Surti, Pataudi and Abid denied him many boundaries (Surti alone was estimated to have saved 40 runs). Catchers as good as Solkar and Venkat a few yards from his heels made him acutely conscious of the risk of giving a bat-to-pad chance and the care taken robbed his play of freedom. Keith received less of the strike because of the number of maiden overs kept out by Lawry, who was thinking mainly of a long first-innings lead to offset having to bat last on a worn wicket. Yet the mightiest hit of the day was a six off Prasanna which Lawry swung over midwicket, heaving himself off his feet.

In $2\frac{1}{4}$ hours Lawry ground out 25 of the first wicket's 81. Recalled in the last hour for a second stretch from the northern end, Prasanna deceived the tall left-hander into cutting at a ball that, instead of turning away, came on to be chopped into the stumps. Prasanna and Bedi greeted Ian Chappell with such well-flighted spin that even this agile mover took half an hour to create an opening for his first run. Not since they found Laker unplayable on queer strips in 1956 had any bowler commanded such respect from Australian Test batsmen as Bishan Singh Bedi. Off 144 balls from his accurate left hand they managed only 18 runs. Two-thirds of the Sikh's 24 overs were scoreless. Two edges past slip in the forties so eroded Stackpole's confidence that Keith averaged only one run an over of Australia's stumps score : 93 off 57 overs in 190 minutes.

Realising that loss of the initiative is one of the surest ways to lose a match, Chappell and Stackpole, summoned up their most enterprising footwork to disturb the spinners' length and line, especially Bedi's, as more than 45,000 packed the stadium to watch the third day. Nineteen runs off the day's first dozen overs gave the game a trend Australia needed. Skipping forward to drive, Chappell was bowled by Prasanna for 31 of an 83 stand. As Ian has no superior, if an equal, at such strokes, it takes an exceptional ball to beat him.

Stackpole's fourteenth four helped him toward 103 in 280 minutes – a long time for a man of his inclinations, yet outstanding in two ways : against keen fielding Keith made the lion's share of Australia's 167 for three wickets and nobody else in the match could reach a century (In the five Tests only three other Australians were to make hundreds : Paul Sheahan, 114 at Kanpur, Chappell's wondrous 138 at Delhi and Doug Walters'

102 at Madras. India's sole century was 137 at Kanpur by tiny, talented Gundappa Viswanath, a 20-year-old student playing his first Test).

Stackpole's attempt to on-drive Prasanna for six fell into Surti's hands. If capture of two of the foremost Australian batsmen in two overs might suggest that Erapalli Prasanna, an electronics engineer, was bringing some laboratory secret into his off-spin bowling, Redpath's nimble footwork disrupted its working. Ian's fourth-wicket stand of 118 with Walters (48), Australia's only century partnership of the match, put their side 14 ahead and kept Bedi waiting until after tea for the first of his three wickets, a rolling slip-catch by Venkataraghavan. Thirteen fours in Redpath's fine 77 were among shots that moved one critic to write: 'Redpath's innings contained more strokes than one had seen in three Tests between New Zealand and India.' It ended with a full-length dive by Wadekar at silly-leg to dismiss Redpath off Venkataraghavan with the kind of catch the wiry Victorian can take himself in this exposed position. Venkataraghavan followed up by getting Sheahan (14) lbw. Though McKenzie drove Prasanna straight for six, the persistent off-spinner finished with five for 151 in 49 overs in a total of 345. Averaging 108 balls an hour, India's bowlers kept the Australians below 30 runs per 100 balls.

Their fieldsmen deserved high praise, but this could not be bestowed on field-setting which hamstrung the game by crowding the on side with six men (at one time seven) for Prasanna. When Lawry, retaliating, gave off-spinner Mallett six on-side fielders and no slip, he was the first Australian captain to resort to such negative placings for many years.

A modest lead of 74 seemed to grow like Jack's beanstalk as Johnny Gleeson winkled out India's batsmen, backed up by Mallett and Connolly. Hampered by a strained thigh and batting with a substitute runner, Sardesai could not last long against Gleeson's spin on a pitch helping turn. An undetected leg-break bowled Mankad and unrecognised wrong'uns screwed from the bats of Pataudi and Borde to legtrap fieldsmen. Trying to break up the spin combination, Engineer drove Mallett but McKenzie caught him at long-off. Wadekar, a left-hander sorted out Gleeson's double-dealing spin well enough to bat two hours without flurry. Surti stayed with him 40 minutes in the best

E   129

partnership of the innings, 28 – prompting a theory that Gleeson was less effective against southpaws. Lawry swung Connolly into action to dismiss Surti and Abid Ali lbw.

Only three wickets remained when Venkat held out 50 minutes as Wadekar's partner, reviving the dismayed crowd's hope that India might yet score enough to have a chance if Australia slumped on the last day. Venkataraghavan, a mechanical engineer whose six-syllable name is pronounced with accent on the rag, is called 'Wenkie' by his team. He is a taller, quicker and flatter off-spinner than Prasanna, for whom he is an alert snapper-up of leg-trap catches. Improving with every match, Venkat was destined to become India's vice-captain at 25.

He tried to square-cut an off ball from Connolly as it went through to wicketkeeper Brian Taber. Indian writers described an appeal for a catch as half-hearted. One report referred to it as 'feeble', but the Laws of Cricket are not concerned with volume. More to the point, bowler and wicketkeeper did not appeal – the question was raised by mid-on, silly-leg and second slip. Umpire Shambu Pan signalled Venkat out.

The disconcerted batsman's hesitation and a radio criticism of the decision touched off a riot 40 minutes before the end of the fourth day. Over their transistor radios the crowd heard a former fast bowler, Devraj Puri, telling the outside world that, in his view, the bat had been nowhere near the ball. Drawn into this, his broadcasting companion, former Test wicketkeeper Madhav Mantri, replied that he was against expressing an opinion about a decision 'from this far out' (they looked along the wicket from the top floor of the clubhouse). Mantri, an uncle of Gavaskar, pointed out the umpire, the sole judge, was in the best position. The broadcast was in English, a language generally understood by the crowd, though that did not preclude the possibility that excitable hearers ascribed deeper meaning to some of the words heard.

The feeling around the ground seemed to be that the Australian captain would have been a sporting hero had he cancelled the appeal, as the Bombay crowd had seen Gary Sobers do in a Test two years earlier. In the 1967 case Kunderan played at a ball turning to leg and, as Sobers picked it up at leg-slip with a characteristic loose flick of wrist, the expectant bowler, Gibbs, uttered some sound that the umpire took to be an appeal. The umpire gave Kunderan out. The batsman gaped, flabbergasted. Telling the umpire it was no catch, the West Indian captain had the decision reversed.* Back in 1921, when Ted McDonald left the wicket in the Oval Test, thinking he was bowled, the bail had been dislodged by the wicketkeeper. Lord Tennyson called him back. Lindsay Hassett recalled Jack Nel at Durban in 1950 because he thought he had interfered with Nel's running between wickets. After Cyril Washbrook was given out lbw at Christchurch in 1951, N.Z. captain Walter Hadlee asked the umpire to bring him back because he was sure the ball touched the bat first. Trevor Goddard recalled English captain Mike Smith at Johannesburg in 1965 after leg-slip fieldsman Peter van der Merwe had thrown his wicket down.

Lawry's standpoint, for better or worse, has always been not to take anything out of the umpire's hands (except perhaps a ball!).

Depressed by the failure of most Indian batsmen, the downcast Bombay crowd felt that a questionable decision at that stage was too much. Before you could say Venkataraghavan, mob fury exploded in scenes unprecedented in the city's cricket history. More than imagination ran riot. Protesting spectators hurled hundreds of soft-drink bottles, stones and oranges on to the outfield. Owners of the most powerful arms flung bottles more than a pitch-length into the arena, causing Connolly's two deep fieldsmen behind the wicket, McKenzie and Walters, to shift out of range.

As the game went on without Venkataraghavan, and Connolly bowled to the new batsman, Prasanna, demonstrators set fire to hessian around the tennis courts behind the East Stand. Others heaped hundreds of smashed chairs on a fire and set parts of the North and Bombay Cricket Association stands alight. Awning coverings were soon ablaze. Smoke blew over the ground and, with half an hour to go, the scorer was unable to follow the game from the pressbox near square-leg. Walking to the middle with his scorebook, elderly scorer Jehangir Irani reported his difficulty.

* Captaining the World XI against Australia in Sydney in 1972, Sobers scooped up a shot by Stackpole in the gully. An umpire signalled the batsman out but Sobers waved to indicate that the ball had touched the ground before his hands reached it.

Like Hutton at Georgetown, Lawry was determined to continue, so umpires Shambu Pan and I. Gopalakrishnan suggested that the scorer go to a part of the ground where he could see the play and their signals. Irani had been followed forward by *Indian Express* reporter G. K. Menon, who had no right to enter the field but apparently felt the scorer needed support in convincing the umpires. 'Stop the game,' Menon called. 'We can't see the game. Smoke is getting in our eyes.' The umpires told him to leave. Exasperated by interruptions which might rob his team of time to win, Lawry barked a reproof, to which Menon retorted in kind.

Nearby fielders Mallett and Gleeson brusquely insisted that Menon get off the field. That Mallett, so quiet that his nickname is 'Rowdy', and Gleeson, a character who sees humour in most situations, should have spoken gruffly was evidence of the acute tension caused by the riot. As Menon left, fresh spurts of flame crackled around one roof. A seething mass of people flung their weight against the wire-mesh barricade in front of the East Stand. As it rocked, the Australians watched in alarm, ready to bolt for the clubhouse if it gave way. Picking up bottles, policemen flung them back over the wire. As the bottles smashed on the concrete, showers of broken glass quickly drove the crowd away. Two stands were cleared while fires were put out.

As McKenzie began his run-up to bowl, a stone larger than a marble fell across his track. He went back to start again, trusting that the powerful thrower had run out of ammunition. It was just as well that the batsmen were defending, as no fielder would have liked to chase a ball hit near the trouble-spot.

Hundreds of refugees from the smoking East Stand crowded in front of the clubhouse sightscreen. Normally, batsmen would step back from the wicket until it was cleared but evidently they recognised that this was beyond the umpires. Neither batsman appealed against the screen being obscured or against smoke enveloping the stadium. Perhaps they felt it was no time to find out how the agitated crowd would react, or that defeat was so inescapable that even justifiable delay could not reprieve India. Had any visiting side been at the wicket in a losing position, I wonder would they have batted on or appealed?

Policemen suppressing the riot from the field were mainly 60 to 70 yards from the wicket but on a few occasions some might have come as near as 40 yards. Test play had never gone on in such a situation before, causing people other than the rioters to feel that the umpires should suspend the game.

I think fair-minded opinion would sympathise with batsmen trying to play bowling amid such alarming disturbances, yet a worse wrong would be done if mobs felt they could stop a match because their country's team looked like losing.

The Times of India's widely respected sports editor, K. N. Prabhu, called it a day of infamy for Indian cricket. One passage from his report: 'It is to the credit of Lawry and his men that, amid din and uproar, they stood their ground and carried on with the game as best they could. And Wadekar, too, held his ground, phlegmatic and unperturbed by the dismal turn of events on and off the field. It is a novel and sad state of affairs that violence latent in our public life should spring to the surface on our cricket fields. It was an explosive situation . . . The major casualty was the fair name of Indian cricket. And Bombay cricket.'

When Mallett bowled Prasanna five minutes before stumps the last man, Bedi, partnered Wadekar at 125.

On police advice, the Australians stayed on the field for 20 minutes while the riot squad tried to clear intruders from the members' reserve. Squadmen carrying mesh shields escorted the players to the clubhouse; Mallett and Stackpole had armed themselves with stumps, just in case. Manager Fred Bennett came out to help in the escort. A bottle flying over his shoulder struck Gleeson behind the right ear after the bowler walked off beside Taber a few paces ahead of the umpires. The blow knocked Gleeson to his knees. Two policemen lifted him to his feet and he walked into the clubhouse unaided. The blow raised a lump but did not break the skin and had no after-effects. (Wag of the team, Johnny had joked a little earlier about some of the members having better arms than the mob! I think he would be in favour of drinks at grounds being sold in light cartons, like milk.)

From clubhouse balconies a couple of wicker chairs were dropped on the Australians. One fell on Lawry. With the humour his friends know – he usually allows the public no glimpse of it – Bill said 'I don't think it was meant for me but for Pataudi'. (He was the first Australian international hit by a chair since

one struck Kangaroo winger Ken Irvine on the head at Perpig-
nan, Southern France, in 1969.)

In a final paroxysm of frenzy, bottles broke every window
of the teams' dressing rooms, so the players were hurriedly
shepherded deeper into the building's shower and toilet block
while the riot squad went into action against the throwers. In
clearing away the last rioters squadmen suffered so many cuts
and gashes that the dressing room looked like a casualty station.

Among 50 people hurt seriously enough for medical attention
were a number of children with legs cut by broken glass, as well
as policemen and an Indian reserve, Ashok Gandotra (who
played in the second Test at Kanpur a week later). When
another reserve, Sunil Gavaskar, 20, next came to Brabourne
Stadium to practise he found his gloves spattered with blood.

Lawry later expressed admiration for the umpires, who had
not been daunted by the riotous demonstration.

The two captains agreed to go by figures kept by All-India
Radio's scorer on the top floor of the clubhouse, where visibility
was clear.

Former Test captain Lala Amarnath said in the *Indian
Express*: 'I have never witnessed such an ugly scene in Bombay
before. The public unnecessarily dragged Lawry into the controversy, as he had nothing to do with the umpiring decision.'
Conveying deep regrets to the Australian skipper, Indian Board
president A. Ghose said: 'Such incidents tend to blacken the
image of our country.'

Arguments ensued about how much blame should be laid
on the broadcast comments. Blaming one of the four commentators for provoking the crowd by questioning the umpire's
decision, the Cricket Club of India banned any broadcast of
running commentary on the fifth day, but reversed that decision
after All-India Radio pointed out that it was committed to pro-
vide an international hook-up for listeners in other countries.

Coming to Devraj Puri's defence, radiomen contended that
spectators were in uproar before his comment on the umpire's
decision. Support for them came from listeners in Delhi who
insisted that it was a broadcaster's duty to inform the radio
audience of the facts as he heard and saw them. Lieutenant-
Colonel C. P. Chaube said he heard a mighty roar of protest
from the crowd as Venkataraghavan was adjudged out, then

Devraj Puri's comment that the bat was nowhere near the ball. Chaube added: 'To say that his remark upset the public is to believe that spectators were otherwise blind to the occurrence. Later I heard Devraj Puri say "It would be better to abandon the game rather than excite the crowd further today" . . . No batsman could concentrate amid the pandemonium. It was far from sportsmanship to insist on continuing the game. No wonder the Bombay thousands shouted: "Aussies go home !" ' (A week earlier they had been garlanded with jasmine and marigolds at a Bombay reception).

C. S. A. Swamy said in the *Sunday Standard* many factors contributed to the low type of partisan spectator getting out of hand: the nature of the appeal and the decision, the broadcasters' question and answer – intended for listeners outside but heard over transistors by spectators, some of whom were probably only waiting for some excuse to give vent to pent-up feelings over high admittance charges, sticky weather and the poor fare dished out . . . The prevalent rate of one run in two minutes must be hard on the broadcaster but he should not pass on his irritation to listeners. Swamy added: 'If the intention is to keep out all controversial remarks, a code of mike conduct for objective coverage can be evolved and broadcasters groomed – in which case the words commentary and commentator should go out and broadcast and broadcaster be substituted.'

Another listener, K. S. Pednekar, went beyond actual words to tone of voice: 'I think Indian commentators get slightly excited when an Australian batsman is out. When an Indian batsman is out this happy excitement is absent. The commentator shall do well if he does not share emotions of the spectators.'

Freelance writer Arvind Lavakare, a qualified cricket and table-tennis umpire in Bombay, declared in the *Times of India:* 'Unless we all wake up, shameful scenes at Eden Gardens, 1967, and Brabourne Stadium, 1969, will cease to be isolated incidents. It does not require a professional psychiatrist or psychologist to determine that the roots of the riots at the Brabourne lay basically in the excess discomfort thrust upon the majority by authority. To take your seat on concrete layers an hour or two before play, then to sit through the sun and all for $5\frac{1}{2}$ hours without a break even to go to the toilet, is a modern torture inflicted on Bombay's East Stand . . . In the Bombay Cricket Association and North

Stands and elsewhere it is no secret that thousands sneak in. Such overcrowding and official apathy towards comfort cannot keep emotions bottled for all times. A solitary incident can ignite wrath uncontrollable. Umpire Pan's decision did precisely that. . . .'

Criticising the CCI for not doing more to prevent the nuisance of transistor radios, Lavakare says sending some official around once every hour to silence them is not the way to stop the menace, nor are notices hung in corners. Evidently he would make it a punishable offence to have a transistor audible at a Test ground. He advocated stern action : not only 100 detectives to confiscate radios but 'with powers to pronounce sentence of a day in prison, with a fine of 100 rupees.'

Urging the Board of Control to promote and uphold the fair name of Indian umpiring, Lavakare went on : 'It is no use issuing angry press releases when some Bob, Tom or Harry Simpson ridicules our umpires. It is no use merely submitting apologies to foreign captains when an umpiring decision lights a fire in the stands.' He recommends that the Board impartially determine the best two or three umpires in the land and appoint them for all five Tests. He described 400 rupees (£30) in fee and allowances as meagre for $27\frac{1}{2}$ hours standing in a Test and pointed out that, while cricketers and officials were given free air passages, umpires had to travel by train. Chiding them for doing little to raise their own status and dignity, he added : 'For certificates from fair-skinned captains they will immolate their self-respect by picking up Lawry's cap, thrown down unsportingly and unbecomingly. . . .'

All bottled drinks were banned from the stadium on the last day. Removal of wrecked and charred chairs left many forlorn gaps in the East Stand. The ground was half empty, but in any other city, except Calcutta, would 20,000 have attended to see the expiring twitches of a match in which defeat for the home side was yawning a couple of hours ahead?

Bedi stayed with Wadekar 45 minutes while the last wicket added 12. Driving at top-spinner Stackpole's eighth ball, Wadekar was caught for 46, the only man to get past the twenties in a total of 137. It was India's lowest innings of the series, the outcome of a pathetic rate of $1\frac{1}{2}$ runs an over which told of the batsmen's inability to break the initiative held by Australia's bowlers for more than five hours.

Australia needed only 64 to win but Surti injected some excitement for the faithful 20,000 by getting both opening batsmen in his first two overs without the aid of fieldsmen. Bowling at his fastest the 'Poor Man's Sobers' splintered the off stump of Lawry (2), trapped Stackpole (11) lbw three balls later and bumped a bouncer over Walters. Though they found Bedi hard to get away – only 11 off nine overs – Chappell and Walters steered the Australians to their first win in Bombay, where previous teams had drawn two Tests and lost one. The win by eight wickets was the foundation stone for their side's 3–1 success in the 1969 series.

The flavour of victory had been soured by a demonstration against Lawry. After joyful noises when Surti bowled him, the crowd booed the Australian captain from the field. Cricket historians said it was the first time this had happened to a visiting player on any Indian ground. Before the major cause of their displeasure – the incidents involved in Saturday's riot – Bill was already no hero with the onlookers. A few hours before the disturbance he had tried to squeeze in another over by McKenzie before lunch. When the umpires signified that it was time for lunch the crowd had seen him throw his cap on the ground apparently in pique – an action that gave the 40,000 more to talk about in the interval than the play.*

* While Lawry was being booed in Bombay 2,000 anti-apartheid protesters in Britain, mainly students, were clashing with police at the Welford Road rugby ground, Leicester, where the Springboks were playing East Midlands. Several people were injured and nine demonstrators were arrested. The disturbance was one of a chain of incidents that preceded a Government request to the Cricket Council to cancel the South African cricketers' tour arranged for 1970.

Bombay. Nov. 4, 5, 7. 8, 9, 1969. Australia won by eight wickets.

INDIA 1st innings — 2nd innings

	1st innings		2nd innings		
D. N. Sardesai b McKenzie	20	c Taber b Gleeson	...	...	3
F. M. Engineer c Redpath b McKenzie	19	c McKenzie b Mallett ...	...	28
A. V. Mankad b McKenzie	74	b Gleeson	...	...	8
C. G. Borde c Chappell b McKenzie	2	c Redpath b Gleeson	...	...	18
Pataudi (c.) c Lawry b Gleeson ...	95	c Stackpole b Gleeson	...	...	0
A. L. Wadekar lbw Connolly ...	9	c McKenzie b Stackpole	...	46
R. F. Surti st Taber b Gleeson ...	4	lbw Connolly ...	...	...	13
S. Abid Ali c Stackpole b McKenzie	3	b Connolly	...	...	2
S. Venkataraghavan c Taber b Connolly	2	c Taber b Connolly	...	9
E. A. S. Prasanna not out	12	b Mallett	...	...	3
B. S. Bedi c McKenzie b Gleeson ...	7	not out ...	...	...	1
B 15, lb 4, nb 5	24	Lb 4, nb 2 ...	...	...	6

Total off 135.4 overs (7 hrs. 40 mins.) 271   Total off 90.2 overs (5hrs. 10mins.) 137
Fall: 39, 40, 43, 188, 239, 245, 246, 249, 252, 271.
19, 37, 55, 56, 59, 87, 89, 114, 125, 137.

Bowling.	Balls	Runs	Wkts.		Balls	Runs	Wkts.
McKenzie	174	69	5	... ...	96	33	—
Connolly	186	55	2	... ...	120	20	3
Gleeson	214	52	3	... ...	192	56	4
Walters	36	13	—				
Stackpole	18	8	—	... ...	8	0	1
Mallett	180	43	—	... ...	126	22	2
Chappell	6	7	—				

AUSTRALIA 1st innings — 2nd innings

	1st innings		2nd innings			
W. M. Lawry (c.) b Prasanna ...	25	b Surti	...	...	...	2
K. R. Stackpole c Surti b Prasanna	103	lbw Surti	...	...	...	11
I. M. Chappell b Prasanna	31	not out	...	...	...	31
K. D. Walters c Venkat. b Bedi ...	48	not out	...	...	...	22
I. R. Redpath c Wadakar b Venkat.	77					
A. P. Sheahan lbw Venkataraghavan	14					
G. D. McKenzie c Borde b Prasanna	16					
H. B. Taber c Surti b Bedi	5					
A. A. Mallett not out	10					
J. W. Gleeson c Borde b Prasanna...	0					
A. N. Connolly c sub Solkar b Bedi...	8					
B 4, nb 4	8	B 1	...	...	...	1

Total off 169.4 overs (9 hrs. 25 mins.) 345   2 wkts. off 26.5 overs (1 hr. 30 mins.) 67

Fall: 81, 164, 167, 285, 297, 322, 322, 337, 337.   Fall: 8, 13.

Bowling.	Balls	Runs	Wkts.		Balls	Runs	Wkts.
Abid Ali	108	52	—	... ...	18	14	—
Surti	54	23	—	... ...	24	9	2
Venkat.	186	67	—	... ...	6	2	—
Bedi	376	74	3	... ...	54	11	—
Prasanna	294	121	5	... ...	54	20	—
				Mankad	5	10	—

Runs per 100 balls: India 31, Australia 35.
Balls per hour: India 108, Australia 106.
Runs per over: India 1.8, Australia 2.9.

Umpires: Shambu Pan, I. Gopalakrishnan.

Chapter 13

WOE, CALCUTTA!

CALCUTTA is no place for those who want a quiet life. It is down at the opposite end of society's seesaw from the Buckinghamshire churchyard where Thomas Gray penned his lines far from the madding crowd's ignoble strife. Take five million loins, bind up many of them with dhotis and you have the Bengalis, crowded in an industrial metropolis as populous as Sydney and Melbourne combined. You don't have to be a sharp-eared student of current affairs to hear rumblings of West Bengal's political volcano. They open up deep fissures. The raw nerve of the time is exposed here, painfully. Extremists commit political murders. In periods of legislative impasse the State has come under Federal Government control.

In December, 1969, Communist propagandists plastered posters in the city, thickest near the Eden Gardens cricket ground, claiming that Doug Walters had taken part in the forces that fought in South Vietnam. 'Go home Walters!' the posters blared. This lie about a well-liked young sportsman staggered the Australian players. Two years of compulsory service in the Army had not taken Walters outside Australia. The only weapon Doug had borne outside his homeland was a cricket bat, never guilty of anything more vicious than a square cut. The lie was nauseating to a team from a country largely unaware of what most of the outside world thought of Australia's involvement as America's ally in war in South-East Asia. It was 18 months before the Pentagon Papers brought to light a dismal catalogue of political and militarist misconception.

To the shocked Australian players it was inexplicable that untrue posters and a misleading newspaper report could prompt 3,000 protest marchers to demonstrate outside their hotel, the Great Eastern, and that in the morning the team should find the front windows boarded up. Travelling sportsmen often know little

"The troops are coming out to inspect the crowd . . . !"

about political ferments. Even consciousness that they were visiting a State where pro-Peking candidates had polled well at elections would hardly have helped the Australians feel less hurt by signs of public antagonism. Since incidents at Bombay, newspapers were increasingly critical of captain Bill Lawry and his demeanour on the field. In the preceding Test umpire I. Gopalakrishnan had told him to stop running on the Delhi pitch in the second innings and the crowd had jeeringly accused him of using unnecessary force with his bat in flattening spots on the wicket.

Memories of the Test holocaust at Eden Gardens three years earlier spurred the authorities into extraordinary precautions for the Australians' Test match. Chief Minister Ajoy Mukherjee called in units of the Eastern Frontier Rifles, a conference of police and army chiefs arranged for them to be on standby in the Eden Gardens area and the Home Ministry rostered nine extra magistrates for duty in Calcutta. India's Delhi victory by seven wickets, squaring the rubber one-all, encouraged hopes of another win against the redoubtable Aussies. When over-enthusiastic Calcutta crowds pressed close, hindering practice, police dispersing them beat them with long staves. In this inflammable atmosphere team manager Fred Bennett demanded full protection for his players and was assured that 3,000 police would be placed around the ground. Hessian awnings that normally shade sections of the crowd from the sun's heat were abolished as a potential fire risk – a precaution that contributed to trouble on the fourth day. As players reached the ground scalpers were demanding 40 rupees (about £3) for passes officially sold at eight rupees.

The weight of things on his mind did not impair Lawry's judgment of the wicket. Winning the toss from the Nawab of Pataudi, he became the first visiting captain to send India in. The Indians never really recovered from having Farokh Engineer and Ajit Wadekar smartly caught in McKenzie's first 13 balls on a misty morning. Five slipfielders were watching expectantly as 'Garth' seamed the ball and made it lift from a moistish track.

In an hour the athletic West Australian's three for 11 off eight overs justified his skipper's decision before the first drinks brought a rest for Garth and relief for the batsmen. It was the deadliest opening spell Bengalis had ever seen in a Test. How much catching counts has seldom been better demonstrated than by Stackpole's holding of both opening batsmen at second slip (Keith finished with four in the match) and footballer-cricketer Eric Freeman's high interception of Wadekar's glance. On the opposite flank from his normal spot Chappell picked up Pataudi at leg-gully off Mallett's off-break. Taber's three catches included the wicket that mattered most, Gundappa Viswanath, at 20 already the finest batsman in the side.

Only 5 feet 2 inches, Viswanath looked like a prep boy among prefects when, with two out before a run came, he entered to face McKenzie bowling at his top. Stunned by India's opening disasters, the crowd found their voices when the midget twice proved that McKenzie could be driven to the boundary; the first stroke of the bow tells of a master fiddler's presence. The gifted Bangalore college student is inches smaller than Lindsay Hassett and Hanif Mohammad who had shown earlier generations of bowlers that size isn't everything and that timing can achieve more than tonnage – as gifted Sunil Gavaskar reaffirmed later. It was evident in Viswanath's wristy square-drives and on-drives, his cuts late or square, his hooks, his glances and his sweeps. He shaped like repeating his Kanpur century – first player to make 100 for India in his first Test against Australia and the only one to score a Test 100 against Lawry's team. Left-handers have been scooping up a disproportionate share of cricket's honours but the southpaws have yet to produce as tiny a star as the boy from Bangalore, who was awarded a Padma Shri for meritorious service to sport.

Viswanath had made 54 out of 103 when Taber's gloves closed on his attempt to cut Mallett's straight ball. Touched bumpers ended at the same destination when vigorous Ambar Roy cut at one and left-hander Eknath Solkar, 42, swung at another on the leg side. The same gloves collected Freeman's accurate throw from square-leg to run out Prasanna (26) and end India's innings for 212. All-rounder Sreeni Venkataraghavan had yet to emerge as the man to be chosen vice-captain in the next series at the age of 25. Bowling more than one-third of Australia's 97 overs, McKenzie beat bat and stumps more often than he took wickets, six for 67, best supported by Mallett, three for 55. For the 16th time Garth dismissed at least half a Test side. (By the time England's series in Australia ended in 1971

he needed three more wickets to pass the Test record for
Australia, Richie Benaud's 248 in 63 Tests.)

The ball was still rather smooth for spinning when Prasanna
and Bedi took over India's attack soon after lunch on the second
day. Lawry swept Prasanna for six and, chastened by that
indiscretion, left the main burden of scoring on Stackpole's substantial shoulders. Undertaking this with pleasure, Keith drove
a six over long-on and hit five fours in his 41 of Australia's first
65. Stackpole's freely-used square-cut looked to be the most
devastating blow seen in 1969 except for Cassius Clay's left jab.
When Keith attempted a single for an off-drive, Ashok Mankad
nipped across from mid-wicket and threw down the stumps.
Stackpole's surprise at being adjudged run out was understandable when a photographer developed a film of the incident.
Keith had to wait a year to have a similar appeal answered the
other way at Brisbane – one more incident at the bowler's end,
bearing out that an umpire's eyes cannot be as unerring as a
camera.

Heartened by the disappearance of Stackpole, the Indians
applied pressure to Lawry. Three fielders crouched not far from
his lean haunches, ready for any misjudgment of Bedi's left-
hand spin. When the Sikh switched from over-the-wicket to
around it Lawry, 35, was snapped up low by the middle man
of the three, Solkar. A batsman can expect the worst if he puts
a ball above grass-height anywhere near this left-hander. Solkar
made 10 catches in the series and earlier had caught seven men
in one match for Bombay.

Newlywed Bedi's Australian wife, Glenith, was looking on
admiringly from near the pavilion, roughly square-leg. Her
presence seemed to inspire him. When Bishan first met Glen,
a Commonwealth Bank girl, at a Melbourne party in 1968 they
talked about banking until the conversation took a more engross-
ing turn for a couple in their early twenties. Before going to live
in India, Glen made a five-month visit, shopping in bazaars, to
obtain an insight into ways and customs. (Sixteen months after
this Test she figured in a cross-world Stork Derby with Gary
Sobers' Australian wife Prue; each had a son, while their hus-
bands were opposed in a Test at Port of Spain in April, 1971.)

On the third morning Walters and Chappell made a holiday
crowd glad they had packed in early. Walters swung the third

six of the innings over the leg boundary and gave two chances in boldly trying to snap the web being woven by Bedi and Prasanna, founders of the world's best finger-spin attack as the 1970s dawned. Though not as young as Ramadhin and Valentine when the West Indians humbled England's batting as 20-year-olds, Prasanna and Bedi took only a couple of years from their first Test together in 1967 to begin overtaking Gibbs and Sobers as the top pair of finger-spinners in international cricket. Back from the West Indies in 1971 their total stood at 209 wickets in 28 Tests and they had snared 187 as confederates in 21 Tests.

India's pair offer as much contrast in themselves as their bowling does. While a turban covers the Sikh left-hander's scalp sweat sticks strands of hair to the Hindu off-spinner's capless forehead. As Erapalli Prasanna spins the ball into the breeze a silver medal jiggles on a neckchain – not so much evidence of depth of religious devotion, I believe, as a token of good fortune, a Hindu equivalent of a St Christopher safe-journey medal. Puckers between his eyebrows are signs of the thought going on inside as he tries to outwit batsmen with variations of spin, pace, flight and drift – sometimes even a round-arm delivery.

Round-faced Prasanna, six years older than his junior partner, is shorter, looks busier, turns the ball more and usually delivers from over-the-wicket. Subtlety makes him less obviously hostile than Lance Gibbs yet batsmen find he can turn as much as the great Guyanese; both incur pain from worn forefingers. Even batsmen with footwork of a Chappell find it difficult to get to Prasanna and drive the ball with the middle of the bat. When he took his 100th wicket he was the first Indian to do so in 20 Tests, two fewer than leg-spinner Subhash Gupte and three fewer than left-hander Vinoo Mankad, that overworked all-rounder. Prasanna passed 100 wickets in seven fewer Tests than Jim Laker and five fewer than Ramadhin and Gibbs. Lance went on to make himself the first off-spinner to top 200 Test victims.

Bishan Singh Bedi does everything the other way around. After he has rubbed his hand on the earth and pushed a Sikh steel bangle up his right forearm, seven dainty steps bring him on tiptoe around the wicket to deliver from wide out. Compared with Prasanna, his movements are leisurely. The ball loops lazily

Coils of barbed wire being laid around the ground at Headingley, Leeds –
part of the precautions Yorkshire took against anti-apartheid demonstrators
in 1970

Demonstration – with a welcome difference. Crowds swarm on to the ground at Perth, Western Australia, to congratulate Greg Chappell on scoring a century in his first Test – against England, December, 1970

Bouncers: after four bouncers to English opening batsman Brian Luckhurst in one over in Melbourne, Alan Thomson bumped a fifth early in his next over. As Luckhurst ducked, the ball struck him on the back and flew to wicketkeeper Rod Marsh

The Sydney incident, 1971. *Left:* Clutching his scalp when John Snow's delivery struck him, Terry Jenner collapses on the pitch. *Below:* England's captain Ray Illingworth hurries over to the fallen tail-ender

The Sydney incident, 1971 (continued). *Above:* Bowler John Snow and skipper Illingworth argue in no uncertain terms with umpire Lou Rowan. *Right:* A spectator takes a hand – and a handful of John Snow's shirt – after the latter had gone to field on the fence. It was soon after this that Illingworth led off the England team from his hand, at first sight invitingly. Yet would-be hitters find it hard to draw a bead on Bedi. On its way the ball curls and drifts, and when it pitches nobody except perhaps the wicket-keeper knows whether it will turn or not. Batsmen have to watch closely for one that Bishan brings the other way with his arm. Sometimes he makes it dawdle through the air. His flightcraft resembles that exploited by Tony Lock after the ex-Surrey spinner reformed his once-suspect delivery and became Western Australia's heaviest wicket-taker in middle age. Bedi is so accurate he can land the ball on a tea leaf. Backed by a cordon of off fieldsmen hard to pierce, he can bowl economically, as befits the captain of the All-India State Bank XI.

Bedi's easy-going habit of calling everyone Phaji (meaning elder brother in his native tongue, Punjabi) has caused team-mates to make this his nickname. His off-field urbanity gives way to unemotional perseverance as he bowls. It takes a lot to change the facial expression visible between the whiskers and the turban. Whatever Phaji is thinking he keeps well behind wraps.

Absorbing cricket was seen as, against high-quality spin bowl-ing from this pair and Venkat, Walters and Chappell added 101 at a rate of 51 an hour. Then Bedi swung the pendulum of play the other way by getting Walters 56 and Redpath in one over, amid appropriate acclamation. Making a habit of getting Walters, the left-hander was chiefly the bowler who kept Doug waiting until the last Test for a century. Engineer's legside stumping of Walters to break the Calcutta partnership was a gem of wicketkeeping art. When Wadekar dived with one hand stretching for Redpath's low snick, the batsman awaited a decision. All the while Shambu Pan was consulting square-leg umpire J. Reuben crowd noises suggested it was a foregone conclusion. Some of the choicest batting of the year kept the crowd happy after lunch as Chappell and Sheahan lifted the total from 185 to 257 for the fifth wicket. Sheahan began as if his eye was still tuned from the 114 that charmed Kanpur. Excepting Barry Richards, no right-hander since Graveney bats more handsomely than this 6 feet 2 inch Victorian in true form, as Paul's classic straight-drive, on-drive and square-cut soon showed him to be this day. 'Timbers' they call him, because he came from Geelong College – geographically akin to Geelong Gram-mar School, whose bush outpost, Timbertop, had Prince Charles on the roll for half of 1966. From strokes made defending his stumps the ball often finds itself in the outfield.

Sheahan's graceful reach and power and Chappell's range of mobile shots subjected the bowlers to continuous pressure from both ends: loyal Indian critics admitted that for the first time in seven Tests their country's bowling looked beaten, weary, almost bedraggled. Fortune came to their rescue. Sheahan cut Guha to third man, ran one and sprinted off for a second without noticing that his partner was not returning. As he scrambled back he was beaten to the bowler's end when Prasanna's throw was relayed by wicketkeeper Engineer. Exit Sheahan when a high score appeared to lie ahead of him. Run outs have been a factor against his achieving the eminence promised when his 81 at Adelaide in 1967 signalled the advent of no ordinary batsman. Not all have been his fault but in trying to steal a second run against England at Perth in 1970 his imprudent under-estimation of D'Oliveira's throwing arm lost him his place in the Australian XI for the rest of the series.

'Chappelli', the Australians' Italian-style nickname for Ian, was playing the most outstanding innings of the match and probably one of the five best of his career. He showed the Bengalis a complete example of building an innings: a patient first hour on a pitch new to him, merging into swift footwork to take the initiative against good bowling. Two-thirds of his runs came from 16 boundary hits, of which the crowd most admired his late-cut. On pitch where a wicket fell for every $10\frac{1}{2}$ overs and nobody else in either side reached 65, he made 99 without a chance – nothing to encourage the bowlers except one lifted pull of Venkataraghavan that fell safely.

Noises anticipating 100 were being heard when Ian identified the ball Bedi brings in with his arm and moved to play it. Unaccountably, this one turned toward the off and was edged to slipfielder Wadekar. Chappell instantly walked toward the gate showing no sign of inner disappointment at missing a 25th century at the age of 26. The crowd's long applause probably expressed commiseration as well as appreciation.

Following his 138 on a Delhi track with which few batsmen coped, his Calcutta 99 was one of the innings that caused Lawry to nominate Ian as the world's best batsman on all wickets. Several Indians were willing to accept this, though they had not seen Richards or Graeme Pollock and it was almost three years since Sobers had batted in India. (I heard an Australian fan say the captain's remark 'hung an albatross around Chappell's neck' – and so it proved in South Africa.)

The one thing Eric Freeman and Geoffrey Boycott have in common while batting is that both wear contact lenses. Freeman's set seemingly make more balls look like half-volleys, judging by his hard-hit 29 before he was caught in the gully off Bedi.

Long regarded as incapable of batting any better than any other last man, big Alan Connolly (known as 'Al-pal' to his mates) felt the day had come to correct that misapprehension. The 6 feet $3\frac{1}{2}$ inch seam bowler blasted three sixes off Prasanna and a fourth off Bedi, all over long-on or midwicket. Could they have been there to see Alan make 31 in 18 minutes I wonder what would have been the reaction of a group of young men in Melbourne who used to laugh their heads off every time he scored a run. Lala Amarnath said he came like thunder and went like lightning. Connolly's unheralded onslaught lifted Australia to a count of seven sixes in an innings of 335. The only like spectacle I have seen in a Test innings was seven sixes in four hours from the bats of Sam Loxton and Keith Miller off the bowling of Jim Laker, Dick Pollard and Ken Cranston on a July day at Headingley in 1948. Walter Hammond alone hit 10 sixes in his 336 not out at Auckland in 1933.

As they followed Connolly's four soaring hits into the crowd Prasanna's eyes lost their usual happy expression : Australians could not restrain chortles at the sight of half a dozen sixes in an innings off the bowler who had done most to beat them at Delhi. Despite his triumph there his successes attacking with five leg-side fielders in Australia had been obtained with fewer balls per wicket than with the assemblage of six, sometimes seven, on-fielders given him by Pataudi in India.

Until Guha caught the last man off Solkar, India's only wicket-taker at Calcutta was Bedi, seven for 98 off 50 overs in a total of 355 off 143 overs. With grateful eyes, matching the pride in his wife's, his teammates watched the left-hander earn his best Test reward on a day when the Australians took the measure of everyone else. Batsmen in attacking mood could scarcely average two runs an over off Asia's subtlest flighter of the ball. Unable to partner him at their usual level, Prasanna was having his only blank match against the Aussies, though he totalled 51 wickets in his other eight Tests against them.

These are the kind of ups and downs that help to make cricket the game it is: much easier to picture Boycott going for 0 or McKenzie taking no wicket than a reigning Wimbledon champion losing in the first round next time. A Latin pupil might have written *vini Bedi vincit* of a day when there was no hosanna for Prasanna.

On the third consecutive cloudy evening poor light curtailed play by 14 minutes. As on the first day, the umpires allowed two more overs before granting the Indians' appeal. India's batsmen found the umpires less compliant than the Australians, whose appeal on the second evening had been upheld instantly, 75 minutes before time. The holiday crowd streamed from Eden Gardens, noisy with animated chatter. Fascinated by eventful cricket, they had cheerfully endured daylong discomforts in the crush. Their behaviour was all that could have been asked. They were in lively mood, although their national team had been headed by 123. After all, the Indians had been 67 behind at Delhi yet won with seven wickets to spare. Throughout Monday's rest expectations of another enthralling day ran high.

Tragedy struck before the players could reach the ground. Through the night 20,000 had lined up outside in the hope of buying the day's quota of 6-rupee tickets on sale at booths – only 8,000, as all other tickets had been bought in advance by members of cricket clubs. Later arrivals desperately tried to snatch tickets from fortunate buyers. As the hour for play drew near, those at the back impatiently pressed forward. A stampede began. People knocked down screamed and groaned as the mob tramped over them. Police tried to drag some of the fallen from under the milling feet. In an attempt to stop the stampede they charged into the crowd with lathis and burst several teargas grenades. Infuriated, the mob threw stones and soda-water bottles in a pitched battle with the police. Six people were trampled to death and 100 injured; 30 were admitted to hospital and 70 allowed to leave after treatment. It was in no way the players' fault, yet an aggrieved mob stoned the teams' hotel and broke a few windows before police dispersed them. (The same windows were shattered 15 months later when a new Pakistani

High Commission chief arrived while civil war was raging in adjacent East Pakistan.) The West Bengal Government appointed Karuna Ketan Singh, a retired civil serviceman, to inquire into the role of the police in the context of deployment at the ground and action taken. He was asked to recommend measures to prevent such incidents.

On behalf of the shocked Australians, manager Bennett drew up a message of sympathy. Many believe that the loss of life, injuries and the resentment of those who bore the brunt of the police action unsettled a number of the spectators who again strained the ground's capacity (57,000) and that this contributed to later trouble inside.

Everything continued to go wrong for India. While the batsmen were giving McKenzie due respect Australia's second and third pacemen, Connolly and Freeman, took over as the main destroyers of Indian hopes. With the build and belligerence to walk unchallenged into any military academy 'Fritz' Freeman is a fast-medium bowler of high-voltage energy and determination. After having Engineer caught, cutting, in the gully, the Port Adelaide footballer bustled Viswanath into error. As the little student shaped to cut an off ball it ducked back under a bat he desperately tried to switch to defence. The side could not rally from the double setback of losing Viswanath for five and Pataudi for one, again to off-spinner Mallett. In the hope of breaking up a close leg field of three, the captain swept hard but was caught on the boundary. Disappointed patriots who might have condoned such a shot at Kanpur seemed to brand it a miscalculated risk at Calcutta. Half the side had slumped for 93. Ambar Roy stuck with Wadekar for a stubborn hour and a half until Sheahan's electrifying dash in from cover to make a full-stretch catch that only a man with his speed and reach could bring off.

Ever since his Melbourne 99 I have been unable to guess why the bats Ajit Wadekar handles with natural ease have not stacked more runs on to his Test total. This time the quick-sighted Bombay left-hander so curbed his strokes in a dutiful attempt to give the innings backbone that 32 of his 62 runs came in singles. Wadekar saw seven partners fall for 68 before he was ninth out at 159, lbw to the indefatigable Freeman, who shared eight wickets with Connolly.

With Gleeson an onlooker and Mallett the only spinner, Australia's bowling rate slipped back to 95 balls an hour, a long way short of India's 113 balls an hour, but the Aussies batted more like winners by averaging 42 runs per 100 balls to India's 36. So in every way except catching the cricket most worth watching came when the home players were in the field.

India's slump for 161 dismayed a crowd for whom the day had begun sadly with loss of life outside. In the 10 minutes between innings feeling against Pataudi bubbled up like tar on a blistering day, as if the team's leader were somehow to blame. Since his 95 at Bombay in the first innings of the series the Nawab's scoring had dwindled to 0, 38, 0, 8, 15 and 1. As the Indians began fielding, hoots and chants of 'Shame, Pataudi!' came from sections of the crowd. The cries rang discordantly in the ears of Australians who remembered – had the hooters forgotten? – 'Tiger' gamely limping on to the field at Melbourne, Brisbane and Sydney with a torn hamstring as well as one damaged eye, how he knelt at slip between balls, how he batted bravely almost on one leg for more than 330 runs in successive Tests, so that Frank Tyson likened him to Long John Silver.

In the Ranji Stadium section of the stands – this time without the usual hessian sunscreens on the two decks – the occupants downstairs had no protection from anything dropped from the gallery. After desultory potshots, volleys of bottles, stones, and refuse made the downstairs crowd escape on to the field. Nobody knew whether the pelting was prompted by an unreasoning boil-over of disappointment, enmity over some local issue or whether there was more than one cause.

Lawry had hit opening bowler Subrata Guha's fourth ball to the boundary when the refugees from the Ranji stadium swarmed on to the field. Police stationed around the boundary shepherded them along the edge of the field. Lawry and Stackpole waited by the pitch like sentries. In that period an incident occurred that resulted in scathing criticism of Lawry and a chain of events that led to the Australians' bus being stoned in the most alarming scare any cricketers have suffered anywhere.

Versions differ but readers of most Indian newspapers next morning read that Lawry had attacked an Indian photographer. In Calcutta, *The Statesman*, a leading English-language daily said : 'Lawry did something that, to say the least, could be termed disgraceful. A photographer who had wanted to get a close shot of Stackpole and Lawry side by side brought upon himself the wrath of the Australian pinnochio. Lawry, presumably irritated, could not keep his temper in check and knocked over the poor photographer and struck him with his bat. It was a horrible sight, and one was led to wonder what Lawry thought himself to be. Would he have done the same in England or South Africa? Lawry, not quite the most popular of captains, exceeded himself and should be asked to apologise . . .' (Another Calcutta paper's report of an apology was a fabrication, Lawry said.)

Pictures of the photographer lying on the field appeared in *The Statesman* and in the *Amrita Bazar Patrika,* in which secretary Shyamal Bose stated the Press Photographers Association's regret and resentment of Lawry having 'hit a photographer without provocation and abused another while they were taking pictures of him. The photographer was identified as Miran Adhikary of the Bengali daily *Basumati.* In his account of the incident in *The Sun,* Melbourne, Bill said that in trying to protect the wicket he pushed the photographer with his open hand. In the picture of the fallen man Lawry was not holding his bat, but stooping as if to pick it up from the ground.

Nearest witness was Stackpole, and here are his recollections: 'I think it great to play in front of such enthusiastic crowds as those in India and on such a fine ground as Eden Gardens, one of the best I have played on anywhere. This makes it more of a pity that anything should have happened to cause friction before the end of the Test. When bottles and debris were dropped on them, the people had nowhere to go except forward on to the field. Police came across to check the invasion but none of these people came within 50 yards of the wicket. As police were ushering them around the edge of the field, about 20 yards in, the Indian players walked two-thirds of the way toward the dressing-room at the other end of the ground and looked ready to make a bolt for it if things got out of control.

'Twelve or fifteen photographers ran on to the field, each trying to get a scoop angle. Lawry and I tried to get them to leave but they took no notice. Some of them were pestering us to stand in the foreground of pictures of the crowd scene. We thought that a bit much, seeing that by coming on the field they added to confusion already caused with hunted-out spectators and police all over the place. We kept telling them to get off the ground. In his concern about the wicket Lawry took exception to one of the most intrusive of them. After taking a couple of sneak photos this fellow walked away. He was still hanging around so the Phantom went to chase him away. The chap started running, so Bill followed him, prodded him on the backside with his bat and said: "Now get off!" The photographer stumbled and fell. He had a press camera and when he fell I think it dug into his ribs. A couple of others helped him up. Lawry seemed to think he was playing a part but I think he was in pain, not putting on an act.'

Keith paused, then went on: 'At a time like this it's a bit lonely out there, but you realise that the only way to enable the game to be resumed is to stay. I'm sure that if we had gone off and the fieldsmen and umpires had left the field, the police would have been content to quieten things down. Their immediate task was to restore order and they weren't looking any further than that. By staying, we were a reminder that there was an interrupted game to be resumed. When things quietened down we asked the police could they get the people back over the boundary line, so we could play again. In some places they were sitting over the boundary line, the best that police could do with them. We were keen to finish the match that day. Though another day was scheduled, the disturbances raised a doubt whether the match could be resumed then. There was a possibility that masses of demonstrators or other crowds might block the approaches and the team's bus might not be able to get through.'

After 13 minutes the opening pair resumed seeking the 39 runs needed to win. The disturbance had left tension and nobody wished to prolong the game pointlessly. Only five overs in about 20 minutes were needed. When the totals were equal, Lawry said to Stackpole: 'Guha is going to bowl a full-toss to end the match. Don't hit it for four, a single will do.' But Keith could not resist such an offering and his stroke sent the ball rolling to the crowd-fringed boundary.

In the moment of defeat sections of the crowd singled out Pataudi as target for a bitter demonstration. As the players walked off Lawry said to Stackpole: 'We'd better protect Pat.' Turning to the Nawab he said: 'Come with us.' Besides being two of the biggest men on the field, the Australians had bats. They walked each side of Pataudi, who was outwardly calm, although he had ample reason to be terrified by the mob's bitterness. A couple of wicker chairs were dropped on the group and nearby demonstrators spat betel-juice at India's captain before he reached sanctuary in the dressing-room.

'None of the demonstration was against us,' Stackpole said. 'It was against their own side. I think they were most upset because they felt a couple of their batsmen got out to rash strokes, especially Pat's sweep off Mallett which Connolly caught.'

Far-reaching implications of the midfield clash with the photographer and another incident in the Great Eastern Hotel that night were not realised until the Australian team read the newspapers next morning.

Reports that McKenzie and Redpath had assaulted Indian pressmen after the team's celebration dinner caused incredulous derision all the way from Melbourne to Perth and back. Two men less likely than good-natured Garth and gentlemanly Redders to lay a finger on anything except bat and ball could not be found in the touring fifteen or, for that matter, on the whole Australian continent – not even in the Society of Friends. News that they were away from the hotel at the time quickly cleared their names in Australia – where their reputations made it least necessary – but thousands of Indians misled by the first report saw no correction and may still misjudge these two sportsmen.

With Australian touring sides a private team dinner to celebrate winning a series is a regular thing – as regular as match results allow, anyway – whereas it seems India's custom is for a formal dinner, with high officials making speeches well into the night. This chasm between customs added disastrously to the day's antagonisms because there was no one to bridge it. Lawry was feeling the lack of Australian reporters a severe handicap – a barrier to getting the team's viewpoint known to Indian pressmen. The absence of liaison in the pressbox resulted in more than 20 Indian newspapermen turning up and having to be told to leave because the dinner was private. They retired to the hotel's liquor permit room but later men with cameras knocked and entered a bedroom shared by Freeman and Mallett. When they failed to heed the tired bowlers' request that they go, 14-stone

Freeman forcibly put them out and telephoned to have them removed from the hotel.

Coming on top of assorted versions about the Bombay riot, and Lawry's brush with the photographers, it would be hard to imagine anything more cumulatively damaging to the team's image than for people to read that Australian players had assaulted Indian pressmen. Lawry must have felt he was carrying more weight than an Everest expedition Sherpa.

Police had escorted the Australians everywhere but no escort was considered necessary on the six-mile bus ride from the hotel to Dum Dum airport. As the bus climbed a hill outside Calcutta the players were taking little notice of their surroundings when a loud noise like an explosion shocked them. Stones were crashing against the sides of the bus, cracking and starring the windows. Through one partly-open window came a stone bigger than an orange. It missed Gleeson, who was sitting on the opposite side of the bus, by a hand's span.

'We were badly scared,' players said, 'and we dived for cover to the floor of the bus, wondering what would happen next. The most frightening thought was that stones might break through the driver's window, knock him out, and leave the bus to career out of control. Fortunately, little or no glass flew about inside the bus, as the windows did not shatter. We have no idea who the throwers were, except that we had passed a ricefield. When the bus passed out of range and we looked back from the top of the hill we saw about 100 Indians waving their arms. At the airport we saw the police chief. He was astonished when we told him the bus had been stoned.'

After the Press Photographers' Association threatened a protest strike about the pitch incident, members wore black armbands while taking pictures at the next game at Bangalore. Here the Australians ran into a different kind of trouble – a danger of becoming the first international side to be beaten by a zone team. Led by Jaisimha, who declared both innings, South Zone had a side of almost Test strength, with exceptionally good bowlers in leg-spinner Chandrasekhar and off-spinner Prasanna. Jai's second closure, 249 ahead, left only 170 minutes to get Australia out. By taking six wickets for nine in eight overs Prasanna brought about the fall of the eighth wicket at 53, and the crowd of about 20,000 were dwelling on victory. Lawry was no longer thinking about runs – and who can put them out of mind more completely? – as he and Gleeson resorted to every ruse and stratagem to get through the last hour. Even a woman in a gay sari walking by the sightscreen gave the captain an excuse to step back from the wicket as the bowler approached. He told the umpire the sari was distracting him.

With only 10 minutes to go, the disappointed crowd began pelting coconut husks, orange peel and apple cores at the South Zone fieldsmen. So much debris was falling on the field that umpires Nagaraj Rao and N. S. Rishi called off play five minutes before time and the players ran into the pavilion.

The uneasiness of the team, scarcely knowing what to expect next after the stoning of the bus, was equalled by alarm caused in Australia by reports of riots and rock-throwing. Several ex-players supported a suggestion to cancel the remaining Test, in the belief that it would expose the team to undue risks. Photographers boycotted the Australians' arrival in Madras for this match but manager Bennett's on-the-spot assessment was borne out when the Test was played and won without cause for anxiety.

In fact, uneasy moments for captain and manager had begun two months earlier at their first press interview in India, when they were questioned about scornful comments on Indian umpiring by the 1964 captain, Simpson, which had drawn a tart rejoinder from India's Board of Control. *Indian Cricket* editor P. N. Sundaresan, a writer of standing, put reactions in his country this way :

'Though they tried to explain away the remarks, there was no doubt the public had already been prejudiced to some extent against them . . . The tour might still have gone smoothly had only Lawry known how to take things with a smile. This is not to question his serious application to Test cricket or his being a stickler for rules. But it did little credit to him to resort to tactics like rubbing the ball on the ground to take the shine off, as he did in the Delhi Test, or make a scene when an appeal was negatived . . .

'Behind wild stories about crowd behaviour that created much adverse comment abroad lies the Indian spectators' approach to the game. A Test match in India is more of a

carnival and vast crowds create problems because of limited
accommodation. With a big crowd clamouring for admission
outside the grounds, a law and order problem is not uncommon . . .

'Test stars evoke as much glamour as cinema stars, wherever
they go a crowd follow and they are mobbed for autographs.
This curtails the players' freedom of movement and creates
in them a fear for personal saftey. Both local and visiting
cricketers have to suffer this . . . It must have been exaspera-
ting for the visitors to have received so much attention from
the cricket-mad public but a more amiable captain than
Lawry could have earned its goodwill.'

It would be misjudging Lawry (a man few outsiders under-
stand) to think him stonily heedless of Indian crowds' feelings,
especially when hooting and hissing while he had the strike
ceased when his partners faced the bowling. When Jack Fingleton sent an article adulatory of Lawry to *The Hindu*, Madras,
before the final Test, Bill found time to write a letter thanking
him on behalf of himself and his team. The article could not
reverse a current that had been two months gathering way. An
otherwise well-behaved Madras crowd heckled Lawry, who complained that the noise upset his concentration. The umpire said
he was powerless to quieten the barrackers, whose shouting,
whistling, trumpeting and drum-beating swelled louder at signs
that they were having an effect on their quarry.

Yet Madras people lined the streets, clapping and cheering the
Australians, leading to the conclusion that the average Indian
spectator was not antagonistic to the team as a whole.

The captain's dramatic account of tour incidents stirred the
Indian Board to protest to its Australian counterpart that many
of Lawry's statements were exaggerated, baseless and deserved
condemnation. The Australian Board replied with a literary
composition couched in terms to placate Indian officials,
yet loyally pleading in extenuation the tremendous pressure
on an international captain on an overseas tour, where
events occur completely different from those to which he is
accustomed.

Back home in Victoria after more worries in South Africa,
Bill could at last unwind in familiar surroundings. Yet events

proved that destructive urges have no geographic or racial boundaries. Because fires had damaged a dozen Victorian schools while he was away patrols of parents were being formed to guard many schools. In New South Wales, vandals lit fires in 42 schools in six months.

The urge to throw something is by no means monopolised by the world's exasperated have-nots. In Victoria's pastoral western district, where Mercedes and Jaguars were almost as thick as sheep to the acre, graziers opposing a higher levy pelted Wool Board chairman Sir William Gunn with eggs, fruit and vegetables.. A former Rugby forward, Sir William stands 6 ft 3 ins. and weighs 250 lb. How could they miss such a target? Making light of stains streaking his jacket, he rumbled: 'Be all right – it's wool.'

Three stones hit English Rugby League winger Johnny Atkinson on the back as he played at Wagga. Three League clubs in Sydney suburbs banned cans and bottles from Penrith Park, Belmore Sportsground and Brookvale Oval. When world middleweight boxing champion Nino Benvenuti lost to Tom Bethea at Melbourne Velodrome a half-filled can cut the referee's forehead and well-dressed ringside patrons hurled a hail of cans back at the bleachers.

At the height of the nickel boom attendants and police at Sydney Stock Exchange had to call for reinforcements to stop skirmishes in the visitors' gallery. After the Federal Parliament passed a Public Order Bill in 1971 police in the national capital made Canberra's biggest mass arrest of 187 students who refused to disperse after an anti-war demonstration. During the Springboks seven-week Rugby tour of Australia more than 700 anti-apartheid demonstrators were arrested in five States.

In cancelling the South Africans' cricket tour the Australian Board questioned whether it was reasonable to ask the police to undergo a severe ordeal to enable cricket to be played while other members of the public were deprived of police services. Also was it reasonable to expect international cricketers to perform under such trying circumstances.

Before then both the captains of the torrid series in India had been lifted out of the hot seat. Lawry was replaced 11 months after his return. Pataudi's 10-year reign ended when Wadekar led the Indians in their first victorious series in the West Indies and

England. Just north of Calcutta's airport, less than 40 miles from the East Pakistan frontier, thousands of frightened fugitives from warfare crowded wretchedly into one of the emergency camps that held nine million refugees whose anguish made the misfortunes of a cricket match fade into triviality.

Calcutta. Dec 12, 13, 14, 16, 1969. Australia won by nine wickets.

INDIA 1st innings			2nd innings		
F. M. Engineer c Stackpole b McKenzie		0	c Redpath b Freeman	...	10
A. V. Mankad c Stackpole b McKenzie		9	c Taber b McKenzie	...	20
A. L. Wadekar c Freeman b McKenzie		0	lbw Freeman	...	62
G. R. Viswanath c Taber b Mallett	...	54	b Freeman	...	5
Pataudi (c.) c Chappell b Mallett	...	15	c Connolly b Mallett	...	1
A. Roy c Taber b McKenzie	...	18	c Sheahan b Connolly	...	19
E. D. Solkar c Taber b McKenzie	...	42	lbw Connolly	...	21
S. Venkataraghavan c Stackpole b Mallett	24	b Connolly	...	0
E. A. S. Prasanna run out by Freeman	...	26	c Stackpole b Freeman	...	0
S. Guha b McKenzie	... ...	4	not out	...	1
B. S. Bedi not out	... ...	9	c Chappel b Connolly	...	7
B 5, lb 1, nb 4, w 1	... ...	11	B 6, lb 4, nb 5	...	15

Total off 96.4 overs (5 hrs. 47 mins.)... 212   Total off 77.1 overs (4h. 43m.) 161

Fall: 0, 0, 22, 64, 103, 103, 164, 178, 184, 212.
    29, 31, 40, 90, 93, 141, 141, 142, 159, 161.

Bowling.	Balls	Runs	Wkts.		Balls	Runs	Wkts.
McKenzie	202	67	6 ...	...	108	34	1
Freeman	102	43	– ...	...	156	54	4
Connolly	102	27	– ...	...	97	31	4
Mallett	162	55	3 ...	...	102	27	1
Stackpole	12	9	–				

AUSTRALIA 1st innings			2nd innings			
W. M. Lawry (c.) c Solkar b Bedi	...	35	not out ...	... ...	17
K. R. Stackpole run out by Mankad	...	41	not out ...	... ...	25
I. M. Chappell c Wadekar b Bedi	...	99				
K. D. Walters st Engineer b Bedi	...	56				
A. P. Sheahan run out by Prasanna	...	32				
E. W. Freeman c Prasanna b Bedi	...	29				
H. B. Taber b Bedi	... ...	...	2			
G. D. McKenzie b Pataudi b Bedi	...	0				
A. A. Mallett not out	... ...	...	2			
A. N. Connolly c Guha b Solkar	...	31				
B 4, lb 2, nb 2	... ...	...	8			

Total off 143.1 overs (7 hrs. 33 mins.)   335   No wicket off (5 overs 23 mins.) 42

Fall: 65, 84, 185, 185, 257, 279, 302, 302, 302, 335.

Bowling.	Balls	Runs	Wkts.		Balls	Runs	Wkts.
Guha	114	55	– ...	...	18	25	–
Solkar	55	28	1				
Prasanna	294	116	–				
Venkat.	96	30	–				
Bedi	300	98	7				
Wadekar				...	12	17	–

Runs per 100 balls: India 36, Australia 42.
Balls per hour: India 113, Australia 95.

Umpires: Shambu Pan, J. Reuben.

Chapter 14

BOUNCERS AND BEERCANS

I CAN think of no better term for a shooter than the meanest ball on earth, and that's not metaphorically speaking. Yet the lowest shooters are nothing like so contentious as bouncers that sometimes bruise ribs, raise lumps, gash scalps and leave sickly expressions on the faces of hitherto brave men. Since the dust died slowly down ofter the Battle of Adelaide in 1933 bumpers have not provoked such a disagreeable scene as Sydney saw in February 1971 – incidents that will be discussed long after much eventful cricket in the game is forgotten.

Last of six Tests played in Australia by Ray Illingworth's victorious Englishmen, this match brought to boil-over point an issue that had been simmering and sputtering through almost three months since John Snow's first bouncer to Ian Chappell in Adelaide and Alan Thomson's first to Colin Cowdrey in Melbourne. Episode Six became by far the most dramatic of the series, a Test that had everything except a century. It was marked, and marred, by a bouncer stunning a tailender, an international captain angrily disputing an umpire's ruling in midfield, a drunken onlooker grabbing the shirt of a bowler fielding on the boundary and the first team walk-off in Test history, after incensed barrackers threw empty beercans and a few bottles on to stretches of the outfield.

Few individual bowlers or batsmen have ever dominated a series as Snow did this one. Without being the biggest man on the field – Bob Willis stands 6 feet 5½ inches – Snow was like a swordfish among salmon; to most of Australia's batsmen a more apt simile might be like a piranha among perch, ready to tear strips off their already-wan confidence. His quick bowling allowed batsmen's nerves no chance to recover from stresses imposed by Mike Procter's hostility in South Africa. To mix a meteorological metaphor, something short

of a hail of bumpers left Australia's batting show-
bound.

Dark sideburns descend from this handsome and headstrong
bowler's wavy hair. Semi-stovepipe pants show a couple of
inches of sock above his boots; they look like trousers tailored for
a smaller man. John is the only fast bowler who can turn a
poetic phrase as well as seam the ball either way off the track
or make it prance towards a batsman's chin. His well-muscled
back and broad shoulders combine in convulsive effort – recalling his boyhood hero Keith Miller – often making the ball get
up as nobody else in this series could. Willing to go to almost
any length to get Australian wickets, the 29-year-old bowler
preferred to be short of a length on hard strips, finding that,
unlike English tracks, they helped bounce much more than
seaming. I've seen a lot worse verse than Snow's. In his *Contrasts*
one poem ends :

> On the treadmill rolls
> As the body mindless bowls
> Down paths
> And the wheel which turns
> Is turning much faster than before.

Some of his poetry takes a little longer to sink in than his
bouncer; no batsman likes to feel that sinking in, and they tend
to remember it longer than anything he puts to metre. Like
many another successful speedman in international cricket, he
has a healthy splash of brimstone in his bloodstream.

John Snow is a powderkeg of a bowler with a short fuse – a
fuse no longer than a man's tongue, if that man is an umpire.
Three times in earlier Tests he had been cautioned, by two
umpires. In the second innings in Perth when Lou Rowan asked
him to 'Watch it,' he asked brusquely : 'What for?' and was
told he was dropping too many balls too short in line with the
batsman (Bill Lawry). Soon afterward persistent bumpers made
Ian Redpath sway back direfully and the umpire repeated the
warning. The fast bowler sent along an irreproachable ball
then flung the next down half-way. It reared over the six-foot
Victorian's head and Snow said emphatically: 'That's what I call
a bouncer!' With the second Perth warning, Rowan notified

the captain – the second step Law 46 specifies toward ordering an offending bowler off for the innings. When Illingworth
contended : 'They're not bouncers,' the umpire was heard
to reply : 'Somebody's bowling them from this end and it's
not me.'

Even on such a busy tour I doubt whether England's skipper
forgot his first Melbourne appearance against Victoria having
been greeted with three short-pitched balls in Thomson's first four
balls to him. The second struck Illy's shoulder and the third
bouncer brought a caution from umpire Bob Figgis. Victorian
captain Lawry came from mid-off to ask the umpire why.

Far from being too strict, I thought some of the umpiring
permissive rather than punctilious at times, allowing intimidatory
bowling by Snow and Thomson to pass without visible check.
The point demanded discussion when several overs of the Melbourne Test contained four or more bouncers, including the first
over of the match to Keith Stackpole. Standing in a Test for the
first time, Max O'Connell seemed unwilling to project himself
into mid-picture in his opening minutes as an international
umpire by warning the year's outstanding bowler.

BBC broadcaster Brian Johnston asked ex-captain Lindsay
Hassett how many bumpers in an eight-ball over should an
umpire allow. Hassett : 'As a batsman I'd say two. A bowler
might consider he could get away with three. Four in an over
would have to be questioned.' Two an over was the limit set by
Trinidad umpires after excesses early in England's 1960 series
in the West Indies. Using arithmetic as the test whether bowling
is intimidatory has never seemed the answer to me but a bowler
warned after three bumpers in an over can hardly complain that
justice does not appear to have been done.

With each of four bouncers to Brian Luckhurst's end in Melbourne, Thomson's long-range follow-through to the off side
resulted in his return trek to starting-point taking him around
the Cape, meaning nearer extra-cover than the bowler's umpire,
Rowan. Watching through binoculars I wondered would the
umpire walk across to intercept 'Froggy' with an admonition.
I saw no sign of this, nor anything being said to the bowler
when a fifth bouncer, second ball of his next over, struck the
ducking Luckhurst near a shoulder-blade. According to the
grapevine – not always as reliable as the Central Intelligence

Agency – Alan's cheerful expression changed when he 'got the message'. If so, the Englishmen were unaware of this when four bumpers to Doug Walters in Snow's fourth over in the second innings caused O'Connell to say: 'That's enough!' Nettled, Snow hurled down a fifth short ball but it failed to bounce much more than bail-high. Running from point, Illingworth protested to O'Connell about Snow being warned for fewer bouncers than he said Thomson had let fly in one over in the first innings.

Never encouraged, reporters' questioning of umpires has brought to light some inconsistency of opinion and one relevant fact: some umpires disregard fliers that sail wide of a batsman – a distinction too refined to comfort a man aware that he has been spared only by inaccuracy and that the next bumper may be right on the button. I'd think that is how Luckhurst and Cowdrey felt more than once. For Colin, no doubt it stirred painful memories of his call for padded vests in the West Indies.

Batting eighth in the Melbourne Test, Snow ducked under a couple of bouncers from Thomson; none of the watching fieldsmen raised a smile. When the pair met at an Adelaide reception John ran a finger along Froggy's sandy hair and laconically asked where he'd like it parted.

As the teams were named for the final Test the prevailing impression was that England had missed a chance to be two up through failure to order a follow-on in Adelaide when Australian morale had sunk below seagull level. That reprieve failed to save Lawry's neck from the selectors' block which had been awaiting it for weeks. Next, a fractured left forearm denied England the stable batting of Geoffrey Boycott, heaviest scorer of the series.

Winning his first toss as Australia's captain Ian Chappell, who had never put any opposing side in, sent England in to bat on a pitch prepared in Sydney's wettest summer in 16 years. The 27-year-old skipper followed this up by giving his bowlers the most attacking fields of the series, at times resembling the Benaud touch.

Chappell's fast bowlers, Dennis Lillee and left-hander Tony Dell had difficulty directing the glossy ball along compelling lines, especially the newcomer, Dell, so nervous that he confessed he was unable to see the batsman's stumps for a while. On legs solid as an Epstein statue's, the 6 feet $4\frac{1}{2}$ inch Queenslander scarcely looks a Nureyev in his run-up but uses his height, backed by $16\frac{1}{2}$ stone, to make the ball lift nastily from a fresh track. When Gregory Chappell's sharp catch at third slip helped Dell to his first Test victim, John Edrich (30), the fieldsmen's joy showed how highly they valued the wicket of the stocky left-hander, whose batting is made up of equal parts of skill and sang-froid. In making 33 Keith Fletcher twice could not avoid blows on the left arm and chest, and Dell bruised D'Oliveira on the body before his in-dipper flicked from Basil's bat into the stumps.

Under the general applause greeting Illingworth I was surprised to hear an undertone of boos, like a rumble of far-away thunder while the sun shines overhead. Nothing in the captain's play in Australia warranted such sour incivility from a minority of dubious mental age. Throughout he had impressed me as a practical skipper, a man among men. His team respected his deeper knowledge of the game, his efficiency as a tactician, his Yorkshire fibre. They had the fullest faith in his judgment. No generation gap here, though Illy was 38 and his cream trousers were unfashionably wide. There was room, too, for belief that his captaincy qualities were most evident when England fielded: wisdom in judging which bowler would get most out of the wicket and bring the worst out of each batsman, also where to place fieldsmen for likely catches without forgetting economy. I could only attribute the surly undertone of boos to what Sydneysiders had seen on television of bouncers harrying O'Keeffe in the Melbourne Test, low daily quotas of balls by England's bowlers (average only 98 balls an hour) and a tendency to blame his side for dull stretches in earlier Tests. I believe Illy was well aware of drawbacks in his team's play but where is the Test captain who would risk upsetting his bowlers in mid-series by pressing them to break time-taking habits acquired over years?

An alert infielder, he held every catch he could reach and as batsman he showed more interest than most of his specialists in trying to keep the scoring rate from dozing off. As forward shots sprout as rarely from his play as papaws in Pudsey he puts his faith in hooks, sweeps, squarecuts and back-foot forces through the covers; they did not let him down in Australia. This time four were out for only 69 yet, except for brushing his forelock with his left glove, Illy showed no concern. The best and squarest hooker in the side, he was the only one of England's first six batsman to break up the close fields with which Chappell kept pressure on for 37 overs – nearly half the innings.

Knott was the only partner who lasted long with his captain, and England had lost six for 145 when the 66th over entitled the Australians to a new ball. Orthodox captaincy would have called for it instantly, and Chappell discussed this with vice-captain Redpath as they walked to the other end, but the new skipper thought spinners Kerry O'Keeffe and Terry Jenner were bowling well enough to deserve longer tenure of the creases. Within 11 appreciative overs the pair spun the innings to an end. Jenner rattled the stumps three times in his last four overs, twice with legbreaks and once with a wrong'un that removed Illy, whose 42, topscore, contained six well-hit boundary shots.

For the first time in his life O'Keeffe found his mixed spin supported by a close three-man legtrap, in addition to his captain at slip waiting for an edged legbreak. The deployment rewarded the lean and keen young bowler's quick-armed spin with his first Test wickets: Stackpole's fleshy but swift hands caught Fletcher and Knott at leg-gully and Jenner held Lever at silly mid-on (None was as near as Brian Close stands, tempting extinction, when O'Keeffe bowls for Somerset).

In his breakaway from routine tactics Chappell made much less call on four seam bowlers: brother Greg's medium-pace quota shrank to three overs in the match instead of about 20. Sharing 40 overs this day, the two spinners were entrusted with both ends for 24 consecutive overs, causing onlookers with bygone haircuts to think back to O'Reilly and Grimmett. In an hour after tea the pair provided 144 balls of cricket – 18 overs here, the equivalent of 24 overs in England. Stimulating more verve in his players' response, the new leader achieved the triple distinction of dismissing England in less than a day for their lowest total of the series – all done with 150 fewer balls than it had taken to end any English innings in the preceding Tests. Among ex-skippers who praised this captaincy was the latest recruit to their ranks, Lawry, who said Ian did everything right. I met only one man who qualified this, ex-bowler Bill Hunt who thought it would have been wiser not to try too hard to get the last couple of wickets until nearer the day's end, in the belief that the track would be easier for batting next day.

With only 184 on the board the bowlers knew England was heading for defeat unless they could do something drastic. Snow sounded the tocsin by bumping the first and seventh balls of the innings to crew-cut Ken Eastwood, replacing the deposed Lawry as left-handed opening partner for Stackpole. The newcomer fell to Peter Lever for five when wicketkeeper Alan Knott reached a low legside snick.

Snow turned Australian concern to consternation with a superb over – his best of the series, I'd say – to get rid of the bravest of batsmen, Stackpole, the man whom England most needed to prevent settling in. Following up a blow in the hip region (no bumper) John seamed a couple of balls away from the off stump so sharply that Keith walked along the pitch to give the spot pacifying taps. With outgoers on his mind, Stackpole was left standing by a perfectly pitched incutter that clipped the outside of the off peg as it ripped through. Both openers gone for 13! Rather than send another nightwatchman in, Chappell came in himself with two minutes to go – an action reminding me of the captaincy of his dauntless grandfather, Victor Richardson.

Saturday was election day in New South Wales, but the Test topped the poll, judging by the number of voters carrying transistors tuned to the cricket. In the first hour, calling of two front-foot no-balls scarcely mollified Snow. After the second call he walked sternly to the crease and stared at the ground almost as intently as a Queensland blacktracker. In one such dialogue earlier Snow had asked: 'Where's the footprint?' and the umpire replied: 'I don't need a footprint to tell me where I saw your boot land.'

As catcher and third paceman, Willis, tall as Chips Rafferty, drove a wedge into Australia's batting. Rod Marsh's leg shot off Lever looked to be worth four runs until Willis's exceptional reach and lunging experience as Corinthian Casuals' goalie, enabled him to intercept a catch, otherwise non-existent. Chap-

pell tried to drive a well-up ball with which Bob sent his off
stump cartwheeling. Puzzled, Ian asked his partner had he
unknowingly played across the ball. Four down for 66 made
Australia's position precarious.

After lunch England's quick bowlers put plenty of fire into an
attempt to break Redpath and Walters' fifth-wicket stand.
Squatting under three bouncers in two overs from Lever did
nothing to brace Walters' nerve for facing Snow's greater menace
from the other end. Seeing Doug backing away, yet still aiming
desperate square-cuts at flying balls, Snow pressed his thrustful
attack, unsparingly, as if he wanted to drive Walters not
only from the wicket but off the continental shelf. His last
bumper to Doug was nearer a quarter-pitcher than a half-
pitcher. It was the shortest ball I ever saw John bowl. Yet fortune favoured the at-bay batsmen so much that 18 agitated
runs came off two overs, causing Illy to spell his most dangerous
bowler half an hour after lunch.

Whenever Snow chased a shot near the boundary a rumble
of boos beneath the applause for the shot suggested that had some
onlookers been umpiring he would have been warned for
intimidation.

Cutting boldly on a track still aiding bowlers, Walters gave
chances off Underwood at 16 and Willis at 27. The Englishmen found him harder to catch than Ronald Biggs. At 41 a
foozled drive at Underwood coiled from Doug's boot toward
silly-point. Knott's simultaneous pounce and backward flick
to the stumps – do his heels have radar? – were like magic.
Television playbacks proved that this close decision should have
gone Alan's way, but a run later he stumped the venturesome
Walters off the same bowler.

Redpath, bouncer-harassed yet persevering stoically, drove
well in reaching the first 50 of the Test. Willis, Underwood and
Illingworth's accuracy limited him to eight runs in the next 45
minutes, amid an ungrateful tincan chorus – barrackers' clanking
disapproval of slow scoring by foe or friend. After Derek caught
Redpath's drive and Knott snapped up O'Keeffe off Illy at 178
the last recognised batsman, Greg Chappell, put Australia
ahead of England's 184 with only three bowlers left to help
him.

Sensation was waiting in the wings when, after 2½ hours at grass, Snow was recalled for the 66th over. He took a new ball for the third delivery and completed the over with a legside bumper to Chappell.

Bouncers had become so frequent in the series that less notice was being taken of them than in most Test rubbers I have watched – except by batsmen, among whom familiarity never breeds contempt. Partly, I suppose, because Tom Brooks is an old fast bowler, much of the umpiring was more lenient than in 1961 when four in one over and three in another caused Colin Egar to intervene twice as Wesley Hall bowled to McDonald and Simpson in Melbourne. In Sydney's January Test, 1971, a Snow bumper caused the ninth man, McKenzie, to retire with his mouth bleeding. In the next Test one of several bouncers to the eighth man, O'Keeffe, bruised his chest.

Now in the final Test in Sydney live television showed millions of viewers in Australian cities that three balls in Snow's second over with this new ball were to the ninth man, Jenner. As the first rose toward his ribs Jenner gingerly fended it away with his bat. It ran around the corner for a single, giving Chappell the strike for four balls. Facing Snow again for the sixth ball, Jenner unhappily squirmed out of its way as it reared. Had he stood still, it would have struck him near the left armpit. The over count so far to Jenner: two short-pitched balls, at least one of which an umpire could have classed as intimidatory.

To follow up Jenner's apprehensive wriggle from the sixth ball Snow's field-setting was changed by bringing Willis from mid-off across to the on side. This made four leg-trap fieldsmen : deep-leg (Underwood), leg-gully (Hampshire), close short-leg (Illingworth) and mid-on (Willis). Stepping back, Jenner stared at the reshuffle like a bird transfixed by a snake's mesmerism. Like every cricketer watching, he recognised the field adjustment as preparation for catching a mishit off a bouncer to come. It came. Banged down short, it cut in as it reared toward Jenner's collarbone. As he tried to duck beneath it, the ball struck the left side of his head near the back and rebounded toward cover.

Jenner's collapse on the pitch brought a thunderous hoot from the keyed-up crowd. The outburst reflected a similar sense of outrage to that felt much less demontratively at Trent

Bridge in 1966 when a ball from massive West Indian fast bowler Charlie Griffith struck England's last man, Underwood, on the mouth. The bowler's captain, Sobers, looked upset but waited until they were back in the room before telling Griffith he should apologise. The bowler did so in writing. Disgusted viewers wrote letters to editors. In being spared severe injury Derek was more fortunate than another tailender, Tony Lock, whose left arm was broken at Perth in 1963 by a bumper from Peter Pollock, then at his fastest.

I had been sorry to see Snow, a top-class cricketer, master of the compelling art of quick bowling, add his name to those who have misinterpreted their craft by breaking the once-honoured unwritten law against bouncing the cricket ball at unskilful tailenders. When Alec Bedser, promoted from the lower division to nightwatchman at Leeds in 1948, was hard to shift next day, an exasperated fast bowler, Ray Lindwall, let fly a bouncer which struck Alec on the chest. That night Bill O'Reilly, who was Lindwall's club captain in Sydney, quietly told Ray: 'I hope I never see you bowl another bumper at a bowler.' Trying to duck under bumpers from Freddie Trueman at Edgbaston and the Oval in 1958 New Zealanders Noel Harford and John Sparling retired hurt by blows on the head. England's ex-captain Sir Leonard Hutton commented: 'I do not like to see bouncers bowled at any except the very top-class batsmen – batsmen with the skill and experience to look after themselves in the face of such an attack.' Harford was in the upper half of New Zealand's batting order and Sparling went in eighth. From what I have seen and heard at Test grounds in six countries the principles expressed by O'Reilly and Hutton are much closer to most cricket-goers and players' concepts of fair play than opinions attempting to justify a bullring outlook. Where else more so than in Sydney, the city where selector Edmund Dwyer first proposed in 1952 deleting the words 'standing clear of his wicket' from Law 46, forbidding intimidation of a batsman by persistent and systematic short-pitched balls?

From close-leg, five yards away, Illingworth was first to the stunned Jenner. Hooting and abusive shouts from the Hill continued as the pallid tailender was lifted to his feet. Willis carried the dropped bat as masseur David McErlane and Lever helped Terry walk unsteadily off, blood oozing through his hair.

As Snow turned to walk back for his run-up to bowl to the tenth man, Lillee, umpire Rowan called: 'Before you go, John . . .', seemingly intending to caution him. Snow gave no heed. Nearby players heard the umpire call more loudly: 'Just a minute, John!' The bowler walked on with a muttered remark. Rowan: 'I am not impressed by your performance and am giving you a first warning.' He turned to signal with one finger to square-leg umpire Brooks.

The bowler whirled around, objecting loudly: 'That's the first bouncer I've bowled this over – your blokes have been bowling seven an over.' Illingworth hurried down to support him, looking rather like the Khmer god ·whose glance could set objects on fire. 'What's going on?' he asked. Rowan, a detective sergeant by occupation, repeated: 'I'm giving the bowler a first warning.'

Holding up one finger Illingworth contended it was unfair to warn a man for bowling 'one bouncer in the over.' In the heat of the moment language more likely to be heard in locker-rooms than libraries burst from the warned bowler and the worried skipper hotly taking his part. Not the sort of words that figure in the Sussex sonneteer's poetry, though fairly easy to rhyme with a simple cricket term or two. It was a frustrating moment. No wonder Britain was accelerating moves to enter the Common Market!

Caught between two fires – Snow was baying toward his left ear and the captain toward his right – umpire Rowan waved a hand as if to idicate that this confrontation must now cease. 'Get on with the game!' he said. 'Push off!' They did, after Illingworth turned back and, jerking his thumb toward the pavilion, said: 'We'll see who has the last word on this when we get out there.'

By word and gesture Illingworth had shown he did not class either of the two preceding balls to Jenner as a bouncer. A number of onlookers thought otherwise. Definitions vary. A prison that New York calls a Correction Facility still looks like a jail to most people. In cricket, a thudding bouncer can hardly be mistaken for a length ball, and vice-versa, but when a border-line ball pitches the game suffers if the opinion of the man appointed to judge is not accepted. Spectators were astonished to see an umpire's decision being disputed by a captain from the country that taught the world how to play. King Arthur wouldn't have done it. It was the one action on the tour that Illingworth regretted, as he told *Sunday Express* readers later.

Why should a seasoned, level-headed Yorkshireman blow his cone? Only by travelling with Test teams can you appreciate the countless pressures on a captain's mind through most of his waking hours for several months on end. Illingworth's quota of these was more trying because all except four of his side had suffered injuries. A breakdown of his swiftest bowler, Alan Ward, upset his main strategy. His surest batsman, Boycott, was disabled, left arm in a sling. Illy was the first skipper to cope with six Tests in a series, and a New Year washout resulted in his bowlers having to saddle up for three Tests in the last four weeks. He felt it unfair that the other side's shortest-pitching bowler had, seemingly, escaped warnings of the sort two umpires had given England's fastest bowler. If two repeat warnings this time cost him his main bowler for the rest of the innings and enabled the Australians to square the rubber, he would never hear the end of having let them off the hook in Adelaide by not ordering a follow-on. Though I believe he acted there as his bowlers wished, the blame for letting the Ashes slip would settle on him. This outline is not given in an attempt to justify the inexcusable but I think the culmination of all these factors explains why Illingworth slipped his trolley.

Instead of the on-target bouncer and its hot-worded sequel monopolising weekend headlines they were supplanted by a sensation in which the crowd's hooligan fringe got into the act.

As Snow ran up to deliver the last ball of the dramatic over to the tenth man, Lillee, a crescendo of hoots from many parts of the Hill showed the crowd's wrath at a bumper having knocked down a tailender. There is no way of estimating how many of the 29,684 present joined in, but the hooting was much more impassioned and widespread than earlier Sydney booing of bumpers, such as Miller to Hutton, Lindwall to Compton and Weekes, Hall to Harvey, Loxton to various batsmen.

While the Englishmen had drinks near midfield a dozen cans were thrown from the rowdy lesser Hill at the north-east corner into the vacant outfield, presumably in resentment at the felling of Jenner. Calling to Snow not to go there to field, Illingworth sat down while a ground attendant tossed the cans into a gutter at the foot of the fence. 'Better go to third man,' Illy advised. Snow : 'No, I'll go down.'

As Snow walked to field at deep-leg an indistinguishable tirade of taunts greeted him. He responded in kind, and gesticulated an invitation to anyone who wanted to make something of it. Instead of stopping at his usual spot about eight yards from the excited corner he went close to the fence. Youths and boys leaned across to shake his hand or pat his shoulder. 'Thanks mate, thanks mate !' he repeated to each hero-worshipper. A middle-aged drunk in an orange shirt and white towel hat thrust out a hand but, instead of patting, grabbed his shirt and dragged him against the pickets. 'What the hell do you think you're doing ?' exclaimed Snow. The man would not let go until neighbours hauled him over backwards, aided by a shove from the poet-bowler's right palm. (Asked had the grabber said anything, John said : 'He couldn't speak – he was stoned').

As Snow walked about 15 yards in from the boundary a second wave of cans landed around the stretch of outfield in front of the lesser Hill. Most of them, yards from Snow, appeared to be a renewal of a distorted form of protest but one skidded past John a couple of feet from his right boot. Snow pointed to the cans – there were then six at his end – but nobody could tell whether more would follow and be aimed at him. In case he might need help, Willis loyally ran to join him, only to undo the effect by shouting at the crowd. More cans followed.

Running from midfield toward the pair, their captain kicked a couple of cans toward the gutter and pulled Snow further away. Then he waved an arm to his fieldsmen and, forgetting the umpires, led his team off, apparently feeling his move necessary as a skipper's duty to safeguard his players. (We were not aware until his later statement that a couple of bottles had flown past his and Snow's heads.)

Sitting side by side broadcasting, ex-captains Benaud and Lawry had made a small diversionary bet on the match. Illingworth's disappearance through the gate reminded Lawry of this. Turning to Richie, he said : 'It's a forfeit. Pay up, Benordy !'

The batsmen stayed at the wicket. Lillee, playing his second Test, walked along to Chappell and asked : 'What do we do now?' Greg: 'We stay here until we are told to do something different.'

The umpires walked to the Englishmen's room, where Rowan asked: 'What's going on, Mr Illingworth? Is your team coming back on the field or are you forfeiting the match?'

The captain replied that he had a duty to safeguard his players and said the ground should be cleared.

At the other end a few youths from the main Hill were helping ground staff throw cans into the boundary gutter at 5.10 p.m. when secretary Alan Barnes broadcast through amplifiers: 'The ground will be cleared and the players will return. Clear the field and play will go on!' Mixed boos from the Hill and applause from the reserve greeted that, and were repeated when Illingworth led his team back from a seven-minute sit-in.

Looking on was Colin Egar, who had held the confidence of skippers from four countries before he ceased umpiring in 1970. Asked what he would have done had he been umpiring the Test, Egar replied: 'I'd have been out there getting the outfield cleared while Rowan was in England's room telling them to play or forfeit.'

When Lever bowled the next over Willis was fielding 15 yards in front of the shirt-grabbing spot, Illy having switched Snow to third-man in front of the members' pavilion. As Snow walked 30 paces to begin the following over applause dominated the noises, as if the bulk of the crowd wished to dissociate themselves from the yahoos' can-throwing. (In all, 40 cans and a few bottles were found in the boundary gutters; more than one-third of them were soft-drink cans, causing ground manager Keith Sharp to conclude that boys formed at least one in three of the throwers.)

We heard some booing as Snow ran up but it petered out with the first ball. After this over, his third with the new ball, his end was taken over by Willis. When a shortish ball from Bob struck Lillee in the stomach, doubling him up, some token boos and catcalls came from the still-fuming Hill. Hundreds had left but I should say 20,000 stayed to watch. Greg Chappell was worth watching. It would take more than bouncer incidents, a can-throwing disturbance and a team walk-off to put this 22-year-old cricketer off his game. By Saturday night he had steered Australia to a lead of 51 with three wickets yet to fall.

I learned later that just before the shirt-grab police at the ground were alerted by their chief, Commissioner Norman Allan, who was watching ABC television in his suburban home at Balgowlah and listening to comments by Norman May and Frank Tyson. In reply to my questions Commissioner Allan said: 'A few minutes after the injured batsman fell, the screen showed Snow walking towards the fence, where he was being vigorously booed. Sensing that there would be trouble, I spoke on my hot line to Metropolitan Superintendent Ernest Lynch, in charge at the ground. I said it would be advisable to place police inside the fence in that area, as the crowd was simmering. Police reported there had been a mêlée there a few minutes earlier and they arrested two men for unseemly conduct. Snow, angered by boos and taunts, answered them provocatively. This was indiscreet, of course, but understandable.

'Superintendent Lynch gave the order but before police could be posted inside the fence Snow's shirt was grabbed. After that, nine men were arrested and charged with unseemly conduct, unseemly language or offensive behaviour. No one was charged with assaulting Snow, who laid no charges. When police lined inside the fence the crowd kept its emotions under control and there were no more ugly incidents.'

Noticing that Jenner was recovering from shock, Dr A. B. Corrican asked him: 'Do you think you will feel up to batting again, if needed this evening? If so, I'll have to stitch your head.' He did so and players helped buckle Jenner's pads on again.

Immediately after the dazed batsman was helped off the field vice-captain Colin Cowdrey came to see whether the injury was serious and to express sympathy. Before leaving at the day's end for their motel Snow accompanied manager David Clark to the Australians' room. Snow expressed no regret but asked Jenner: 'How are you?' He brushed his hand across Terry's hair, as if to indicate a glancing blow. Jenner's dark hair was matted with congealed blood at the back and the doctor had warned him not to let water touch the wound area.

One report in London suggested that if this amount of beer-cans justified a retreat there are some parts of the world where no cricket would be played at all. Before Sunday's play, however Illingworth told reporters: 'John Snow was in physical danger. That's why we walked off. Bottles as well as cans had been thrown in his direction. I have seen people hit by bottles and it makes a bloody mess of them. At Port of Spain in 1960 we sat on the ground while bottles were being thrown. They kept on throwing and in the end play was called off. By leaving the field yesterday we settled the whole thing in five to 10 minutes. It could have gone on indefinitely if we had not gone off.'

Nobody could disprove that opinion, though it was the opposite of the stand by another Yorkshireman, Hutton, at Georgetown 17 years earlier. In his snap decision to quit the field Illingworth ran the risk of antagonising more of the crowd than the splinter-group of can-throwing louts who, if any were trying to hit Snow, should have been disgusted with their marksmanship as well as ashamed of their larrikinism. As nothing marred the 45 minutes of play after the Englishmen reappeared, Ray could feel he had not misjudged the situation. His mail supported this view : more than 100 letters expressed regret for the disturbance and did not blame him for the walk-off.

In a letter addressed to the Australian Board of Control Illingworth restated his midfield contention and added : 'The short-pitched ball is a legitimate part of a fast bowler's armoury and, in my opinion, to warn Snow on one such ball was unfair tactics. In my opinion this warning was one of the major factors which caused the subsequent crowd disturbance which in turn led to my having taken England off the field'. The letter was never delivered but each captain filled in a routine report after the match on forms provided by the Board.

Pressmen who tried to interview Rowan had to be content with a cryptic typewritten statement : 'Because of my love of cricket and my respect for the greatest majority of people closely associated with it I have no comment to make. I will not join the group at any wailing wall'. (At the Board's request, however, Rowan supplied a report on the incidents. A copy of this was among information considered by the Cricket Council at Lord's before the warning that players dissenting from umpires' decisions would in future be penalised.)

Applause was the only sound heard as the Englishmen entered the field on Sunday, the third day. A different attendant had charge of the Main Hill sightscreen as the man on duty on

Saturday had been too upset by the disturbance to resume duty at that post.

Bowling from umpire Brooks' end, because of a change of wind, Snow kept the ball up to a length. Nothing more startling occurred in his three overs than an appeal for leg-before-wicket against Jenner, who had returned to the wicket after Knott caught Lillee off Willis. As the appeal was being easily answered, one watching cricketer caused a ripple of mirth by asking : 'How could he be lbw when he was so far away to leg?' Lasting 32 more balls Jenner added 22 runs before Lever bowled him off his thigh for 30. Taking risks as he ran out of partners Chappell 65 had his exposed leg stump hit – Willis's third victim.

England's second innings began 80 runs behind but Luckhurst's dread of a second o was not allowed to cramp his style. He played the bowling on its merits – and as if it had few merits – in making 40 of England's first 60. Mulberry stains from the new ball covered much of his blade while Edrich's bat looked unspotted. Between overs Luckhurst apologised for having so much of the strike. The left-hander's characteristic response : 'Don't worry. You carry on. I'll watch.' After a half-smothered yorker wriggled past the leg peg Brian lowered his bat crossways along the ground to show how he would deal with any more like that one. Flashes from halfway up the Hill caused police to explore the slope for a mirror or shiny lunch tin, without locating the unsporting or negligent culprit. Confident square-cuts helped Luckhurst make 59 of the first 94, putting England 14 ahead before his sweep at O'Keeffe's legbreak gave Lillee a long run for a well-judged catch. Fast bowlers are among the best fielders these days, as Snow, Willis and Lever had shown.

Few people knew what to expect when Chappell handed Eastwood the ball before tea. Ken turned out to be a left-hand wrist-spinner with a penchant for full-tosses. Two minutes before the interval Keith Fletcher 20, tried to place one of these too carefully, Stackpole held the third of his four catches and Chappell's hunch almost earned him a halo. Compelling Edrich 57 to defend against one near the off stick, O'Keeffe saw an edged wrong'un pop in and out of the falling captain's hands as Chappell slewed his body under it in case his second clutch failed.

When not finding gaps, John Hampshire was stinging cover

fieldsmen's hands. Attempting another murderous sweep against O'Keeffe he skied the ball over untenanted ground behind the wicket. When Ian Chappell began racing outward from slip with his back to the wicket it looked a forlorn chance until a delighted yell from the crowd he was facing told of his ankle-high capture of a catch almost as difficult to judge as it was hard to overtake.

Only 85 ahead with four of the best gone – that was the tight corner for England when Illingworth joined Basil D'Oliveira, who in so many Tests for his adopted country has been a cool man in hot spots. Basil's bat of yellower willow looks more natural than the other bleached blades and it suits the play of a batsman observing natural laws rather than cranial theories.

Once as O'Keeffe was running in Illy twisted away from his wicket to look at the leg fielders' positions. A minority of the previous day's hooters started to rumble, inexplicably, and a dozen clots began rapping cans together, irritatingly. Next time Redpath's short-leg position was altered umpire Brooks stood in the bowler's path until all was settled. He also motioned close fielders a few paces back if their shadows fell on the pitch. Recall of Dell and Lillee with a new ball for the last half-hour pained both batsmen, as the towering Queenslander struck Dolly three times on the thigh and waist and a blow on Illy's left knee made the skipper finish the day limping.

While the cricketers relaxed on their rest day, Monday and Bernard Thomas used physio-therapy on the captain's leg, a Central Court magistrate began fining 13 men a total of $700 when they pleaded guilty to offensive behaviour, resistance to arrest or unseemly words. Nearly all between 25 and 18, they included labourers, clerks, students, firemen, a glazier and welder who admitted having thrown two stubby bottles. The magistrate said people were entitled to go to cricket without being subjected to the menace of flying beercans from men acting like hoodlums. The shirt-grabber was not apprehended but one labourer's offensive behaviour consisted of running across the field to shake Greg Chappell's hand at 50; he told the court he was carried away.

Illingworth did not need a runner on Tuesday but he added only four to reach 29 before Lillee hit his left boot. Of 10 appeals for lbw or bat-pad catches in England's innings this was the only one the umpires upheld. D'Oliveira's timely 47 helped the total grow by 93 before Chappell dived to a low snick off Lillee's outswinger, the captain's third catch among the first six wickets. Unable to prevent the last four men from adding 51 to make England 302, the Australians found themselves needing 223 to win. Use of only a light hand-roller was a clue to their thoughts about the state of the track.

Before a run came luckless Eastwood was yorked by Snow who after his second over was the victim of misadventure at the same spot as Saturday's exploits. Against the background of a high stand he misjudged a hook by Stackpole off Lever which would have been catchable had he stood with his back to the fence. Moving forward, John wheeled around too late and, as the ball went over, his outflung right hand jammed between picket-tops. Teeth bared in a sardonic grin of pain, he hurried off holding his torn and dislocated little finger, with a bone protruding. Under general anaesthetic in hospital the finger was repaired and bandaged.

Addition of his outstanding bowler to England's casualty list must have made Illingworth feel like the commanding officer of the Light Brigade at Balaklava. However he and his men felt, they pushed on purposefully with the job of winning the battle. In Lever's third over a model outswinger found an edge and Chappell walked as soon as he saw the ball lodge in Knott's gloves. Placed exactly the right depth down the gully, Dolly held Walters' slash off Willis. With four out for 82 by the 25th over, only two men could lift Australia away from impending defeat, Stackpole and the younger Chappell.

Hooking Dolly, Keith became the only man in the series to be credited with two sixes in a Test but he was steadied by Illingworth who had Redpath smartly caught at leg-gully. In his gentle, wide-trousers jogtrot of eight steps Illy looks innocent as a backyard trundler in slippers, but not to batsmen who have to cope with his on-the-dot length and line plus deceptive drift that sways some balls outward when inward turn is expected. From over the wicket he spun offbreaks into the pads of Stackpole and Chappell, but, unlike Knott, uttered no appeal, simply tilting his head across to calculate whether the ball could have hit the stumps. When Stackpole, attempting a sweep, was bowled behind his meaty legs for 67, top score, eight fieldsmen crowded to pat the broad back of the skipper whose guile had removed the biggest obstacle to an English victory.

As Knott missed a legside chance to stump Marsh an incredulous gasp around the ground was a tacit tribute to the finest wicket keeping by any visitor Australians have seen in my time. This let-off was the gloved genius's only real error in coping with 8,000 balls in the series. (In all the Englishmen turfed 20 chances and the Australians 23.)

For the first time in the rubber here was a pitch on which Illingworth really liked bowling, even with a sore knee. For two-thirds of the innings he held control into the breeze, in one stretch bowling 11 overs straight. On the fifth morning Greg Chappell, 30, aware that quick runs from him were the only hope, advanced to drive the off-spinner but a drifter curved past him. The stumping brought Knott his 24th wicket – a record for any series in Australia – and Illingworth rested with three wickets for 39. The skipper's 160 balls allowed only 18 scoring shots, 10 of them singles. In the last overs Dell averted a hat-trick by D'Oliveira before Underwood ended the innings at 160.

Sportsmen have been known to get up from the floor to win but this is the first time a whole team has quit the scene and returned to carry off the match. Victors by 62 runs, the Englishmen swarmed around their captain and hoisted him on to Hampshire and Edrich's shoulders. Triumphantly they carried off the first skipper for 38 years to have wrenched the Ashes from Australia's grasp Down Under and the only one not to have allowed the Australians one win in a rubber since the 30-hour time limit began there in 1946. Australia's captain and the New South Wales cricket president, Alan Davidson, acknowledged the Englishmen's superiority and congratulated them on fighting back so convincingly after the loss of star players.

Two of these, Snow and Boycott, each had an arm in a sling as they accepted presentations on the field in front of the pavilion. If cricket had judo-style gradings the Black Belt for fast bowlers would surely have been bestowed on Snow. John was so clearly the Man of the Series that I think this award would have been endorsed by any public opinion poll, including those who normally answer 'Don't know'.

Sydney. Feb. 12, 13, 14, 16, 17, 1971, England won by 62.

I. Chappell sent England in.

ENGLAND 1st innings		2nd innings	
J. H. Edrich c G. Chappell b Dell ...	30	c I. Chappell b O'Keefe ...	57
B. W. Luckhurst c Redpath b Walters ...	0	c Lillee b O'Keeffe...	59
K. W. R. Fletcher c Stackpole b O'Keeffe	33	c Stackpole b Eastwood ...	20
J. H. Hampshire c Marsh b Lillee ...	10	c I. Chappell b O'Keeffe ...	24
B. L. D'Oliveira b Dell	1	c I. Chappell b Lillee ...	47
R. Illingworth (c.) b Jenner ...	42	lbw Lillee	29
A. P. Knott c Stackpole b O'Keeffe ...	27	b Dell	15
J. A. Snow b Jenner	7	c Stackpole b Dell	20
P. Lever c Jenner b O'Keeffe	4	c Redpath b Jenner... ...	17
D. L. Underwood not out	8	c Marsh b Dell	0
R. Willis b Jenner...	11	not out	2
B 4, lb 4, nb 2, w 1	11	B 3, lb 3, nb 6	12
Total off 76 overs (5 hrs. 22 mins.) ...	184	Total off 100.7overs (7h. 33m)	302

Fall: 5, 60, 68, 69, 98, 145, 156, 165, 165, 184.
94. 130, 158, 165, 234, 251, 276, 298, 299, 302.

Bowling.	Balls	Runs	Wkts.			Balls	Runs	Wkts.
Lillee	104	32	1	...	...	112	43	2
Dell	128	32	2	...	...	215	65	3
Walters	32	10	1	...	...	40	18	—
G. Chappell	24	9	—					
Jenner	128	42	3	...	...	168	39	1
O'Keeffe	192	48	3	...	...	208	96	3
Eastwood					...	40	21	1
Stackpole					...	24	8	—

AUSTRALIA 1st innings		2nd innings	
K. H. Eastwood c Knott b Lever ...	5	b Snow	0
K. R. Stackpole b Snow	6	b Illingworth	67
R. W. Marsh c Willis b Lever ...	4	b Underwood	16
I. M. Chappell (c.) b Willis ...	25	c Knott b Lever	6
I. R. Redpath c & b Underwood ...	59	c Hampshire b Illingworth	14
K. D. Walters st Knott b Underwood	41	c D'Oliveira b Willis ...	1
G. S. Chappell b Willis	65	st Knott b Illingworth ...	30
K. J. O'Keeffe c Knott b Illingworth	3	c Shuttleworth b D'Oliveira ...	12
T. J. Jenner b Lever...	30	c Fletcher b Underwood... ...	4
D. K. Lillee c Knott b Willis ...	6	c Hampshire b D'Oliveira	0
A. R. Dell not out	3	not out	3
L b 5, nb 10, w 1	16	B 2, nb 5	7

Total off 83.6 overs (7 hrs. 10 mins.) 264 Total off 62.6 overs (5 hrs. 10 mins.) 160
Fall: 11, 13, 32, 66, 147, 162, 178, 235, 239, 264.
0, 22, 71, 82, 96, 131, 142, 154, 154, 160.

Bowling.	Balls	Runs	Wkts.			Balls	Runs	Wkts.
Snow	144	58	1	...	...	16	7	1
Lever	118	43	3	...	...	96	23	1
D'Oliveira	96	24	—	...	...	40	15	2
Willis	96	58	3	...	...	72	32	1
Underwood	128	39	2	...	...	110	28	2
Illingworth	88	16	1	...	...	160	39	3
Fletcher					...	8	9	—

Runs per 100 balls: England 34, Australia 36.
Balls per hour: England 95, Australia 110.

Umpires: Louis P. Rowan, Thomas F. Brooks.

INDEX

Abid Ali, S., 113, 116, 119, 127, 130
Adcock, Neil, 58
Ahmed, Ghulam, 121
Ahmed, Saeed, 103, 104, 105, 106, 107, 109, 125
Ahmed, Younis, 110
Aird, Ronald, 51
Alam, Intikhab, 103, 104, 105, 106, 111, 113
Alexander, Jerry, 55, 57, 58, 62, 64, 65, 66, 68, 69
Allen, Dave, 54, 62, 69–70
Allen, G. O., 27, 29, 30, 36, 37
Amarnath, Lala, 117, 134, 147
Ames, L. E. G., 29, 36, 102, 106, 107, 108, 109, 110
Archer, R., 71
Armstrong, W. W., 95, 96
Atkinson, Denis, 42, 43, 46, 47

Bailey, Trevor, 43, 45, 96
Bannerman, Charles, 23
Bannister, Alex, 48
Bari, Wasim, 106, 107
Barnes, Alan, 173
Baroda, Maharaja of, 77
Barrington, Ken, 21, 54, 59–60, 61, 62, 64, 68, 69, 85, 91, 125
Bedi, Bishan Singh, 74, 75, 113, 114, 118, 127, 128, 129, 133, 136, 137, 143, 144, 145, 147
Bedser, Alec, 45, 169
Benaud, Richie, 22, 45, 52, 64, 125, 126, 127, 143, 172
Bennett, Fred, 133, 141, 149, 155
Bhattacharya, 116
bodyline tests, see Test matches, England v. Australia, 1932–33
Bonnor, George, 97
Borde, Chandu, 80, 125, 129
Borde, Man, 57, 67
Bowes, Bill, 26, 28, 29
Boycott, Geoffrey, 21, 91, 148, 163, 171, 179
Bradman, Sir Donald, 20, 27, 28, 29, 30, 34, 36, 55, 62, 83, 90, 115

Brittenden, R. T., 117
Brooks, Tom, Umpire, 23, 168, 170, 175, 177
Brown, David, 21, 85, 86, 87, 88, 92, 108
Brown, George, 96
Buller, Sid, Umpire, 21
Burge, Peter, 21
Burgess, Gordon, 115
Burgess, Mark, 119
Burke, Jim, 125
Burke, Perry, Umpire, 40, 41
Butcher, Basil, 22, 39, 55, 64, 75, 87, 88
Bynoe, Robin, 74

Camacho, George, 39
Camacho, Stephen, 39, 85, 87, 92
Cardus, Sir Neville, 20
Carmody, Keith, 124
Carter, Hanson, 95
Chandrasekhar, Bhagwat, 73, 74, 75, 154
Chappell, Gregory, 164, 165, 167, 168, 172, 173, 176, 177, 178, 179
Chappell, Ian, 125, 128, 137, 143, 144, 145, 147, 160, 163, 165, 166, 176
Chidambaram, M. A., 77
Christiani, Robert, 46
Clark, David, 174
Cleverley, Donald, 117
Close, Brian, 84, 86, 90, 92, 165
Collins, Herbert, 96
Compton, Denis, 42, 43, 44, 47, 48, 49, 171
Congdon, Bevan, 114
Coningham, Arthur, 113
Connolly, Alan, 78, 125, 126, 129, 130, 131, 147, 149, 153
Constantine, Learie, Baron, 56, 66, 67, 68
Contractor, Nari, 122, 125
Corbett, Claude, 31
Cottam, Bob, 110

Cowdrey, Colin, 54, 58, 59, 62, 83, 84, 85, 86, 88, 91, 100, 101, 102, 104, 105, 106, 108, 110, 118, 160, 163, 174
Cranston, Ken 147
Cricket Cauldron (Bannister), 48
crowd arrangement, importance of, 15*ff*., 75
Cunis R. S., 116, 117, 120

Davidson, Alan, 26, 58, 179
Dell, Tony, 163, 165, 177, 179
Dexter, Ted., 21, 52, 54, 60, 70, 78, 95
D'Oliveira, Basil, 87, 92, 100, 101, 104, 107, 110, 146, 164, 177, 179
Douglas, Johnny, 96
Dowling, Graham, 113, 114, 115, 116, 119, 120, 125
Dwyer, Edmund, 169

Eastwood, Ken, 166, 176, 178
Edrich, John, 85, 101, 103, 164, 176, 179
Egar, Colin, Umpire, 21, 70, 168, 173
Elliott, Umpire, 22, 23
Emmett, George, 97
Engineer, Farokh, 79, 125, 129, 141, 145, 146, 149
England *v.* Australia, 1884, 97–8
Ewart, Tom, Umpire, 41
Evans, Godfrey, 43, 45, 49, 50

Fagg, Umpire, 23
Favell, 59
Fender, Percy, 95, 96
Figgis, Bob, Umpire, 162
Fingleton, Jack, 28, 29, 31, 36, 156
Fletcher, Keith, 107, 164, 165, 176
football, violence of mobs, 13–14, 17, 19
Freeman, Eric, 78, 92, 142, 147, 149, 153–4

Gandotra, Ashok, 114, 116, 120, 134
Ganteaume, Andy, 67
Gaskin, Berkeley, 39, 85
Gavaskar, Sunil, 134, 142
Ghose, A., 134
Gibbs, Lance, 39, 45, 79, 85, 87, 92, 130–1, 144
Gilchrist, Roy, 57–8, 65

Gillette, E. S., Umpire, 41, 47, 49
Gleeson, Johnny, 126, 127, 129, 130, 132, 133, 150, 154, 155
Goddard, Trevor, 131
Gomez, Gerry, 42, 46, 67
Gopalakrishnan, I., Umpire, 132, 134, 141
Grace, W. G., 37, 39
Graveney, T. W., 43, 44, 87, 92, 101, 103, 104, 105, 106, 108, 109, 110, 125, 145
Gregory, Jack, 95, 96
Griffith, Charlie, 59, 76, 79, 86, 91, 92, 168–9
Grimmett, C. V., 27, 28, 165
Guha, Subrata, 74, 146, 147, 150, 152
Gul, Aftab, 101
Gunn, William, 23
Gupte, Subhash, 144

Hadlee, Dayle, 114, 116, 119, 120
Hadlee, Walter, 116, 131
Hall, Wesley, 21, 26, 45, 55, 57, 58, 59, 60, 61, 62, 65, 68, 79, 85, 86, 168, 171
Hammond, Walter, 27, 29, 34, 36, 44, 62, 105, 147
Hampshire, J. H., 168, 176, 179
Harford, Noel, 169
Harvey, Neil, 20, 43, 62, 78, 83, 125, 171
Hassan, Fida, 101
Hassett, Lindsay, 20, 43, 131, 142, 162
Hastings, Brian, 114
Hawke, Neil, 21, 110
Hayes, John, 118
Headley, Ron, 110
Hendry, Hunter, 96
Herbert, Sir Alan, 32
Hobbs, Robin, 64, 110
Holford, David, 85, 87, 90, 91, 92
Hollies, Eric, 117
Holt, John, 47, 50
Hornby, A. N., 33
Howarth, Dick, 113
Howarth, Hedley, 117
Hunt, Bill, 165–6
Hunte, Conrad, 54, 62, 63, 64, 68, 74, 76, 125
Hutton, Sir Leonard, 20, 40, 41, 42, 43, 44, 46, 48, 50, 55, 83, 116, 118, 132, 169, 171, 175

Illingworth, Ray, 21, 24, 54, 62, 64, 68, 69, 160, 162, 163, 164, 165, 167, 168, 169, 170, 171, 172, 173, 175, 177, 178, 179
imperialism, cricket spread by, 15
Indian Cricket (Sundaresan), 75
Indrajitsinh, K. S., 116
International Cricket Conference, 94
Iqbal, Asif, 106
Irani, Jehangir, 131, 132
Ironmonger, H., 27, 28
Irvine, Ken, 134
Island Cricketers (Walcott), 49

Jaisimha, M. L., 78, 79, 80, 113, 114, 116, 119, 120, 154
Jardine, Douglas, 26, 27, 28, 29, 34, 35, 36, 37
Jenner, Terry, 165, 168, 169, 170, 174, 176
Jennings, Jack, 87
Johnson, Ian, 51, 52
Johnson, Tyrrell, 113
Jones, Jeff, 86, 88
Jones, Prior, 67, 77
Jones, W. S., 48
Jordan, Cortez, Umpire, 41

Kanhai, Rohan, 39, 54, 59, 63, 68, 70, 75, 77, 85, 86
Khan, Majid Jehangir, 102, 103, 107
King, Frank, 59
Knott, Alan, 107, 108, 165, 166, 167, 176, 178, 179
Kundaran, B. K., 75, 79, 130, 131

Laker, Jim, 43, 44, 46, 49, 79, 128, 144, 147
Langley, Gilbert, 52
Larwood, Harold, 26, 27, 28, 29, 30, 31, 33, 34, 36, 37
Larwood Story, The (Larwood), 29
Lavakare, Arvind, 135, 136
Lawry, Bill, 21, 22, 35, 114, 125, 126, 127, 128, 129, 130, 131, 132, 133, 134, 136, 137, 141, 142, 143, 146, 150, 151, 152, 153, 154, 155, 156, 157, 161, 162, 163, 165, 166, 172
Lee Kow, E., Umpire, 59, 61, 64, 66

Lever, Peter, 165, 166, 167, 169, 173, 176, 178
Leyland, Maurice, 27
Lillee, Dennis, 163, 169, 171, 172, 176, 177
Lindwall, Ray, 26, 71, 169, 171
Lloyd, C. H., 39, 73, 75, 76, 80, 86, 87
Lloyd, E. L., Umpire, 59, 63, 66
Lock, Tony, 41, 43, 47, 79, 118, 145, 169
Loxton, Sam, 147, 171
Luckhurst, Brian, 162, 163, 176

Macartney, Charles, 33, 96
Macaulay, George, 113
Mackay, Ken, 21
Mallett, Ashley, 126, 129, 132, 133, 142, 149, 150, 153
Mankad, Ashok, 126, 129, 143
Mankad, Vinoo, 74, 126, 144
Mantri, Madhav, 130
Marsh, Rod, 166, 178
Masood, Asif, 103, 106, 107, 108
May, Norman, 174
May, Peter, 20, 42, 47, 48, 54, 59, 63, 65, 66, 67, 68
McCabe, S. 90
McDonald, Colin, 51, 59, 106
McDonald, E. A., 95, 131, 168
McDonnell, 98
McKenzie, Graham, 68, 78, 117, 125, 126, 127, 129, 131, 132, 137, 141, 148, 149, 153, 168
McWatt, Clifford, 39, 47
Mead, Philip, 95
Meckiff, Ian, 23
Melford, Michael, 108
Menzies, Badge, Umpire, 41, 47, 48, 49, 50
Merchant, Vijay, 122, 124
Merwe, Peter van der, 131
Milburn, Colin, 102, 103, 104, 105, 110
Miller, Keith, 69, 71, 87, 90, 126, 147, 161, 171
Modi, Rudi, 78, 80
Mohammad, Hanif, 101, 103, 104, 107, 125, 142
Mohammad, Mushtaq, 101, 102, 104, 107
Murdoch, W. L., 97, 98
Murray, Bruce, 113, 116

Murray, Derryck, 85, 91
Murray, John, 110

Nagendra, M. V., 116
Nawaz, Sarfraz, 103
Nel, Jack, 131
Norfolk, Duke of, 21, 86
Nurse, Seymour, 77, 78, 86, 87, 92

O'Connell, Max, Umpire, 162, 163
O'Keefe, K. J., 164, 165, 167, 168, 176, 177
Oldfield, W. A., 32, 34, 35
O'Neill, Norman, 125
O'Reilly, W. J., 27, 28, 33, 45, 165, 169

Palmer, Charles, 40, 47, 50
Pan, Shambu, Umpire, 130, 132, 133, 136, 145
Parker, Charles, 96
Parkin, Cecil, 96
Parks, Jim, 21, 87
Pataudi, Nawab of (Mansur Ali Khan), 28, 74, 75, 76, 77, 80, 104, 113, 114, 116, 120, 121, 122, 125, 126, 127, 129, 133, 141, 142, 147, 150, 152, 153, 157
Paynter, Eddie, 27, 28, 36
Peate, Edmund, 96, 97
Pierre, Lance, 67
Players of England, 97
Pollard, Dick, 147
Pollock, Graeme, 147
Pollock, Peter, 169
Ponsford, Bill, 31, 32, 36
Prasanna, E. A. S., 113, 114, 119, 127, 128, 129, 130, 131, 133, 142, 143, 144, 146, 147, 148, 154
Prideaux, Roger, 101
Proctor, Mike, 160
Pullar, Geoff, 54, 58, 66
Puri, Devraj, 130, 134, 135

Ramadhin, Sonny, 42, 43, 44, 45, 47, 48, 49, 55, 62, 64, 65, 70, 144
Ranjit Trophy umpires, 80
Rao, Nagaraj, Umpire, 155
Redpath, Ian, 125, 126, 129, 145, 153, 161, 165, 167, 177, 178
Reid, John, 124
Reuben, J., Umpire, 145
Rhodes, Harold, 23

Richards, Barry, 145, 147
Richardson, Victor, 35, 166
Rishi, N. S., 155
Robins, Walter, 21, 61, 67
Rorke, Gordon, 84
Rosenwater, Irving, 97
Ross, Alan, 58, 66
Rowan, Louis, Umpire, 23, 161, 162, 169–70, 173, 175
Roy, Ambar, 116, 149
Running into Hundreds (Barrington), 59
Russell, A. C., 95

Sang Hue, Douglas, Umpire, 87, 88
Santos, Sir Errol dos, 51
Sardesai, Dilip, 125, 129
Sharp, Keith, 173
Sheahan, A. P., 128, 129, 145, 146, 149
Sheppard, Rev. David, 57
Simpson, Bob, 20, 21, 22, 58, 155, 168
Sing, Charran, 55, 60, 62, 64, 68
Singh, Hanumant, 80
Singh, Swaranjit, 58
Smith, Mike, 22, 54, 61, 62, 78, 84, 131
Smith, Sydney, 95
Snow, John, 85, 86, 107, 108, 160, 161, 162, 167, 168, 169, 171, 172, 173, 174, 175, 176, 178, 179
Sobers, Gary, 21, 46, 52, 54, 55, 62, 63, 64, 69, 70, 73, 77, 78, 79, 80, 83, 85, 86, 87, 88, 90, 92, 107, 126, 130, 144, 147, 169
Solkar, Eknath, 113, 116, 128, 142, 143, 147
Solomon, Joe, 39, 54
Sparling, John, 169
Spofforth, F. R., 96
Stackpole, Keith, 92, 114, 125, 127, 128, 129, 133, 136, 137, 142, 143, 150, 151, 152, 153, 162, 165, 166, 176, 178
Statham, Brian, 43, 45, 46, 47, 50, 54, 62, 64, 66, 68, 70
Stewart, Mickey, 110, 111
Stollmeyer, Jeffrey, 42, 44, 46, 66, 67
Street, A. E., Umpire, 96
Subba Row, Raman, 52
Subramanya, Venkatraman, 74

Sundaresan, P. N., 75, 155
Surti, Rusi, 74, 75, 77, 78, 126, 127, 128, 129, 130, 137
Sutcliffe, Herbert, 27, 34, 124
Swanton, E. W., 41, 43, 50, 59
Swetman, Roy, 54, 64

Taber, Brian, 130, 142
Tallon, Don, 117
Tate, Maurice, 33, 113
Taylor, Bruce, 114, 120
teargas, use of, 15–16
television films of police action, 16
Tennyson, Hon. Lionel, 94, 95, 96, 97, 131
Test and Country Cricket Board, 23–4
Test matches
  Australia v. India, 1969
    Bombay, 124–37
    Calcutta, 139–58
  Australia v. South Africa, 1967
    Cape Town, 127
  Australia v. South Africa, 1970
    Cape Town, 23
    Newlands, 22
  Australia v. West Indies, 1955
    Georgetown, 51
  England v. Australia, 1921
    Old Trafford, 94–8
    The Oval, 131
  England v. Australia, 1932–33
    Adelaide, 26–37, 160
  England v. Australia, 1946
    Brisbane, 115
  England v. Australia, 1948, 169
  England v. Australia, 1963, 169
  England v. Australia, 1966–7
    Brisbane, 21
  England v. Australia, 1970–1
    Adelaide, 21, 23
    Melbourne, 164
    Perth, 146
    Sydney, 23, 86, 160–79
  England v. India, 1967
    Leeds, 122
  England v. New Zealand, 1958, 118, 169
  England v. Pakistan, 1969
    Dacca, 102
    Karachi, 100–11
  England v. South Africa, 1965
    Johannesburg, 131

England v. West Indies, 1954
  Georgetown, 39–52, 59
England v. West Indies, 1960
England v. West Indies, 1962, 52
  Port of Spain, 21, 54–71, 105
England v. West Indies, 1965
  Kingston, 23
England v. West Indies, 1966, 168
England v. West Indies, 1968
  Kingston, 83–92
  Port of Spain, 23
India v. New Zealand, 1969
  Hyderabad, 113–23
New Zealand v. West Indies, 1956
  Auckland, 120
New Zealand v. South Africa, 1962
  Cape Town, 120
Pakistan v. New Zealand, 1970
  Karachi, 110
Pakistan v. West Indies, 1958
  Georgetown, 52, 65
  Kingston, 83
West Indies v. Australia, 1961, 20, 26
  Adelaide, 21, 70, 78
  Brisbane, 90
  Melbourne, 78, 168
West Indies v. England, 1969
  Headingley, 22, 23
West Indies v. India, 1967
  Calcutta, 73–82, 130
Thomson, Alan, 160, 162
Thomson, Philip, 50
Through the Caribbean (Ross), 66
Titmus, Fred, 87, 91
Trueman, Freddie, 40, 41, 54, 55, 59, 62, 63, 64, 66, 68, 70, 169
Turner, Glenn, 114, 119
Tyldesley, Ernest, 95, 96
Tyson, Frank, 26, 46, 57, 150, 174

umpiring, 20–4
  apologies to umpires, 21
  dissent from decisions, 24, 175
  neutral, 23
  Sir Donald Bradman on, 20
  Sir Neville Cardus on, 20
  Bob Simpson on, 20, 22
Underwood, Derek, 22, 69, 167, 168

Valentine, A. L., 42, 43, 44, 49, 144
Venkataraghavan, S., 113, 117, 118, 119, 127, 128, 129, 130, 131, 134, 142, 145, 146
Verity, Hedley, 28, 36
violence, *passim*
  in football, 13–14, 17, 19
  in rugby, 13
  reasons for start of, 19*ff.*
Viswanath, Gundappa, 129, 142, 149
Voce, Bill, 26, 27, 30, 32

Wade, Bill, Umpire, 22
Wadekar, Ajit, 126, 129, 130, 133, 136, 141, 142, 145, 146, 149, 157
Wadsworth, Ken, 114, 116
Waite, John, 68
Walcott, Clyde, 46, 49, 50
Walcott, Harold, Umpire, 41
Walker, William, 74
Wall, Tim, 27, 35

Walters, Doug, 128, 129, 131, 137, 139, 143, 145, 163, 167, 178
Ward, Alan, 171
Wardle, Johnny, 43, 44, 48
Warner, P. F., 30, 31
Washbrook, Cyril, 131
Watson, Chester, 55, 57, 58, 59, 60, 61
Watson, Willie, 42, 43, 46
Weekes, Everton, 46, 47, 52, 124, 171
West Indian Adventure (Swanton), 41
White, Crawford, 48
Willis, Bob, 160, 166, 167, 168, 169, 172, 173, 176, 178
Wishart, Ken, 48
Woodfull, W. M., 26, 28, 29, 30, 31, 32, 36, 37
Woolley, Frank, 95, 96
Worrell, Sir Frank, 20, 21, 42, 45, 55, 59, 62, 63, 64, 65, 70, 73
Wyatt, Bob, 27